GERMAN AND RUSSIAN TANK MODELS 1939–45

Mario Eens

CASEMATE
Philadelphia & Oxford

Contents

p.62

PzKpfw VIII Maus

Germany, 1946

SU-152

Eastern Front, winter 1943

p.84

Russian Infantry

p.116

Berlin, April 1945

24

24

Panzer I

Ausf. A

North Africa, 1941

The attraction of doing a DAK (Deutsches Afrika Korps – German Africa Corps) vehicle lies primarily in the weathering possibilities. As with a whitewash vehicle the base color, in this instance gray, is covered by a secondary color to blend it better with the environment. When this second, usually inferior, coat of paint starts to deteriorate because of use and weather conditions, the vehicle/model becomes more interesting.

A Panzer I (no specific type in mind) in DAK colors had been on my "want to do list" for a long time. So when I was given the opportunity to build Dragon's Pz.Kfw. I A with interior I did not hesitate. The model is small, but with lots of character, and the inclusion of an interior would keep me busy for quite a while.

1/35

Dragon

Items used:

- Dragon Pz.Kpfw. I Ausf. A Modified Version w/Interior (no. 6356)
- Aber Pz.Kpfw. I Ausf. A – Vol. 1 Basic set (no. 35118)
- Aber German Clamps and Clasps (no. 48 A02)
- Aber Wing Nuts (no. 35 A26)
- Archer German Afrika Korps Insignia (no. AR35026)
- Archer German Fire Extinguisher Placards (no. AR35266)
- Dragon WW II German Infantry Equipment Set 1 (no. 3807)
- Lion Roar Brass Pipe 0.6 mm round (no. LT0025)
- Magic Sculp
- Modelkasten Pz. I A (SK-70)
- Modellbauwelt 2m Stabantenne Wehrmacht (no. MBW 35002)
- M.V. Products Realistic Light lenses for Models (no. LS 27)
- M.V. Products Realistic Light lenses for Models (no. LS 128)
- Royal Model Horns for German tanks WWII (no. 277)
- Schatton German Early MG13 for Pz.Kpfw. I (no. 3520)
- Spare parts box
- Verlinden Productions German Divisional Insignia/Wehrmacht (no. 232)
- Verlinden Productions German Equipment Markings (no. 917)
- Plastic card, strip, rod and tubing, copper wire, foil wrapping of Swann Morton blades, Balsa Wood, brass strip and a Punch & Die set.

Construction

SUSPENSION AND RUNNING GEAR

This version of the Dragon Panzer I A kit has some improvements over previous releases. The first one to come across in the instructions concerns the wheels. Instead of being entirely produced in plastic, they have been reworked to include brass rims to go on either side of the wheels and thus add more depth and scale thickness to that area. Typical for Dragon though is that the original full-plastic wheels are still included in the kit. They will make another nice addition to the spares box. Although the running wheels are sandwiched between the suspension arms, I did not glue the latter together until final assembly as being able to remove the wheels would make the painting stage much more enjoyable. Equally, most of the rest of the suspension and running gear was left unglued.

While the Magic Tracks supplied with the kit look excellent, I did replace them with Modelkasten tracks as I prefer workable track links – this makes the construction and painting process a lot easier.

INSIDE LOWER HULL

Construction of the lower hull is pretty much straightforward. The interior is quite complete and looks good when assembled. I did add a few details to the transmission and driving mechanism using plastic strip, rod and copper wire, but most of it is obscured once the model is assembled. Knowing that it's there does offer piece of mind though. More detail was added in the form of bolts along both sides of the hull (you can line them up with the bolts on the outside), a plastic strip running along the left hull side which represents a channel for conduit, supports on the driver's seat, a couple of Aber wing nuts on the rear wall and straps and buckles on the boxes for the flares (at least I think they are flares).

Before adding the floor to the hull, I glued some plastic strip to the bottom through which I drilled a hole. A brass pin was then inserted and secured with glue. This pin enables me to mount the model on a pin vice which makes handling the model in the painting stages much easier. The pin and strip are hidden once the interior floor is added.

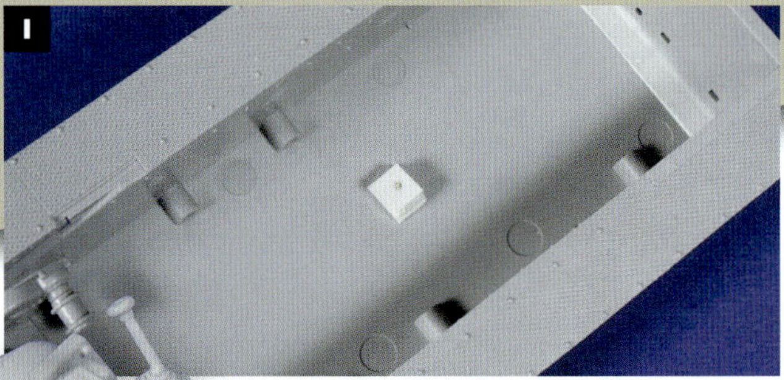

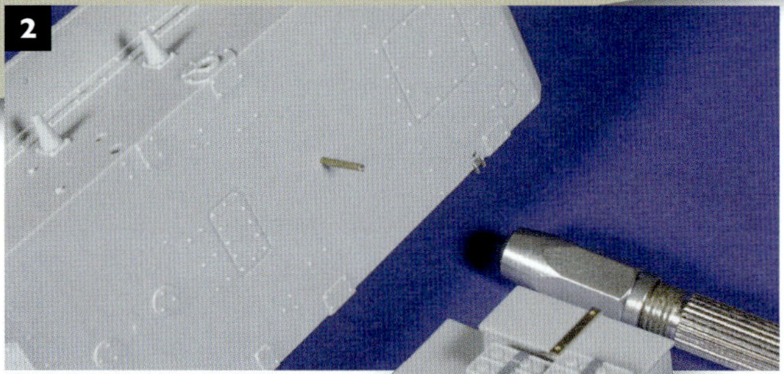

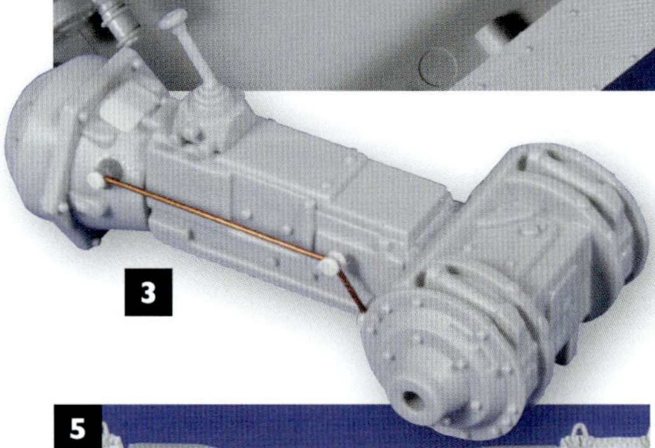

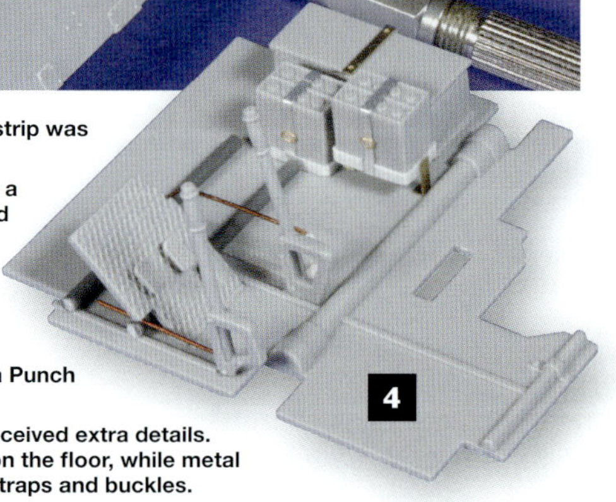

1. Before adding the floor, some plastic strip was glued to the hull bottom.

2. A brass pin was then inserted through a hole drilled from underneath and secured with glue. The pin can then be inserted in a pin vice, which makes it easier to handle the model during the painting stages.

3. The transmission was detailed with some copper wire and plastic strip and a Punch & Die set.

4. Other features in the lower hull also received extra details. Plastic rod was used to add some bars on the floor, while metal foil and copper wire was used to make straps and buckles.

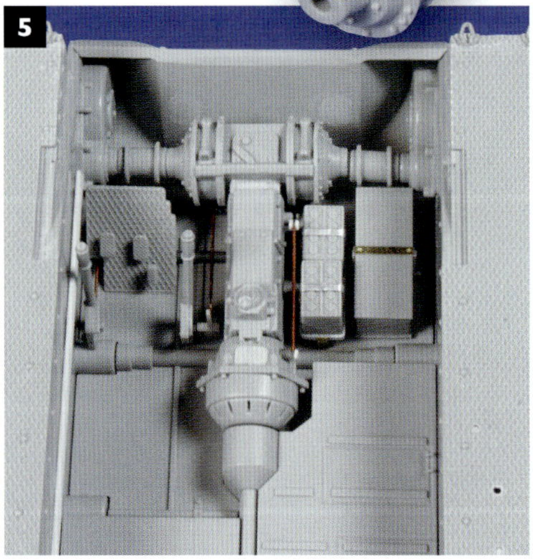

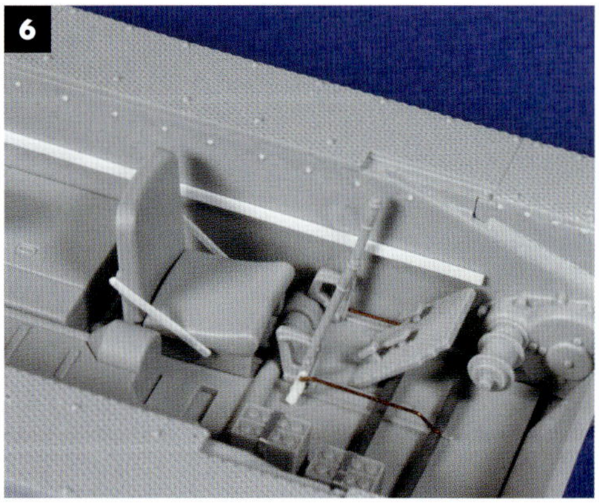

5. The transmission, floor (two parts), and seat form the lower parts of the hull. The plastic strip will represent a conduit channel along the lower left hull side.

6.The floor parts installed. A series of bolts was added along the inside of the lower hull. They can be lined up with the bolts on the outside. Some sink holes need to be filled with putty. The plastic strip represents a conduit channel for electric wires.

INSIDE UPPER HULL AND TURRET

The upper hull needs a bit more attention as Dragon have produced this thin armored vehicle with a double, over-scale, thick skin. The armor plates (front, sides and back) are to be positioned round an interior structure that is molded to the front glacis plate. As I obviously wanted to show off the interior, I needed to find a way to get the armor plate in the doorway in the correct scale thickness. Removing the entire inside skin is one option, but I soon cast this idea aside as this would enlarge the inside space, meaning that I would have to rebuild all internal fittings that are positioned against this inner skin as they no longer would have the correct depth. The only remaining option is to thin the armor on all visible areas around the door. After thinning to scale the edge of the door on the left armor plate using a file, I started assembling the outer skin using the inner skin as a template. First both side armor plates were glued to the front plate. Then I added the roof, and finally the back. While assembling the outer skin, I kept checking that it fitted over the inner skin. Next I removed the section of the inner skin at the doorway by cutting it with a scalpel. Then, to blend the remaining edges with the thin outer skin, I used a file to bevel them. Also, the vision ports (W7) on either side of the door needed to be beveled from the rear to sit flush with the armor plates. As there was no specific Aber detail set for the Dragon model when I started building it, I used the basic set designed for the Tristar kit. Although parts for the vision ports are provided in the Aber set, I decided to stick with the plastic Dragon parts as they would fit the thick inner skin better. Only the rear vision port (D19) received some photo-etch parts as the mechanism to open it is not provided in the kit.

The only internal fitting mounted to the side armor plates that now needs replacing is the triangular box situated beneath the door. As explained above, because of removing the inner skin and thus enlarging the inside, the original kit box was no longer deep enough to span the width of the fenders on which it rested. Some plastic card and thin copper wire were used to create a new one.

One prominent feature that I also found missing from the kit is the dashboard. Again, this was easily fixed with some plastic card and a Punch & Die set. Some photocopies of dials were punched out and added for realism. The reason why the dashboard is not included in the kit in the first place is probably because it is almost entire invisible when the hull is closed. Anyway, knowing it's there adds peace of mind. I also added two handles made from copper wire over the driver's position and two gasmask containers from the spares box against the rear wall, as these too were missing from the kit. All internal fittings were painted separately and added later.

Both hatches in the hull had the molded detail removed and thinned to scale. Detail was replaced with plastic strip, brass tube and photo-etched parts. The cushion on the turret hatch was padded with a layer of Magic Sculp. The turret itself only needed a few details adding, such as bolts made with a Punch & Die set, a handle and a spring.

Before final construction on the outside of the model started, the inside was of course painted and weathered – more on that later, when I explain step by step how it was done.

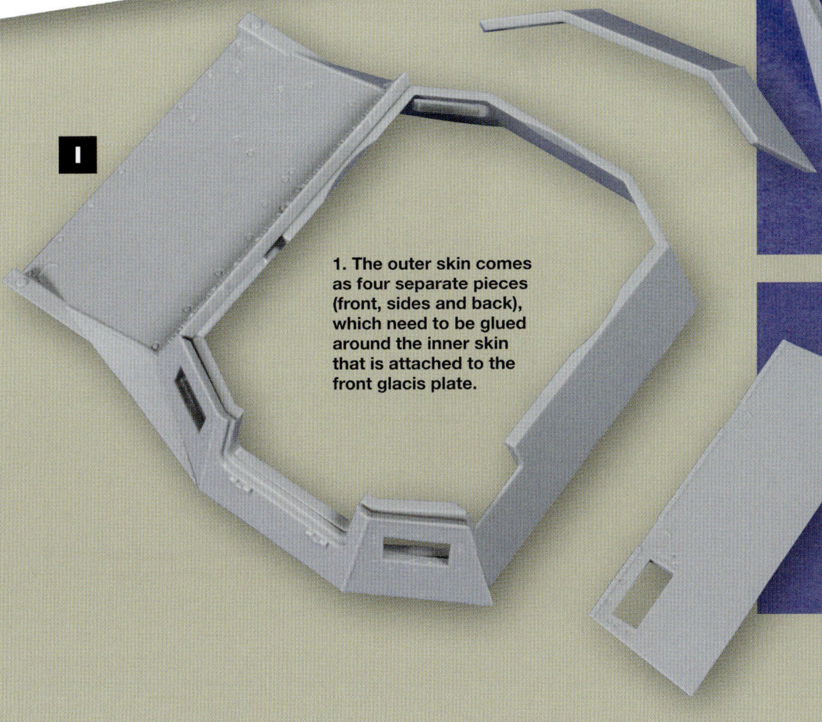

1

1. The outer skin comes as four separate pieces (front, sides and back), which need to be glued around the inner skin that is attached to the front glacis plate.

2

2. The door opening in the outer skin was thinned and brought to scale by filing it down.

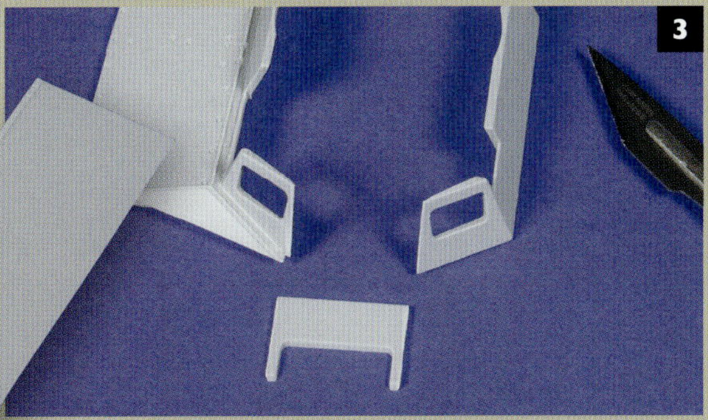

3

3. The inner skin had the part around the doorway removed by cutting it with a scalpel.

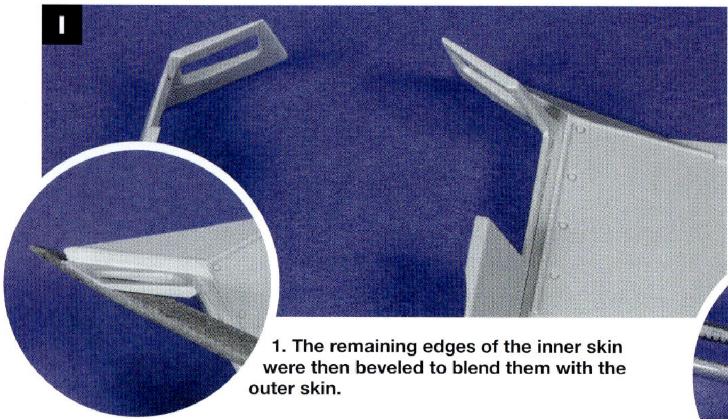

1. The remaining edges of the inner skin were then beveled to blend them with the outer skin.

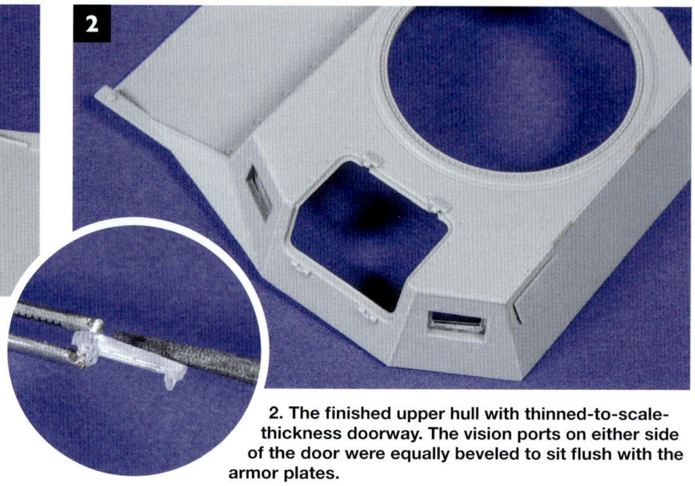

2. The finished upper hull with thinned-to-scale-thickness doorway. The vision ports on either side of the door were equally beveled to sit flush with the armor plates.

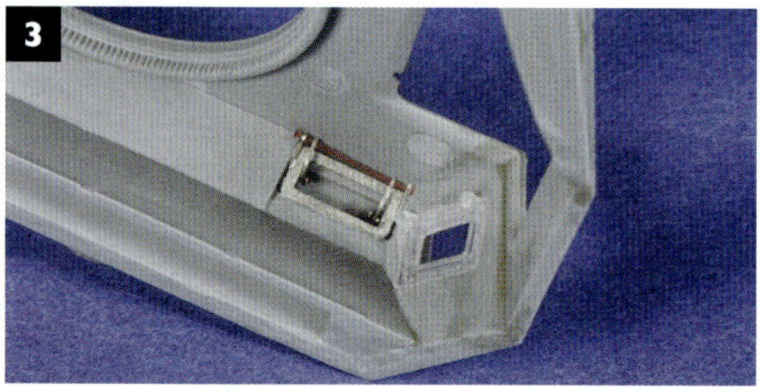

3. Inside upper hull. The side vision ports sit flush with the armor plates. The rear vision port was constructed from Aber parts and plastic rod.

4. A hole in the inner skin needs to be filled with plastic card.

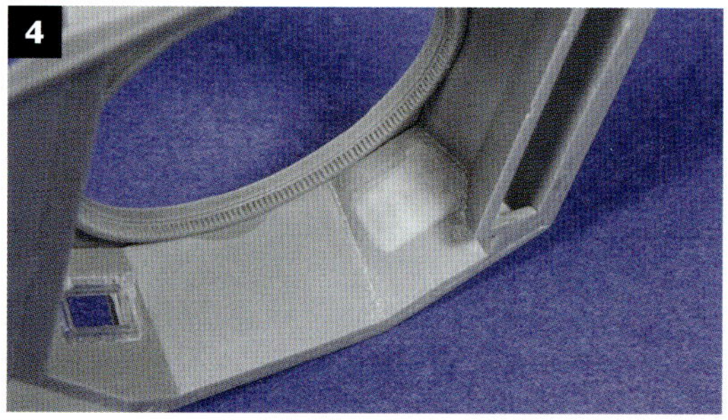

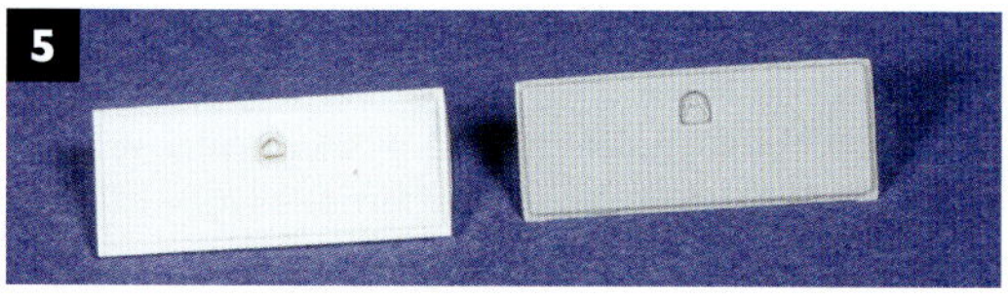

5. The storage box situated underneath the doorway needs to be replaced by a deeper item, as the original kit part now no longer fits.

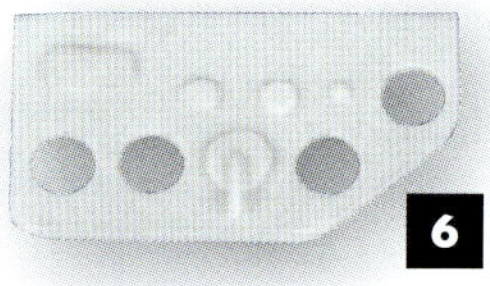

6. As a dashboard is not provided in the kit, I scratch-built one from plastic card.

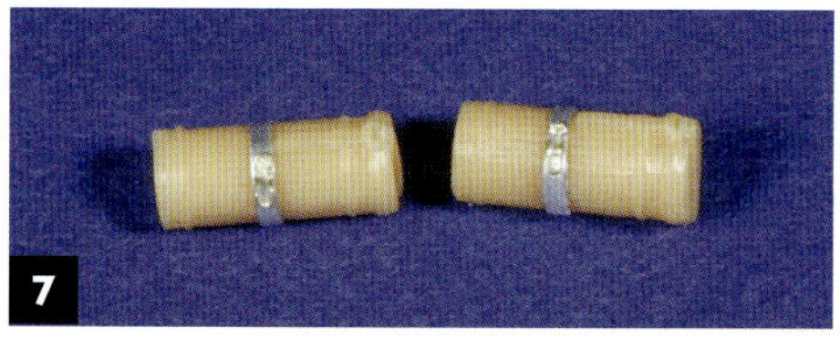

7. Also missing from the kit are two gasmask containers for the crew. They were taken from Dragon's WW II German Infantry Equipment Set 1 and detailed with metal foil and an Aber clamp.

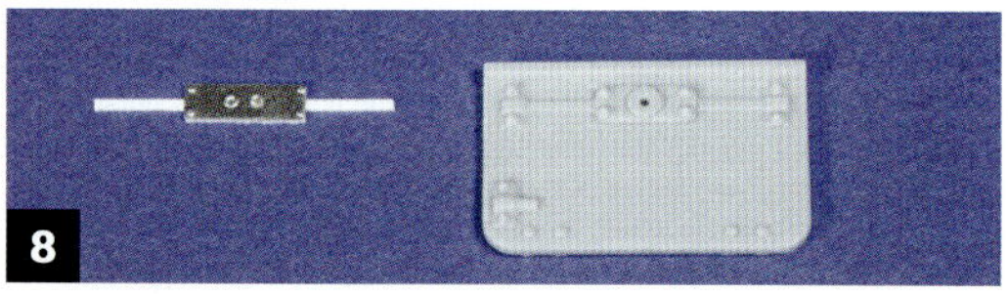

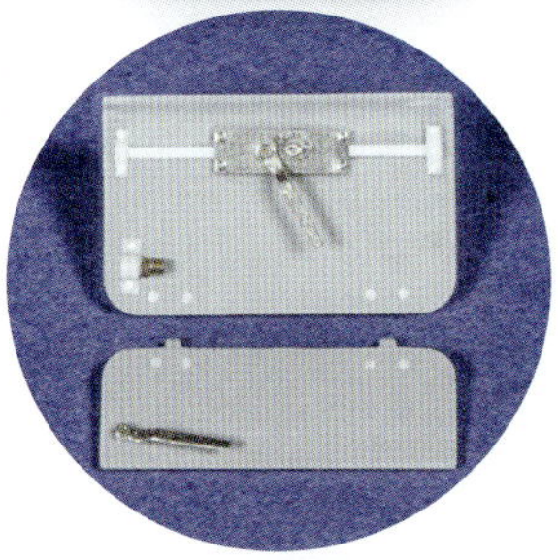

8. Aber parts and plastic strip were used to make a new locking mechanism.

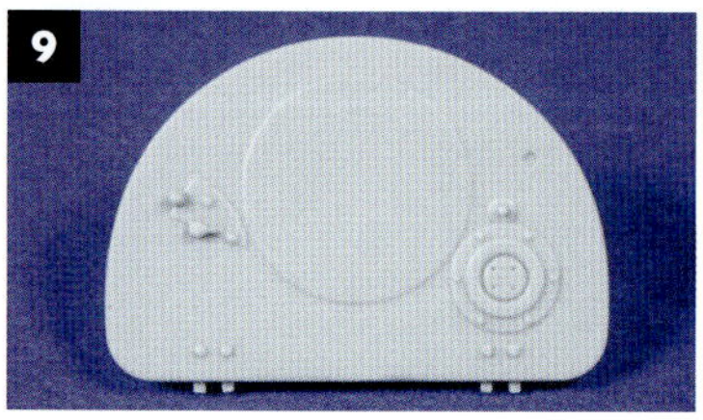

9 & 10. The finished detailed hatch. Magic Sculp was used to add volume to the padding, while the locking mechanism was replaced with Aber parts.

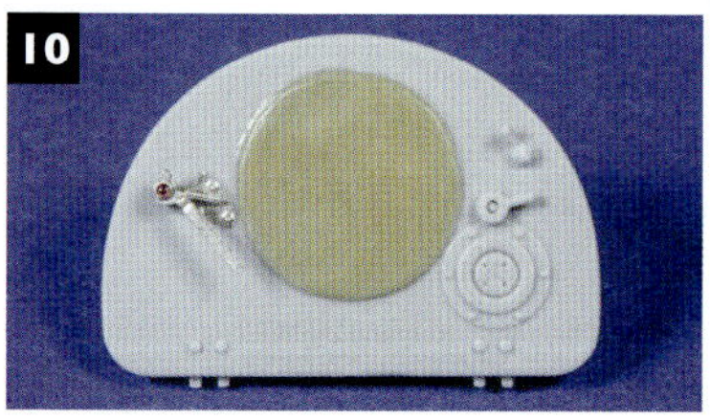

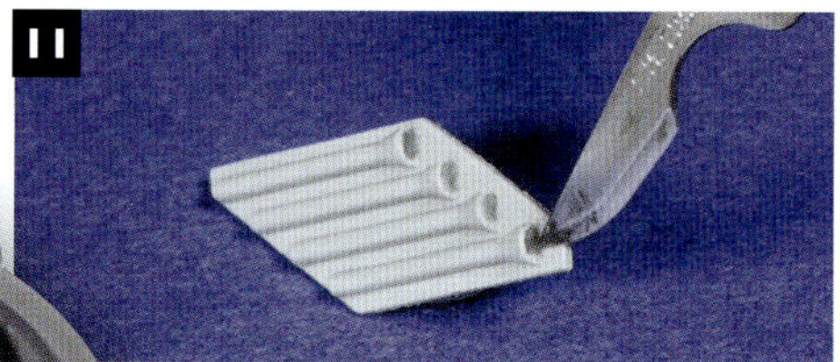

11. The tubes for holding signal flags were thinned at the edges to bring them to scale.

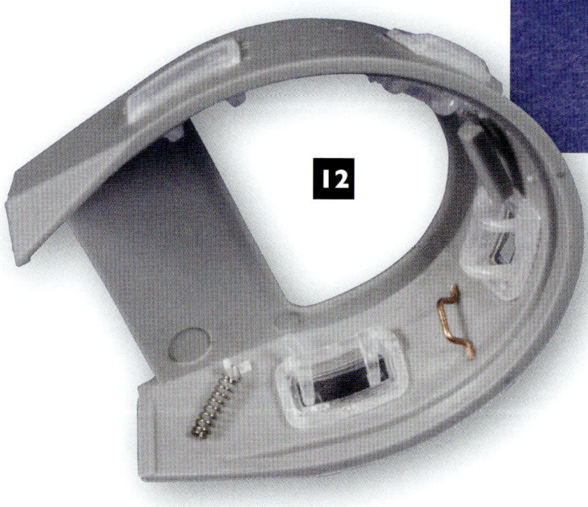

12. The inside of the turret was detailed with a copper handle, bolts and a spring.

OUTSIDE UPPER HULL AND FENDERS

The molded weld seams on the hull outside look rather square on the edges, so I rounded them off by scraping the edges with a scalpel. Missing, or partly missing, weld seams were recreated with Magic Sculp.

The gutter above the driver's vision port, which lacks the shape of a gutter, was reworked by cutting off the bolts, shaping it with a scalpel and adding new bolts made with a Punch & Die set.

As the fenders supplied in the kit are very well detailed I felt it unnecessary to replace them with photo-etched parts. Leaving off the front removable mudguards just meant that thinning the front edges with a file was enough to bring them to scale thickness. Because I left off the front mudguards, I also needed to remove the molded pin in the front catch. Careful cutting with a scalpel did the job and there was no need to replace the whole assembly with photo-etched parts. At the same time the molded conduit for the lights was removed from each fender and side parts B20 and B21, again by carefully cutting them off with a scalpel. I find a fine, round-headed scalpel (no. 15c) works best. The conduit was later replaced with copper wire. For better realism, the lights were drilled out with a round-headed drill bit and M.V. Products lenses inserted.

The tool holders on the fenders were soldered together for better strength. All tool clamps were taken from Aber's 1/48-scale tool clamp set as they are more to scale than the oversize 1/35-scale variants.

The fire extinguisher on the left fender had all the molded detail removed and replaced with photo-etched parts. However, as the extinguisher is too long for the holder, the latter needed to be extended. To do this, I cut the base in half and soldered a length of scrap photo-etch, cut from the frame, between the two halves.

As with the extinguisher, the jack on the right fender had some molded detail removed and replaced with photo-etched parts and scratch-built items. The crowbar was made from brass wire. A piece of plastic rod wound with copper wire replaced the kit's air outlet (D3), while the plastic horn was replaced with a resin casting from Royal Model. The antenna base was reworked with plastic rod and photo-etching and the antenna itself is a brass Modellbauwelt item that was shortened to the correct length.

Both exhausts had the molded pipe removed and replaced with a length of thick copper wire wound with a thinner variant. Although I first thought the pipe on the exhausts was a rubber hose, the photos I used for reference material showed different. Whether this is an original feature or a result of restoration, I'm not sure – I have seen photos of Panzer I exhausts with rubber hoses. The outlet of the exhaust was drilled out and refined. To give the exhausts the characteristic thin rim on both ends, I temporarily removed the exhaust outlet and then used a flat-nosed drill bit to mill out the center and leave a thin rim around the edge. The exhaust outlet was then glued back in place. Braces to hold the exhausts were made from plastic strip as the photo-etched items included in the kit didn't seem to fit very well. Photo-etched grills to cover the exhausts are also included in the kit, but I replaced them with the Aber parts as they are more nicely detailed and seem to be more to scale.

For a good result, the armored cover on the rear deck really needs to be soldered together, as gluing it makes it too fragile.

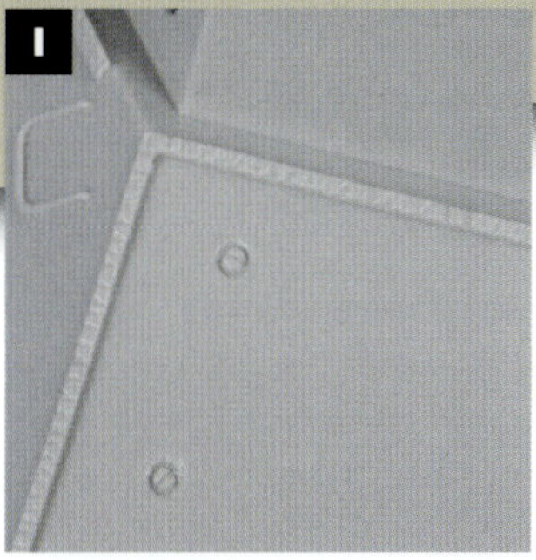

1 & 2. The kit's weld seams are a bit square in shape. I rounded them off by scraping the edges with a scalpel.

3. Missing welds were recreated with Magic Sculp.

4. Molded location indicators were removed all over the model.

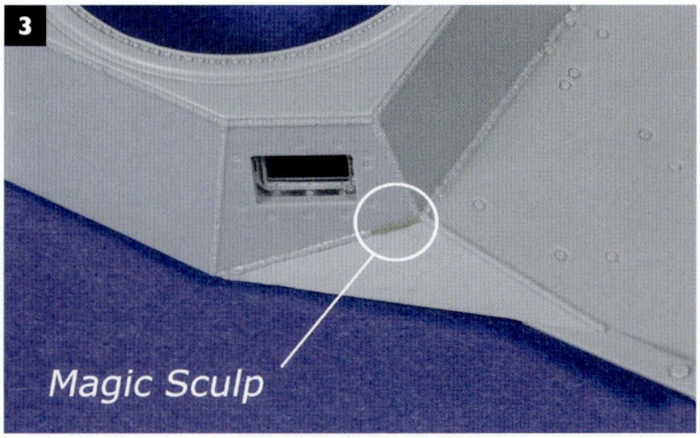

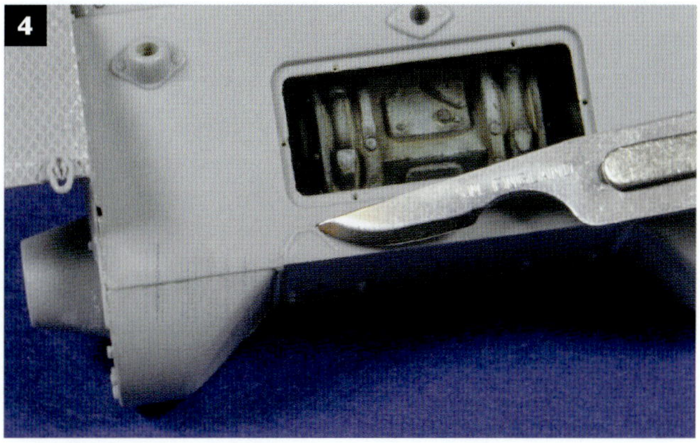

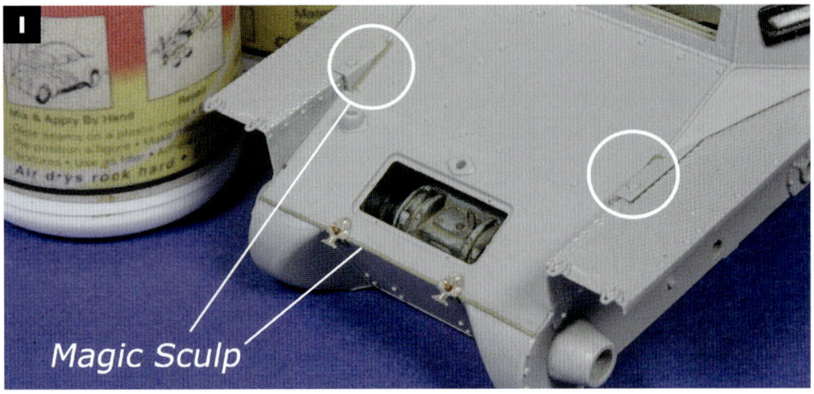

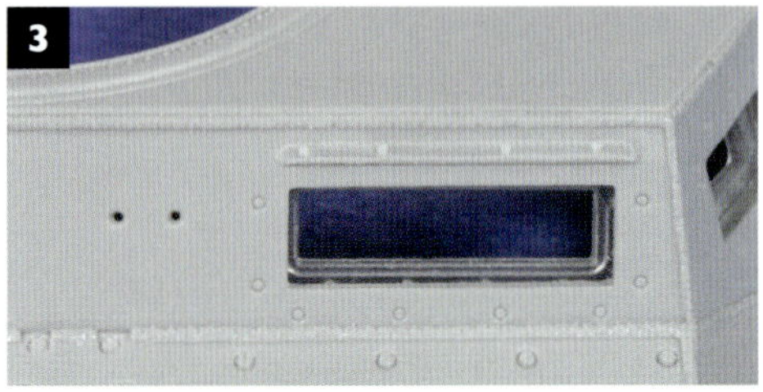

1. The weld seam on the front on the glacis plate and other missing welds were again recreated with Magic Sculp.

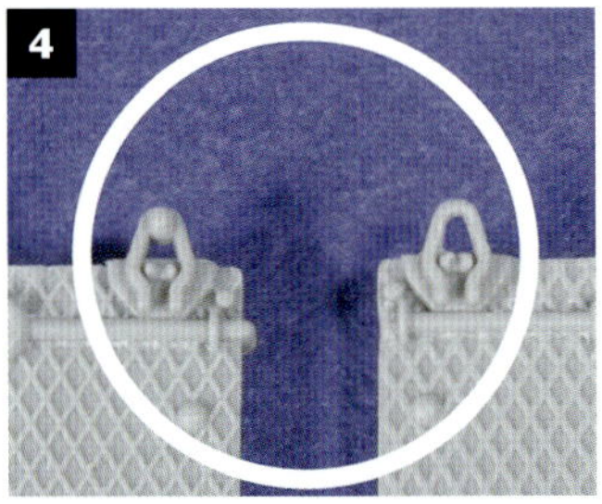

2 & 3. The bolts were removed and the gutter carved with a scalpel. New bolts made with a Punch & Die set were then added.

4. The molded pins in the catches on the front of the fenders were carefully removed with a scalpel. On the left, the original kit part; on the right, the part with the pins removed.

5. The molded conduits for the lights on the fenders were carefully removed with a scalpel.

6. The vertical parts of the front fenders (B20 and B21). Part B20 has already had all molded details like conduit and bolts removed. Conduit and bolts will later be replaced with copper wire and bolts made with a Punch & Die set.

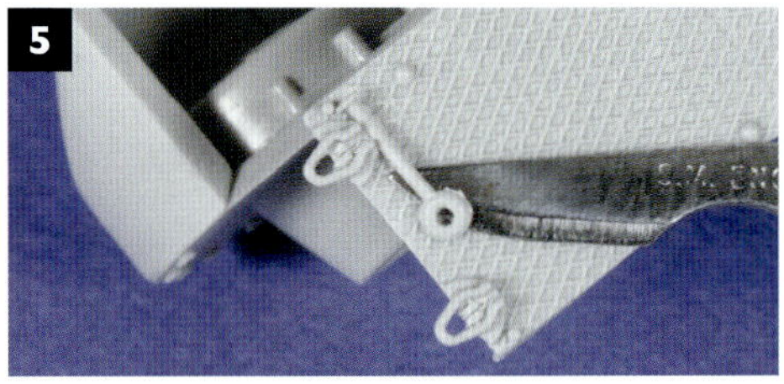

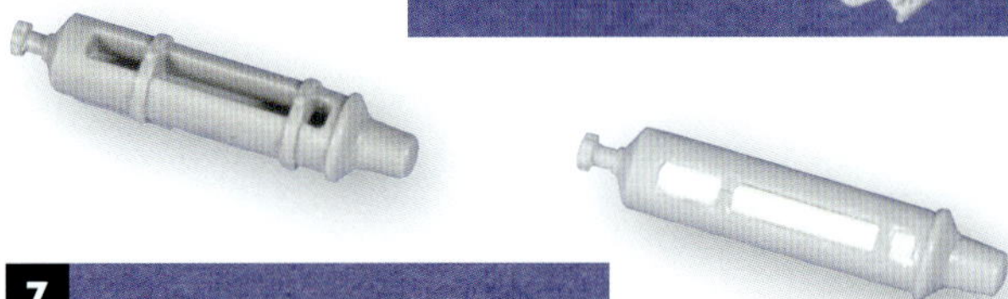

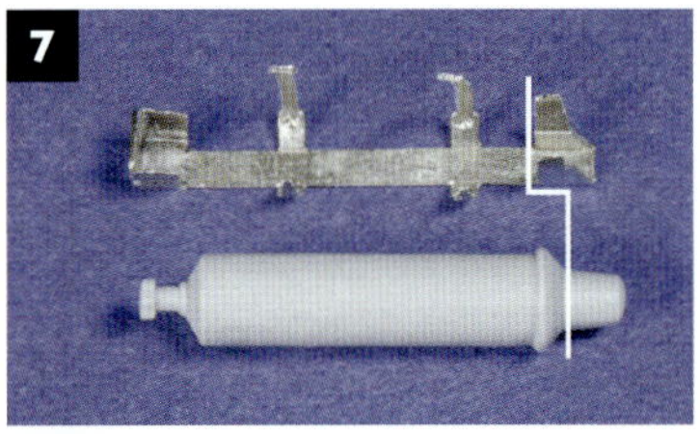

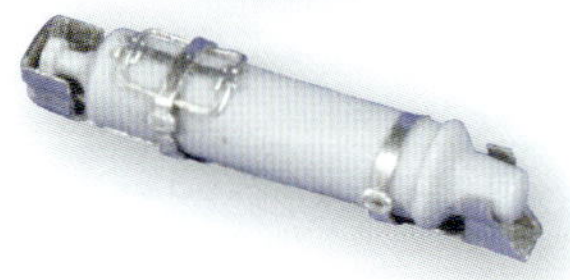

7. The fire extinguisher as offered in the kit. All detail was removed and the gaps in the rear were filled with plastic strip. The extinguisher is a bit too long to fit into the Aber holder provided for the Tristar kit. To lengthen the holder, it was first cut in two. Next, a scrap piece of photo-etch cut from the frame of the set was soldered in between the two parts of the holder. The extinguisher now fits the holder. The straps are closed and the assembly is ready for painting. The whole assembly will only be added to the model after painting.

8. The lights on the fenders were drilled out to take lenses. To drill out the lights, you need to start with a small diameter drill bit, gradually moving to the larger sizes. Finally, different round-headed drill bits were used to get the desired shape.

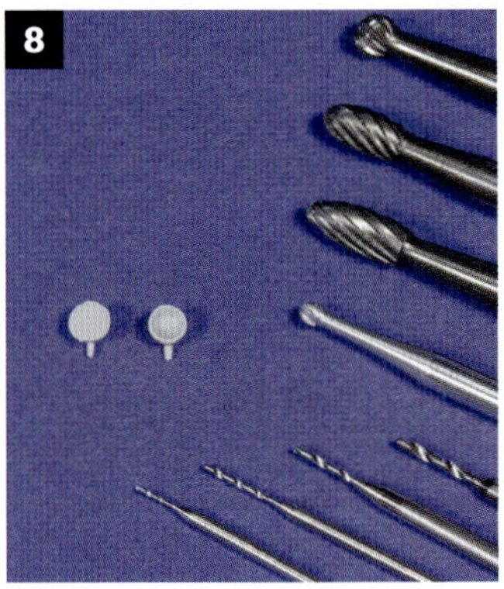

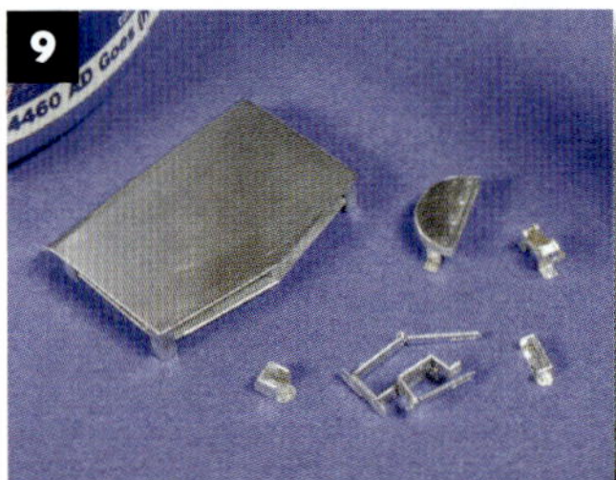

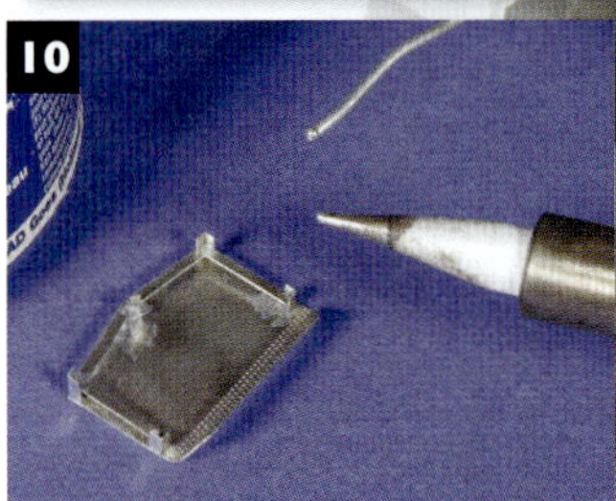

9. Most of the small photo-etch parts were soldered together for better strength.

10. The armored cover on the rear especially benefits from soldering, as it is too fragile to be glued.

1. The left front fender with all the tools and fire extinguisher in place. The tool clamps for the shovel and axe were taken from a 1/48-scale set as they look more to scale.

(Below) The finished jack. Missing bolts have been removed, location seams have been removed and detail added with copper wire and Aber parts.

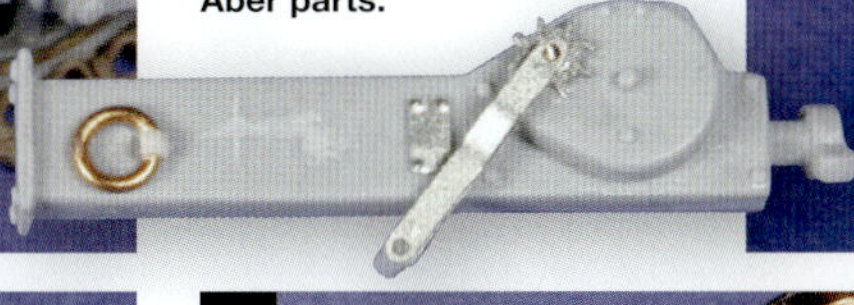

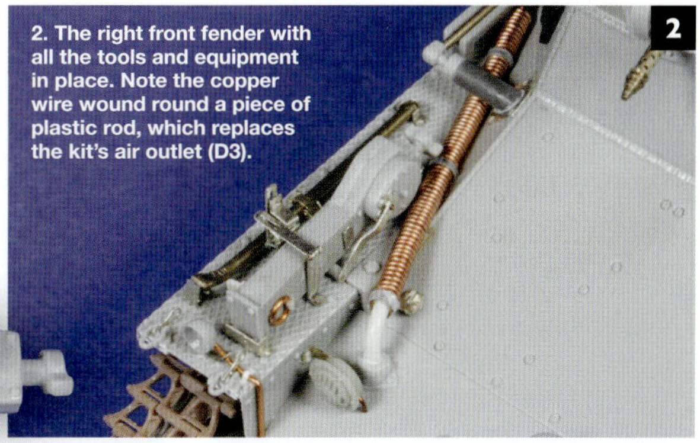

2. The right front fender with all the tools and equipment in place. Note the copper wire wound round a piece of plastic rod, which replaces the kit's air outlet (D3).

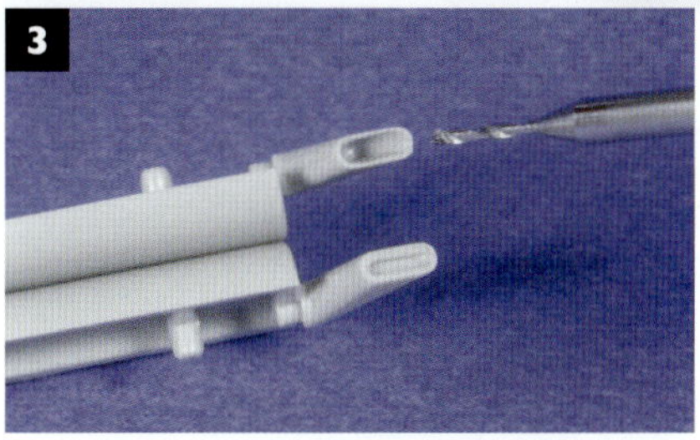

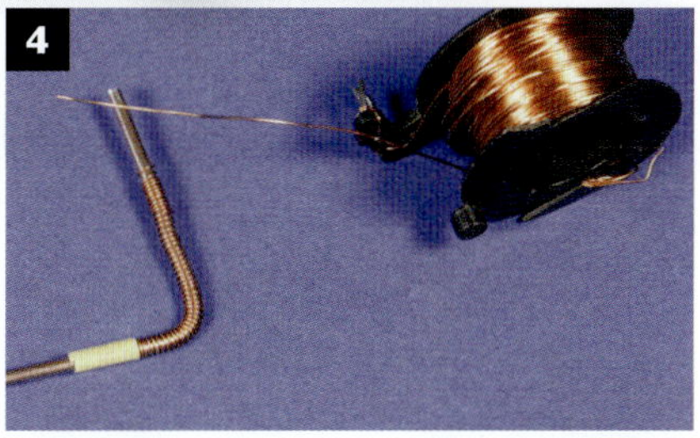

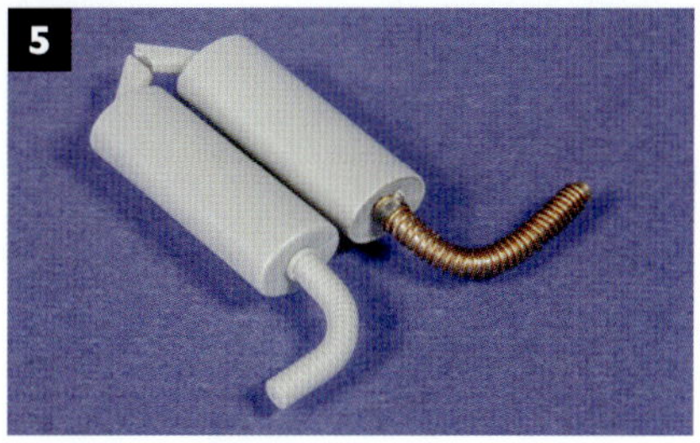

3. To create the typical rim on the ends of the mufflers, the exhaust pipe end was temporarily removed. Then a flat-nosed drill bit was used to mill out the center of the surface, leaving a thin rim on the edge.

4 & 5. The kit exhaust pipes of the kit have been replaced by bent copper tube, onto which copper wire has been wound and glued.

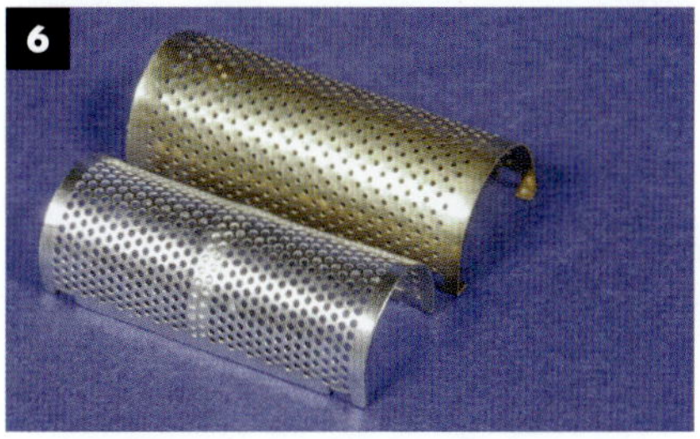

6. Comparing the Aber exhaust cover to the Dragon kit offering. The latter is much larger and less refined.

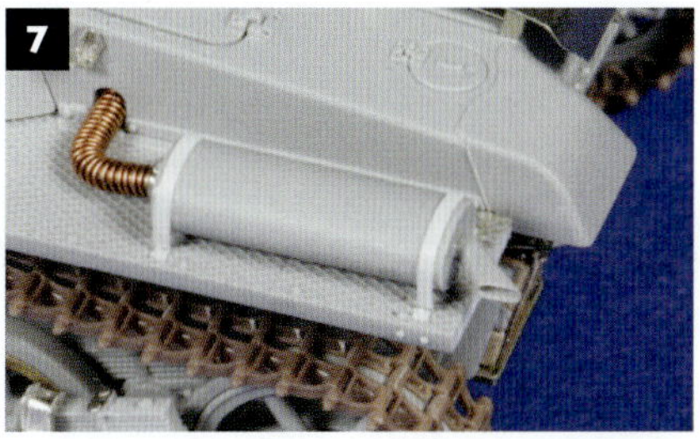

7. Plastic strip was used to make the braces to hold the exhausts.

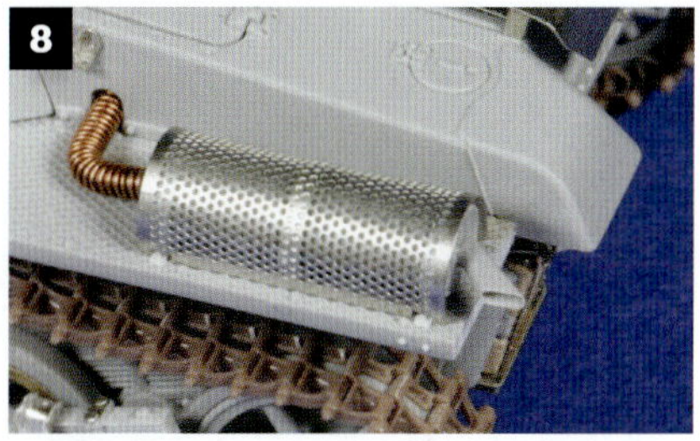

8. The left exhaust with the mesh in place. The same will be done to the right one.

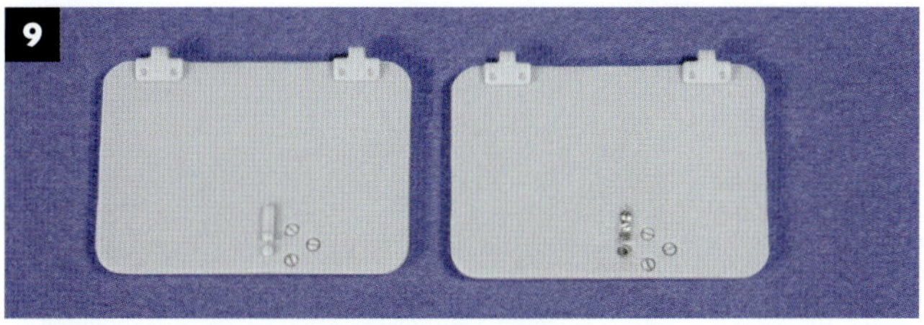

9. Comparison of the hatches in the rear deck before and after detailing.

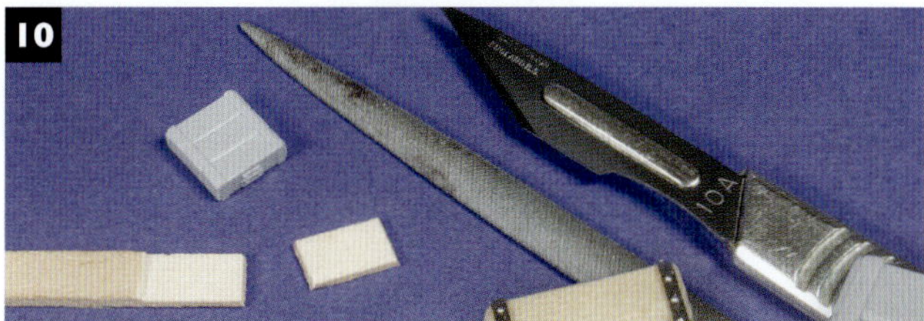

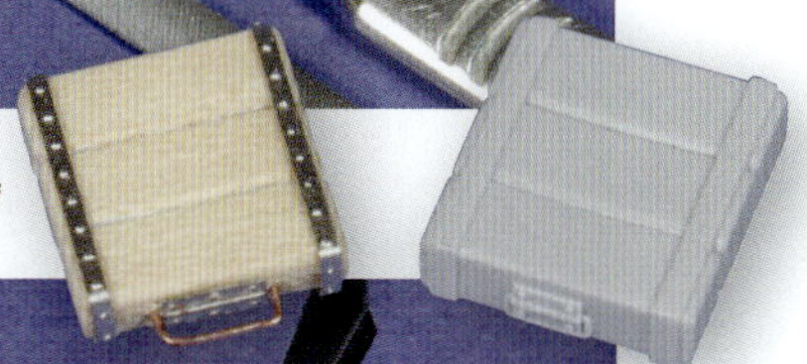

10. The wooden block for the jack was made from scratch using strips of wood cut to the correct size.

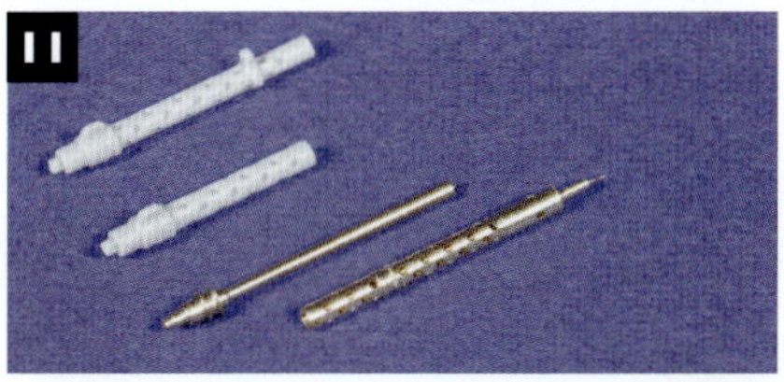

11. Brass turned items by Schatton replaced the molded kit items. Note how the barrels differ in length.

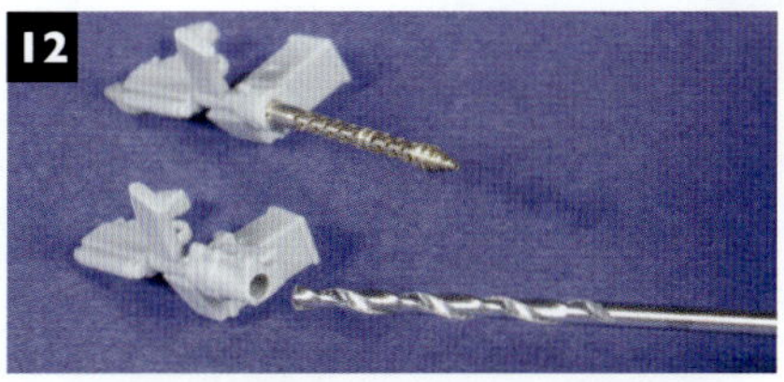

12. The machine guns need to be drilled out to take the Schatton barrels. Make sure you measure first how deep you need to drill.

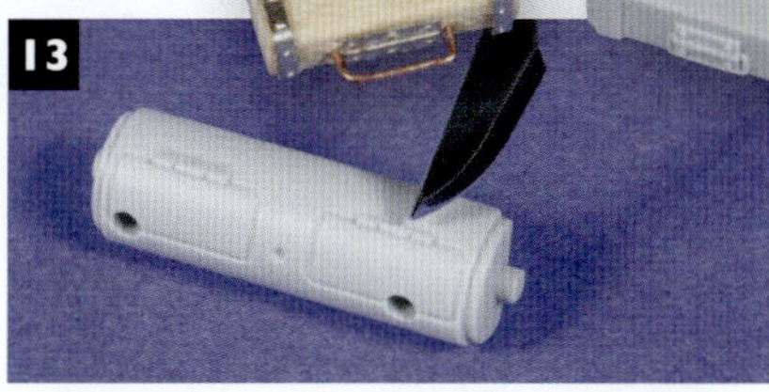

13. The hinges on the gun mantlet were refined by reworking them with a scalpel.

OUTSIDE TURRET

In the turret, the machine-gun barrels were replaced with brass items produced by Schatton. The reason why is obvious, as they are much more refined than the plastic kit items. They come with a separate barrel and outer perforated casing. To make them fit, the holes in the gun mantlet need to be drilled through, as well as the bodies of the machine guns inside the turret (J3 and J4). However, before doing any drilling, make sure you first measure how far each of the kit barrels sticks out of the mantlet so you can calculate how deep you need to drill to insert the replacement barrels. Note how the barrels don't line up.

Also, on the gun mantlet the molded hinges above the barrels were refined by cutting them with a scalpel.

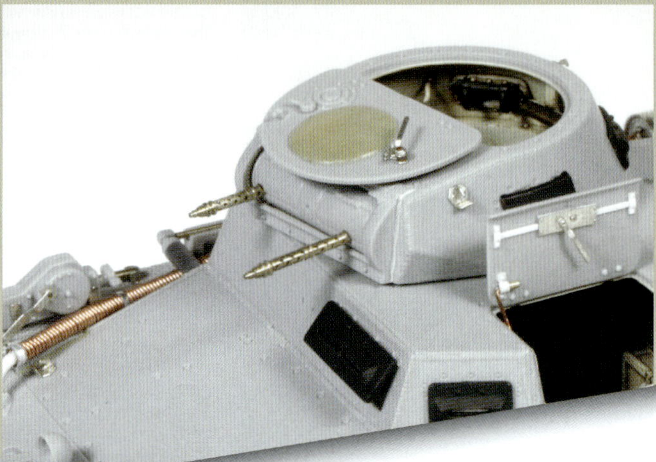

Above, right and below left. The right fender. Aber parts and plastic rod were used to rework the antenna base. The antenna itself is a shortened, brass-turned 'Modellbauwelt' item. The crow bar is made from brass rod. The horn is a resin casting from Royal Model.

Below. The left front fender with all the tools and fire extinguisher in place. The tool clamps for the shovel and axe were taken from a 1/48-scale set, as they look more to scale.

Above, below and bottom. Left-side views showing the side hatch. A flattened piece of copper wire is used to lock the door in the open position.

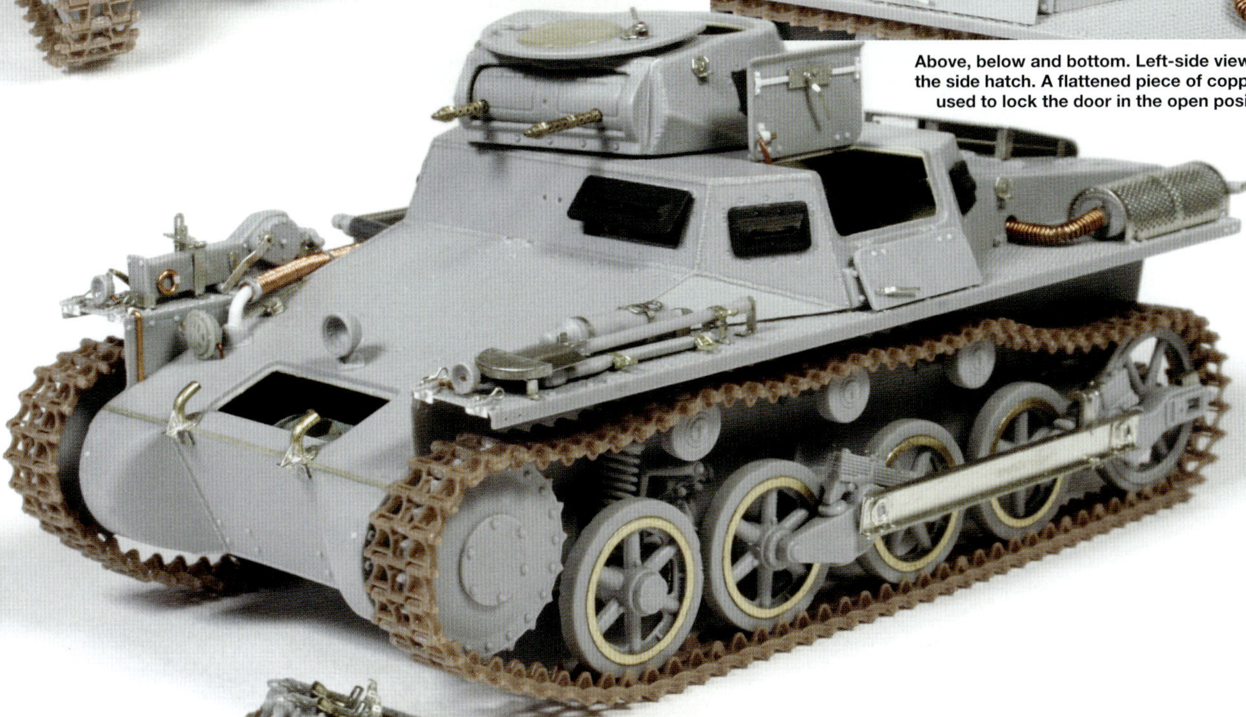

Painting

HISTORICAL REFERENCE

The interior color of German military vehicles has been the source of many discussions. Good reference material seems hard to come by and many a model has ended up with an overall white interior. Usually those white interiors are based on restored vehicles in museums. The original colors, however, were quite different. Also, depending on when the vehicle was fabricated, it received a different interior finish.

During the first years of World War II, the official paint scheme for tank crew compartments consisted of two colors, which were to cover the red primer entirely. A yellow color called Elfenbein, or Ivory, (RAL 1001) was to cover the upper part of the compartment, while a gray-green color (RAL 7009) was used to cover the lower part.

Even though no record has yet been found to substantiate a change, it seems that the Elfenbein, which is a light, lemon yellow color, was at some point changed to a light beige.

In late 1942, it was ordered to stop using the gray-green color and leave the lower part of the vehicle in the original red primer. Later, in September 1944, another order was issued to stop painting the upper interiors in Elfenbein and to leave them in red primer entirely. However, because of complaints from the crews, the use of Ivory paint was officially reinstated at the end of 1944.

Also of note is that all workable parts in the upper part of the interior, like machine-gun mounts, handles, vision ports, handwheels etc., were painted black. The inside color of crew hatches was painted the same as the outside base color, as an ivory hatch would draw too much attention.

More detailed information, including references to modeling paints, can be found at the following Internet link:

http://byrden.com/panzers/Colors/index.html

PAINTING THE MODEL INTERIOR

Painting the interior started with airbrushing the lower parts first, as this seemed to be more logical and would make the job of masking for the second color easier.

Color references on the above-mentioned website suggested that Humbrol Matt Russian Blue (no. 115) is an almost perfect match for the gray-green color for the lower parts. Alas, as with many colors in their range, this color is no longer being produced by Humbrol. However, I was lucky enough not to have to search for an alternative as I was donated a jar of the color by a friend who still had it in stock (thanks, Herman!)

After masking the lower parts and all areas that needed to stay paint free, I mixed the beige color for the upper parts following the suggested colors on the website, Humbrol Gloss Ivory (no. 41) and Satin Oak (no. 71). All workable parts were hand-painted with Vallejo Black (no. 950). Because of the different finishes of the paints used (matt, satin, gloss), I decided to give the entire interior a coat of Humbrol Satin Varnish (no. 135) to make it look uniform.

Weathering the interior commenced with a dry-brush run over the lower parts with the base color, Matt Russian Blue (no. 115), mixed with some Matt White (no. 34). This lifted out the detail and created variation in the base color on the larger areas. When dry, all details and crevices were outlined with a dark color mixed from Humbrol Matt Black (no. 33) and Matt Brown Bess (no. 170). This created more depth and gave a first impression of dirt and grime. To tidy up some of the outlining effects and freshen up the base color on the details, I then had a second dry-brush run with Matt Russian Blue (no. 115) mixed with Matt White (no. 34). For the same reason, the beige color on the lower parts was dry-brushed with a mixture of Satin Oak (no. 71) and Matt White (no. 34).

More dirt and grime, paint chippings and rust effects were then added with a variety of oil paints. The colors used were Lamp Black, Van Dyke Brown, Burnt Sienna, Raw Umber, Burnt Umber and Gold Ochre.

Oil paints were also used to recreate dust effects. Naples Yellow mixed with some Raw Umber was filtered over the lower parts where dust would gather naturally.

Edges and corners prone to scuffing, especially on the floor, were metalized with lead and Karismacolor Silver pencils.

The commander's canvas seat, the driver's leather seat, the leather padding of the commander's headrest and padding on the machine gun, plus the radio and gasmask containers, were all painted with Vallejo acrylics.

For the Red Cross on the first aid kit, I used a VP dry transfer that was cut in half, had part of the middle section removed, and was then added on either side of the vertical locking bar of the frame.

Although most of the interior is virtually impossible to view once the hull is closed, I had a fun time painting it.

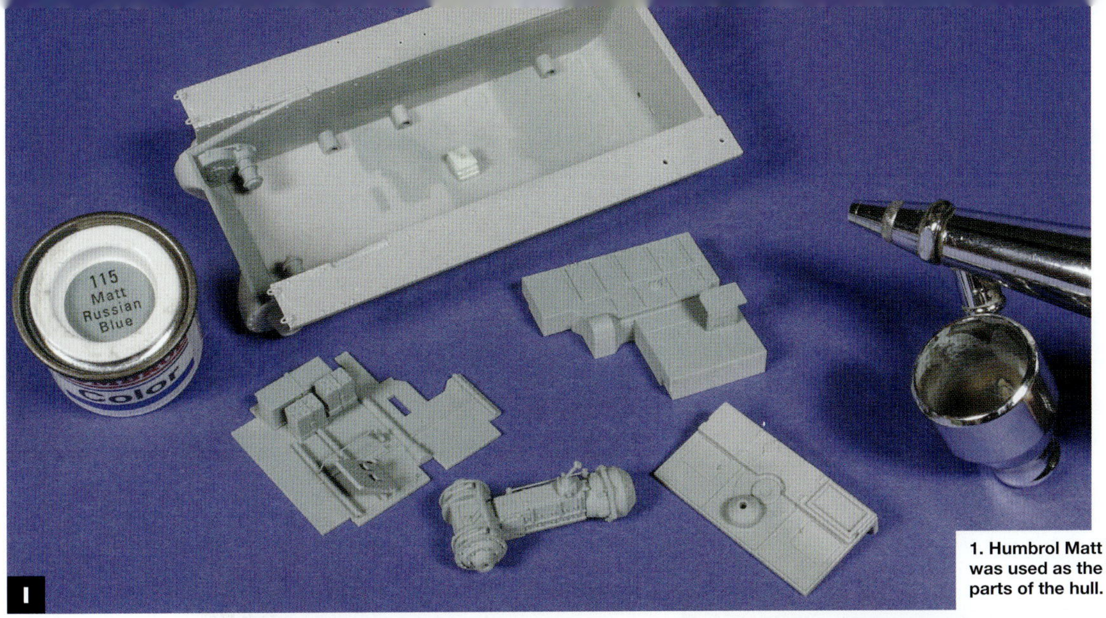

1. Humbrol Matt Russian Blue (no. 115) was used as the base color for the lower parts of the hull.

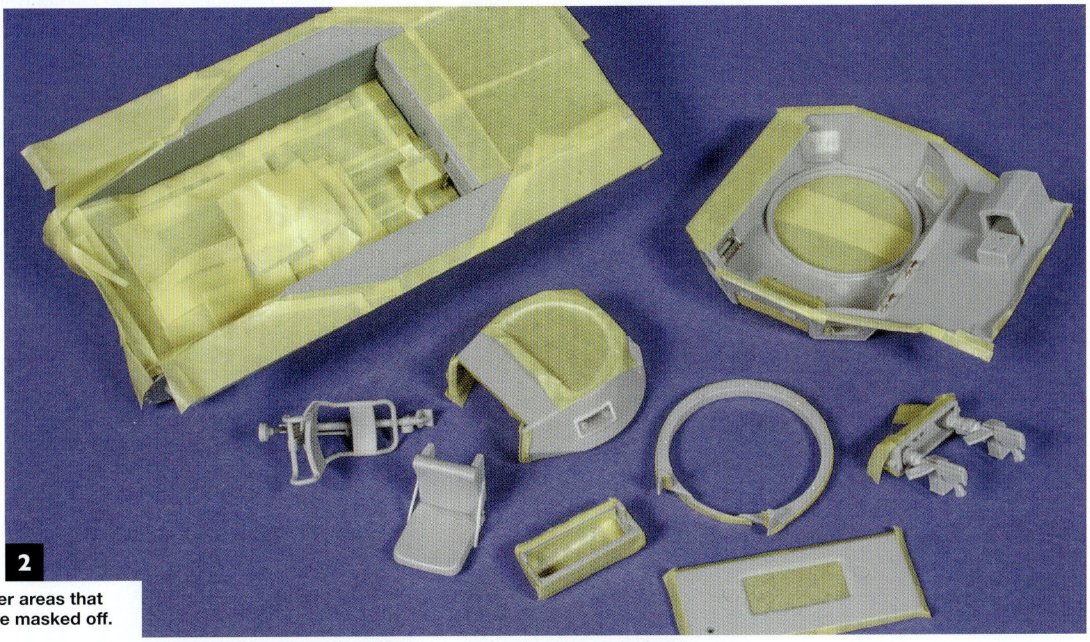

2. Next, the floor and other areas that needed to stay clean were masked off.

3. The rest of the interior was then airbrushed with a mixture of Humbrol Gloss Ivory (no. 41) and Satin Oak (no. 71).

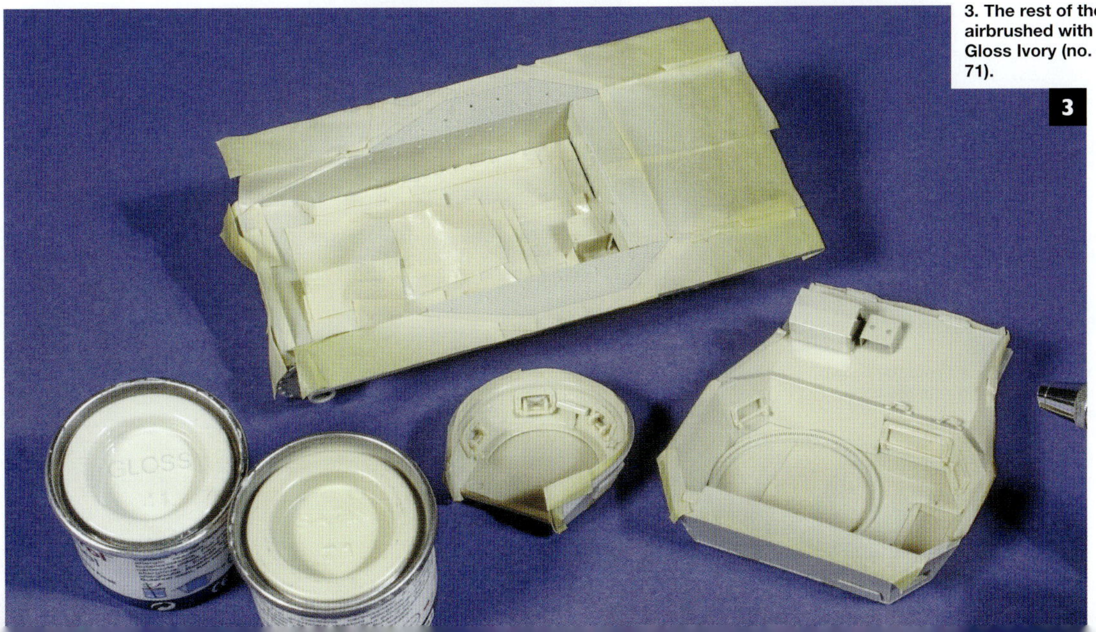

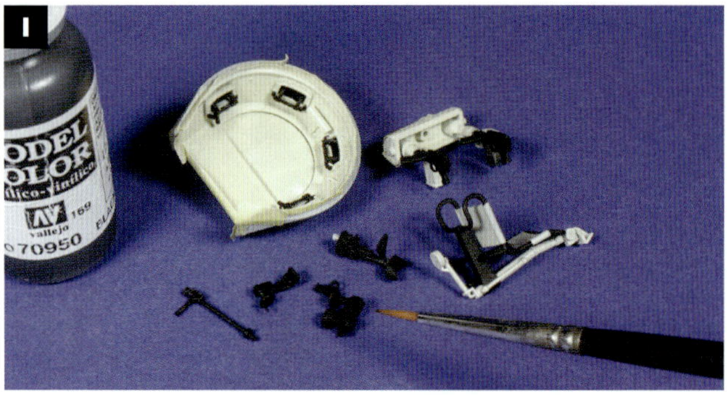

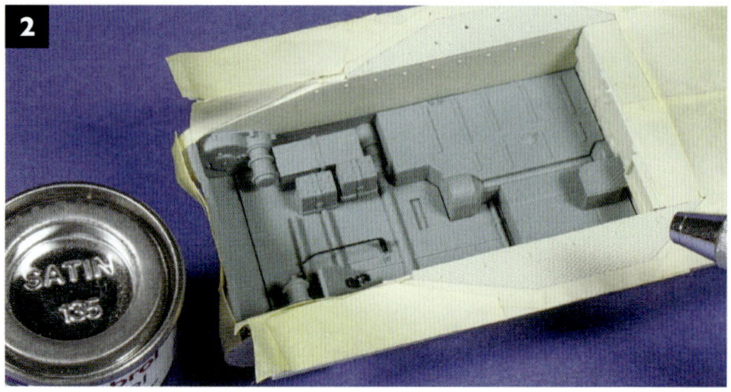

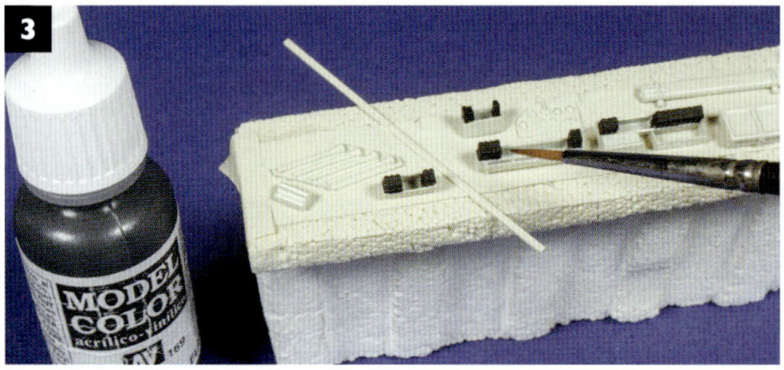

1. All movable parts were hand-painted with Vallejo Black (no. 950).

2. Because of the different finishes of the paints used (matt, satin, gloss), the entire interior was given a coat of Humbrol Satin Varnish (no. 135) to make it look uniform.

3. Small internal fittings were airbrushed separately. Details were hand-painted with Vallejo acrylics. As with the rest of the interior, all separately painted internal fittings were given a coat of Humbrol Satin Varnish (no. 135) to make everything look uniform.

4. The lower hull interior with the basic paints on.

5. First off, the floor and transmission received some dry-brushing with the base color mixed with some Humbrol Matt White (no. 34).

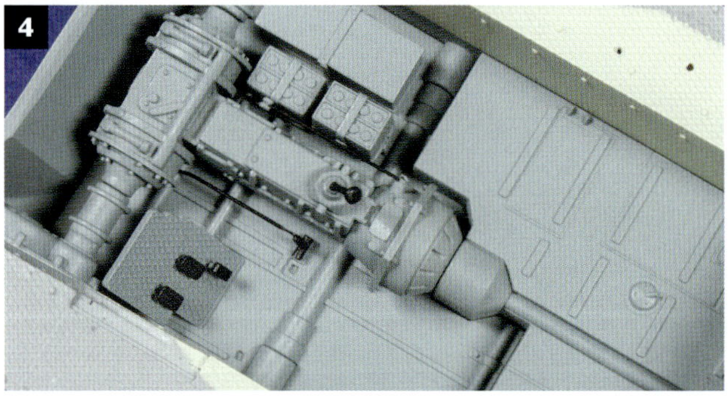

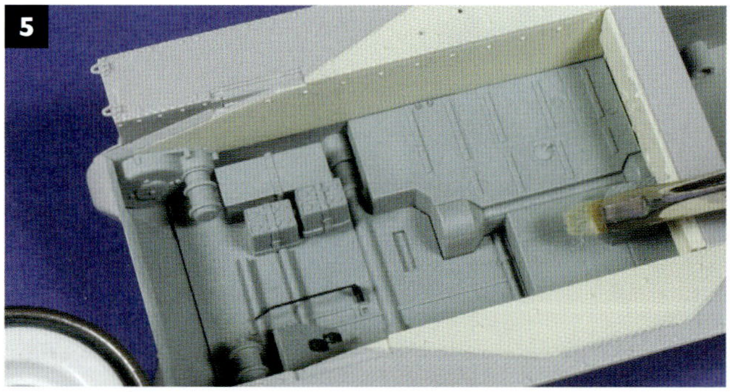

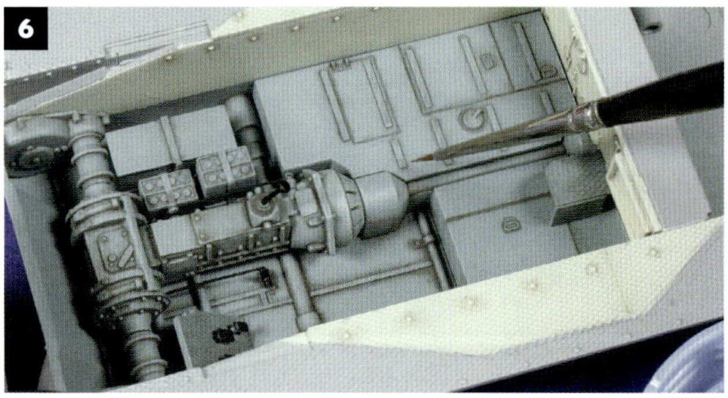

6. Next, all details were outlined with a mixture of Humbrol Brown Bess (no. 170) and Black (no. 33) to create a sense of depth.

7. Then a second dry-brush run was carried out to tidy up any unwanted effects of the outlining stage and to freshen up the colors.

8. The rest of the interior was also outlined with the Brown Bess and Black mixture, and dry-brushed with the base color with some Matt White added.

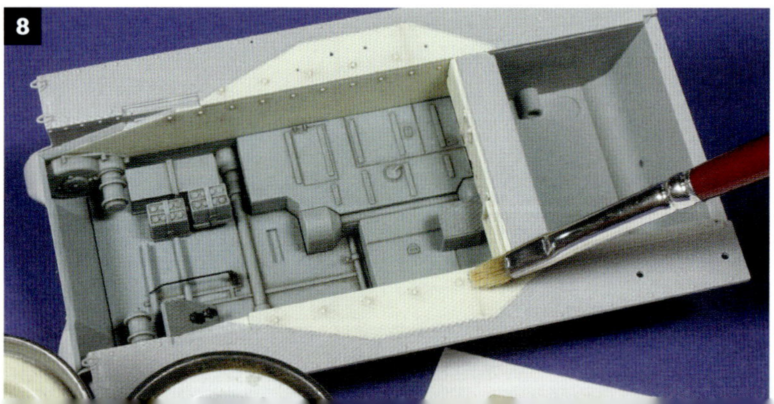

Above. Various oil paint colors were used to weather the floor and lower areas and add dirt, paint chippings and rust effects. The colors used were Lamp Black, Van Dyke Brown, Raw Umber, Burnt Umber and Gold Ochre.

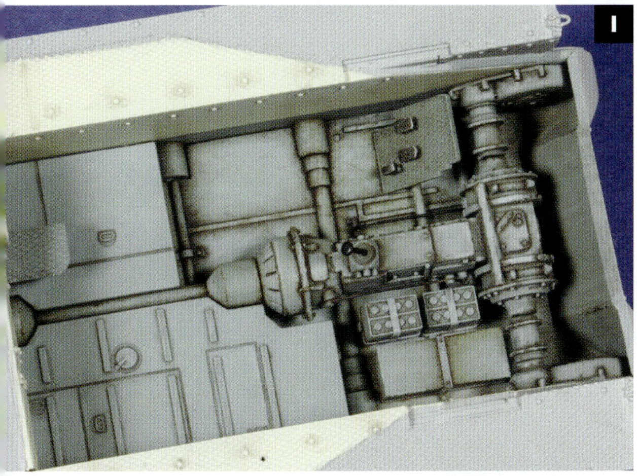

1. The lower hull interior with part of the weathering finished. The rest of the floor was finished in a similar way. Burnt Sienna was used as an extra color.

2. Dust was added to the floor with a mixture of Raw Umber and Naples Yellow oil paint. The small internal fittings have been added.

3–5. Views of the lower hull and transmission. Oil paints were used extensively for the weathering.

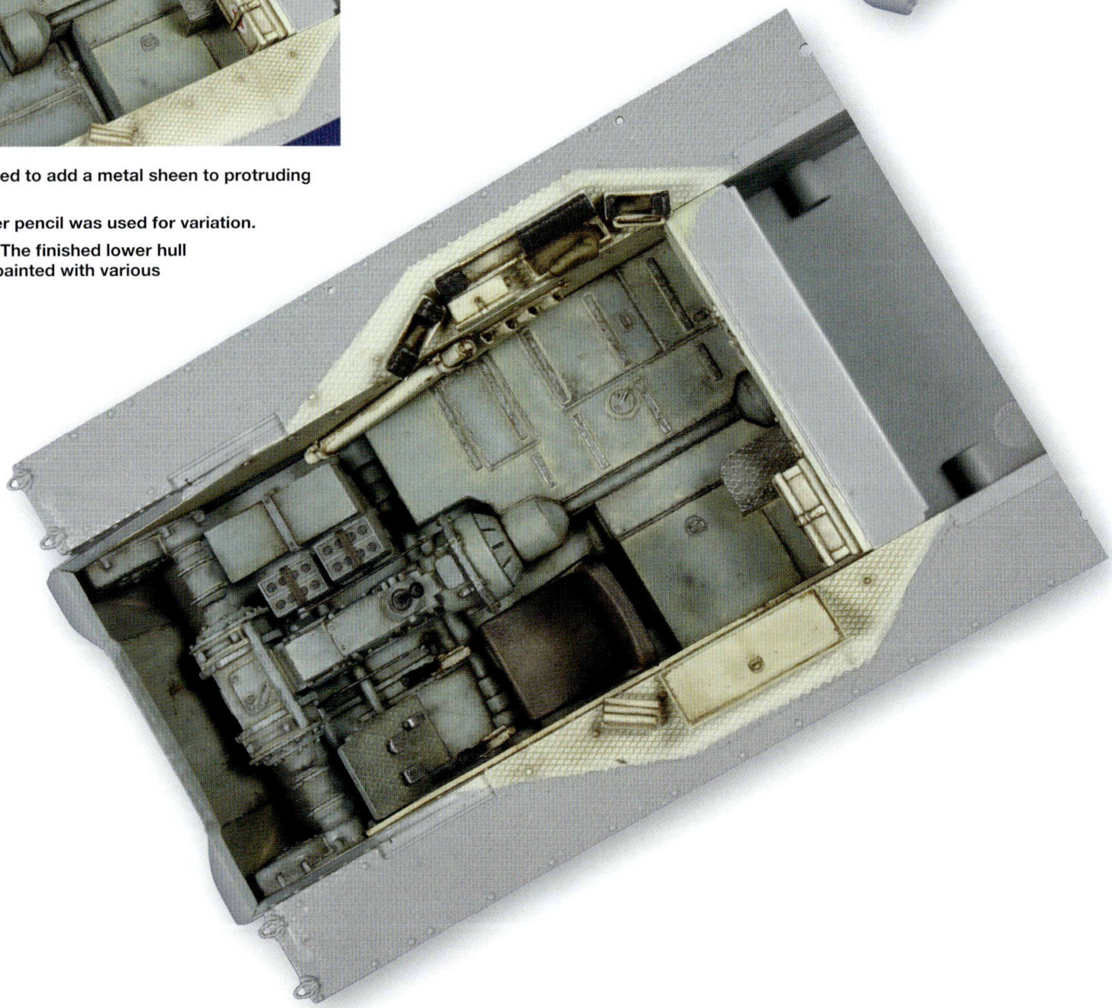

1. A lead pencil was used to add a metal sheen to protruding features and edges.

2. A Karismacolor Silver pencil was used for variation.

Above right, and right. The finished lower hull interior. The seat was painted with various Vallejo colors.

Right, and below. The finished dashboard, front and rear. The tape holds the dials in place.

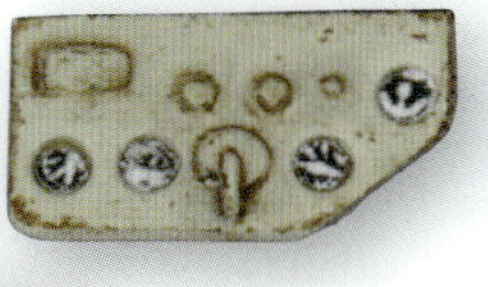

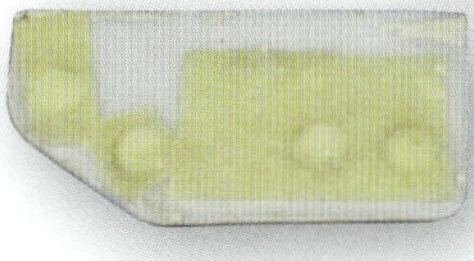

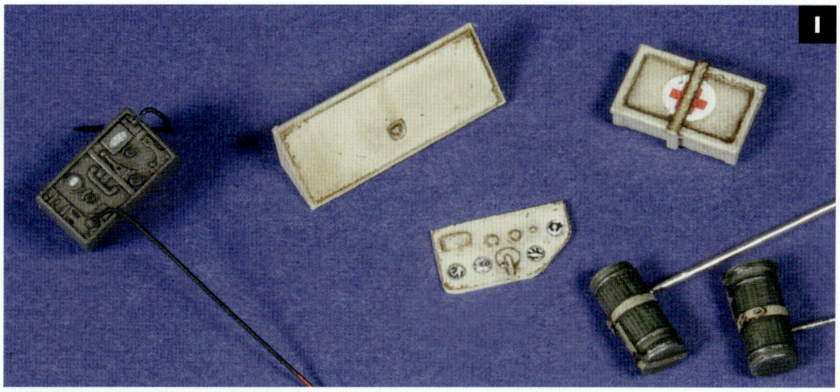

1. Some of the internal fittings ready for installation. The Red Cross is a VP dry transfer.

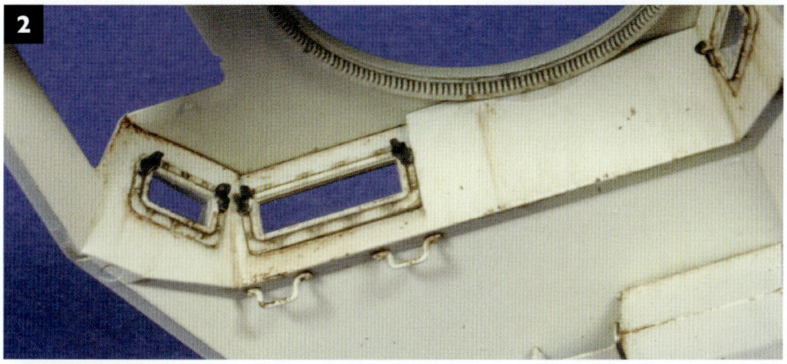

2. The upper hull interior. Note the two handles made from copper wire. Again, oil paints were used extensively for weathering.

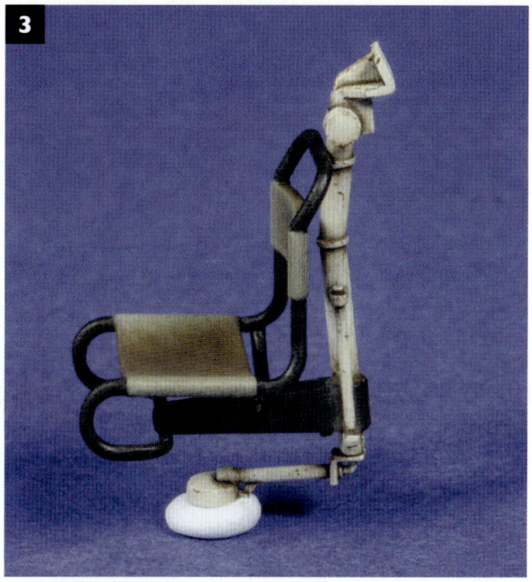

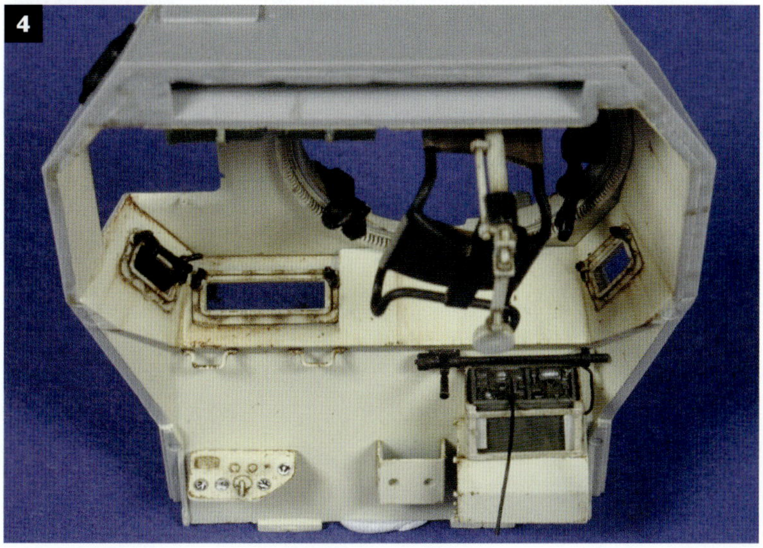

3. The commander's seat ready for installation. The canvas was painted with Vallejo acrylics.

4. The upper hull interior with internal fittings added.

5. The machine-gun assembly seen from the inside.

6. The turret interior.

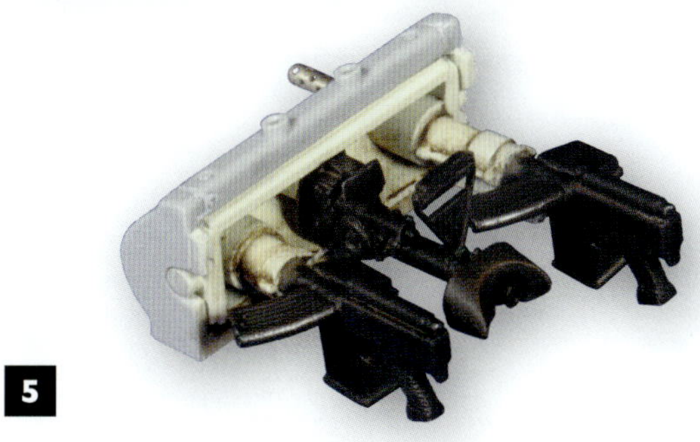

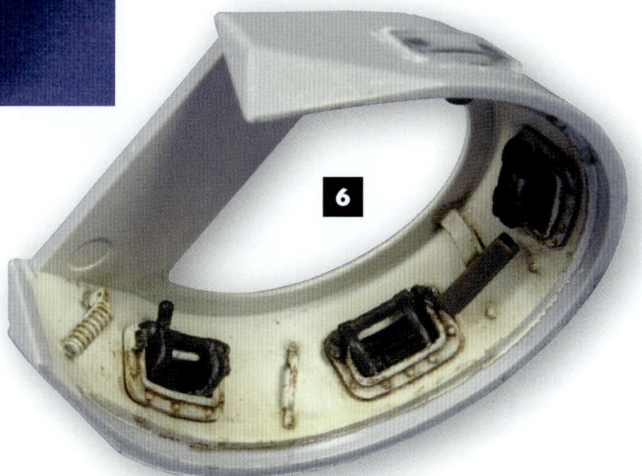

Painting

THE EXTERIOR

After masking off the interior, a coat of Humbrol Matt Tank Grey (no. 67) was airbrushed on to serve as a base color. This was followed by several thin layers of Matt Brown Yellow (no. 94), leaving the original gray base color visible in certain areas that would be more prone to use and wear. The final airbrush work consisted of a layer of Humbrol Satin Varnish (no. 135).

To get more definition of the gray base color and suggest more wear of the sand-colored camouflage overspray, I dry-brushed various areas and details where the paint would deteriorate faster due to use by the crew and weather conditions. Using the dry-brush technique gives you a lot of control over how and where you want the gray base color to appear.

For those who are not familiar with this technique:

1. Take some of the paint gathered at the bottom of an "unstirred" jar of paint. It's important not to stir the paint for dry-brushing.
2. Place the paint on a piece of card and let it settle for a few moments so the oil is soaked up by the card.
3. Use a clean, dry brush (preferably wide; the size depends on the area you are working on) and dip it in the paint.
4. Wipe the brush on a piece of kitchen paper or a cloth to remove most of the paint.
5. Gently move the brush over the model and you'll see a subtle effect of paint appearing.

Gradually building up the effect results in a much more realistic finish. Don't rush it!

Next, as before with the interior, all details were outlined with a diluted mix of Humbrol Matt Black (no. 33) and Matt Brown Bess (no. 170) to create a sense of depth. To blend the paint and clean up any unwanted effects, I always keep a larger, clean, moist brush at hand.

With the dry-brushing technique you get a softer, more general effect. To further bring out the gray base color, I then started adding chipped-paint effects with a fine-pointed brush. The key principles to successful chipped-paint effects are working to scale, composition and variation – in other words, don't make the chippings too big, put them in logical places, keep them interesting to look at and don't use the same sort of chippings over the entire model. If you do, the model will look very boring and unrealistic. To get this stage right it can take quite some time, but it is worth it in the end. If not done well, it can ruin an otherwise good-looking model.

To give the chippings a more 3D effect, you can add highlights, or sometimes even shadings. Even more so than with adding regular chips, it is important to keep the highlights very controlled and in scale. The highlights should be finer than the actual chippings. Overdone highlights will just make the chips look unrealistic instead of giving them a 3D effect. Adding highlights to all chippings doesn't look good either. A well-balanced mix works best.

On the lower hull, I used Humbrol Matt Brown Yellow (no. 94) for adding the highlights. Once I turned to the upper hull, though, I switched to Naples Yellow oil paint as I felt it gave better results. Furthermore, it was also used to add scuff marks and highlights to certain details. As per the inside, dirt and rust effects were created with various oil paints. In this instance, I used Raw Umber, Burnt Umber, Burnt Sienna and Sepia. Humbrol Matt Brown Yellow (no. 94) was in turn used to create the dust effects all over the outside hull.

Although I'm used to using Humbrol and oil paints to recreate rusty

1 & 2. Before getting out the airbrush, the interior was masked off. Humbrol Matt Tank Grey (no. 67) was used for the base coat.

3. This was followed by an overspray of Matt Brown Yellow (no. 94). In areas where the paint would be more subject to wear, the gray was left more visible.

exhausts, I got hold of Lifecolor's acrylics Rust and Dust set. Besides two dust colors the set contains four rust colors ranging from a dark brown to an ochre yellow color. In fact, they look very similar to the colors I normally use. Hence, I went about this in the same way I would usually do, which is to start with the darkest color first and then put on consecutive layers finishing with the brightest color. When first putting on the layers, I tried to keep varying the general tone of the mufflers. It was only in the later stages that I started going back and forth between the different colors to try to get a more defined result. The trick to working with acrylics is to build them up gradually and keep the paint thin. To finish off, a bit of Mig Productions Black Smoke (no. 23) is used to simulate soot in the exhaust pipe.

The mesh covers for the exhausts were aged by giving them the oil paint treatment.

To bring out the antenna holder on the right fender, I decided to give it an all gray color. When working on a model, I often use acrylics to base coat or paint small details or accessories as this enables me to proceed quickly to the next stage. To give the antenna holder a bit of a different shade of gray to the overall basecoat gray on the model, I hand-painted it with Puravest Dunkelgrau. As it is made of wood, I decided to chip the base color and simulate bare wood using Lifecolor Tropical Tan 2. In one respect, chipping with acrylics is more difficult than with Humbrol or oil paints as it dries faster and there is no time to make corrections. However, in this case I could easily correct any unwanted effects by just painting them over with the Dunkelgrau base color.

It's always nice to add a bit of color and thus further interest to a model. Here I used some Red Primer on the rim of the opening in the hull to get access to the transmission. Humbrol Matt Scarlet (no. 60) toned down with some Matt Brown Bess (no. 170) works very well. This combination was also used sparingly on other details, like the edges of vision ports, handles on the hatches, etc.

The transmission itself received some further oil paint weathering with Raw Umber chippings and Lamp Black grease stains.

The machine guns in the turret received a basecoat of Vallejo Black (no. 950), after which they were gently dry-brushed with Vallejo SS Cam. Black Brown (no. 822)[1]. Using a lead pencil, the edges were then accentuated to create the illusion of metal. Other edges and areas on the model which would get rubbed frequently due to use or weather conditions, and would thus buff up, were given the same treatment.

---

1 Vallejo has changed the name of this color to German Cam. Black Brown (no. 822). Also, the tone of the color itself is darker than the original offering.

4

5

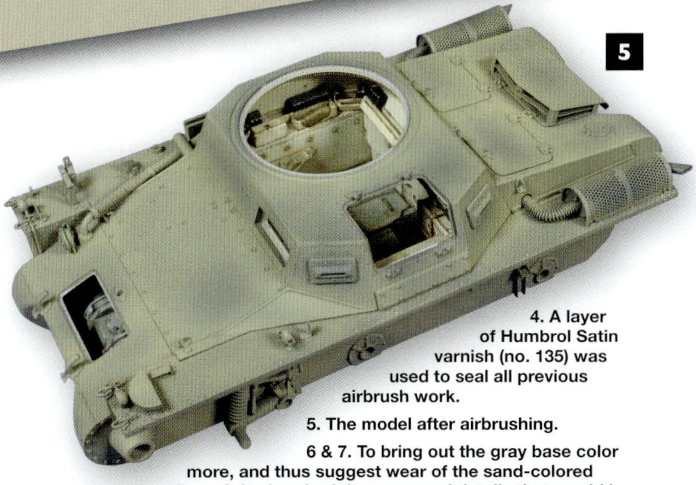

4. A layer of Humbrol Satin varnish (no. 135) was used to seal all previous airbrush work.

5. The model after airbrushing.

6 & 7. To bring out the gray base color more, and thus suggest wear of the sand-colored camouflage, I dry-brushed the areas and details that would be more affected by crew use and weather conditions. Dry-brushing is a great technique, and it needs to be built up gradually to get the best results.

6

7

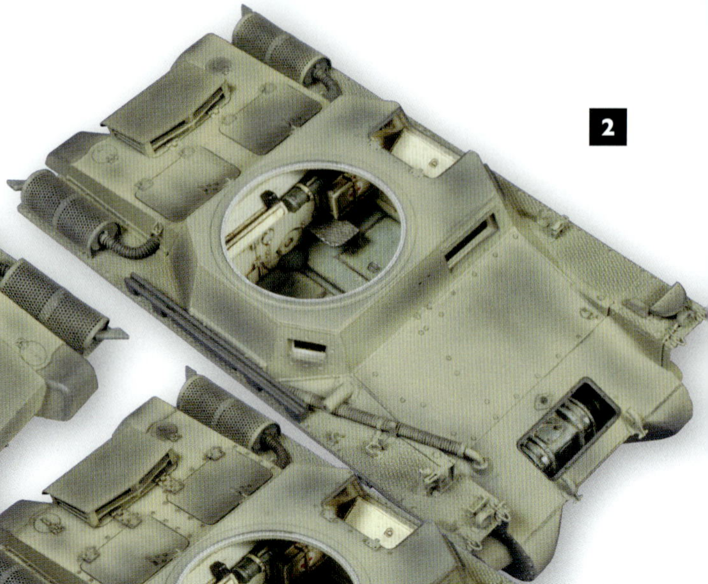

1 & 2. The model after dry-brushing with Humbrol Tank Grey (no. 67).

4. The model after outlining with the Brown Bess and Matt Black mixture.

3. As before with the interior all details were outlined with a Humbrol Matt Brown Bess (no. 170) and Matt Black (no. 33) mixture to create depth.

5. Next, chipped-paint effects and scratch marks were created with a fine brush and the gray base color. This process will take a considerable amount of time, but needs to be done carefully as it means a lot in determining the final look of the model.

6. The rear deck after adding chipped-paint effects and scratch marks with the gray base color.

7. To create a 3D effect on the chipping, random chips were highlighted by adding light-colored chip marks. On the lower hull, I used Humbrol Matt Brown Yellow (no. 94).

8. Matt Brown Yellow was also used to create dust effects on the outside hull.

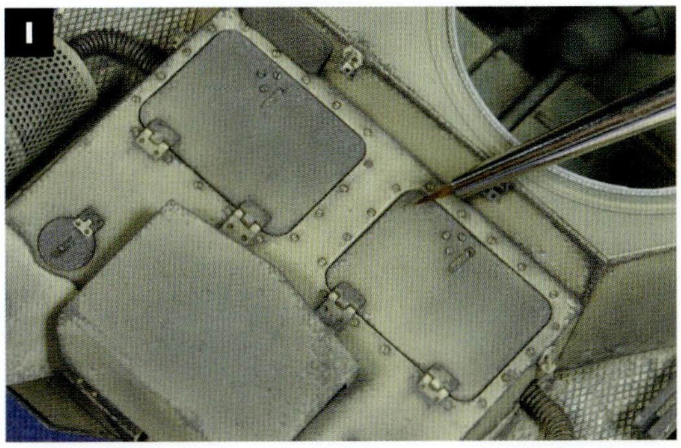

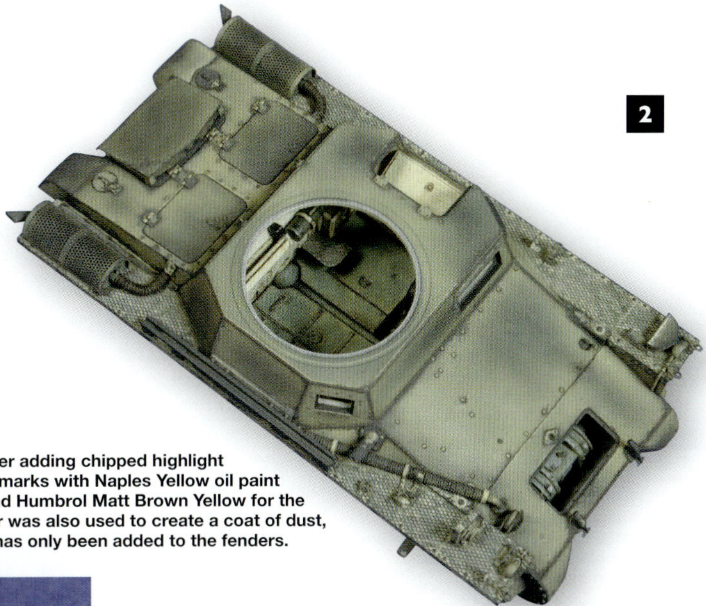

1. On the upper hull, I switched to Naples Yellow oil paint to create the highlight chipping, scratch marks etc. as I felt this gave better results than the Humbrol Matt Brown Yellow.

2 & 3. The model after adding chipped highlight effects and scratch marks with Naples Yellow oil paint for the upper hull and Humbrol Matt Brown Yellow for the lower hull. The latter was also used to create a coat of dust, which in this stage has only been added to the fenders.

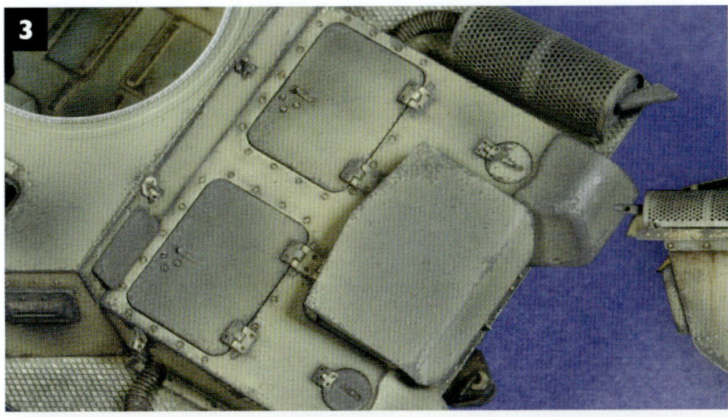

4. Rust and dirt streaks were created with Raw Umber and Burnt Umber oil paint.

5. For variation, some Burnt Sienna was also used.

7. A mixture of Humbrol Matt Brown Bess (no. 170) and Matt Scarlet (no. 60) was used to recreate a Red Primer color.

6. Localized and controlled filters with Raw Umber oil paint were added to vary the Yellow base color. Burnt Umber oil paint can also be used for variation.

8. The same color combination was used sparingly to add little touches of Red Primer in selected places.

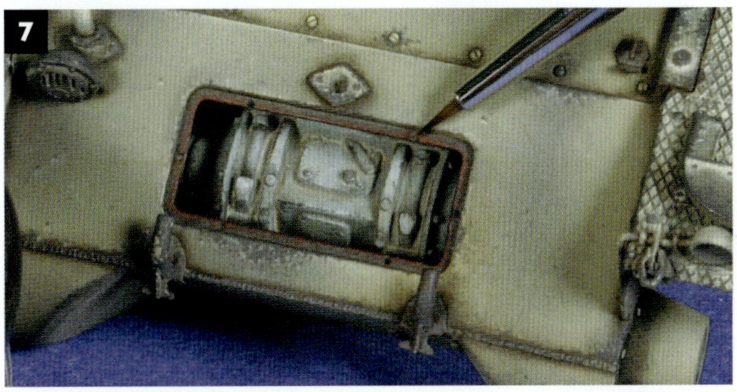

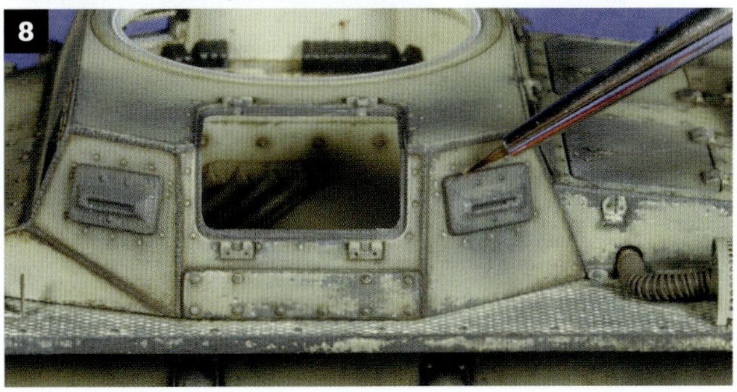

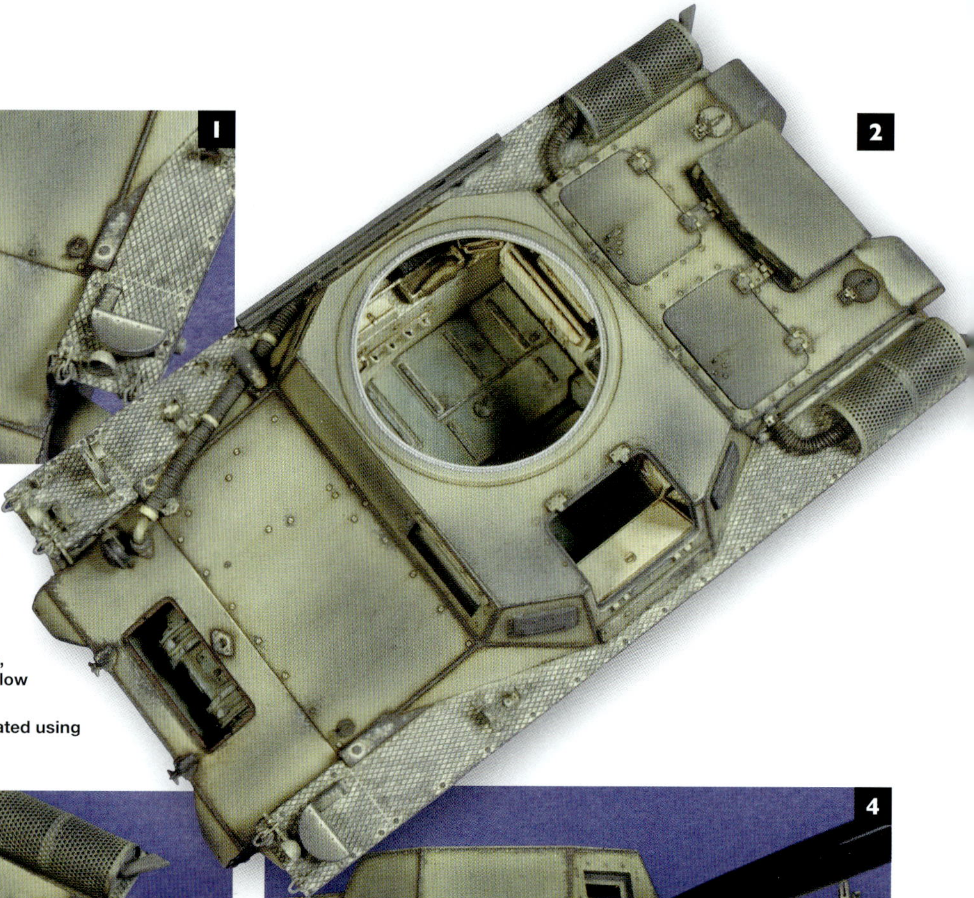

1 & 2. The model after adding rust and dirt streaks with Raw Umber and Burnt Umber oil paint and adding localized and controlled filters, mainly with Raw Umber oil paint, to vary the Yellow base color. Selected Red Primer touches have been added as well.

3. The rear deck after adding rust and dirt streaks with Raw Umber and Burnt Umber oil paint and adding localized and controlled filters, mainly with Raw Umber oil paint, to vary the Yellow base color.

4. Dark shadows, grease and oil spills were created using Sepia oil paint.

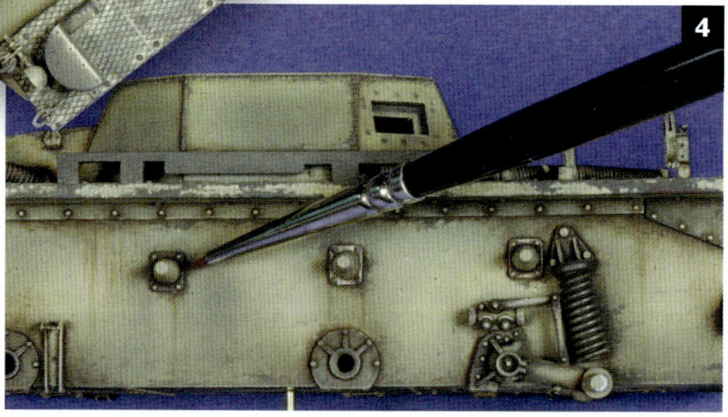

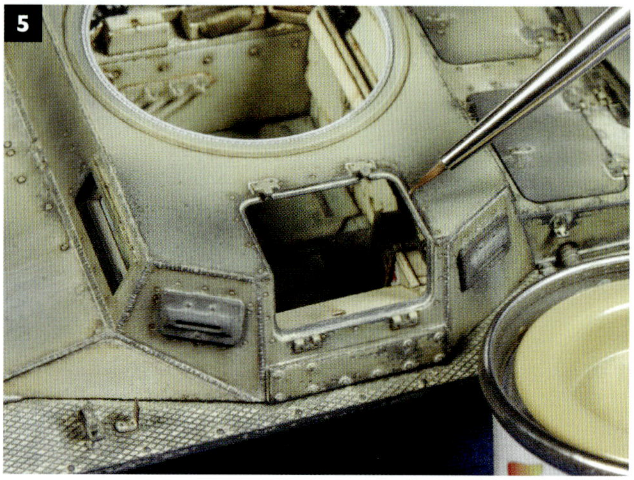

5 & 6. As on the fenders, the rest of the hull was dusted with filters and washes of Humbrol Matt Dark Yellow (no. 94).

7. The rear deck after adding dust with filters and washes of Humbrol Matt Dark Yellow (no. 94).

8. The lower hull received the same dust treatment as the rest of the model.

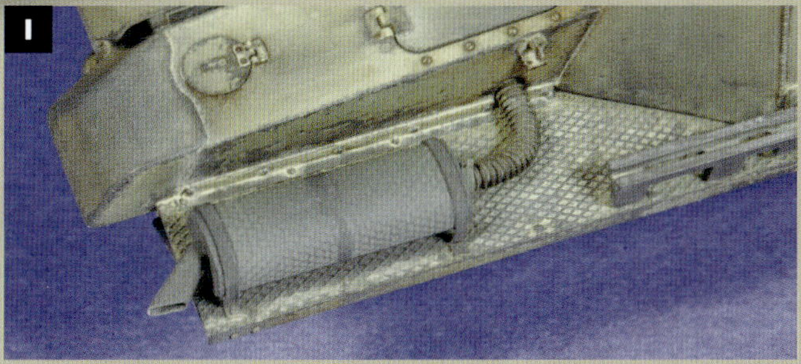

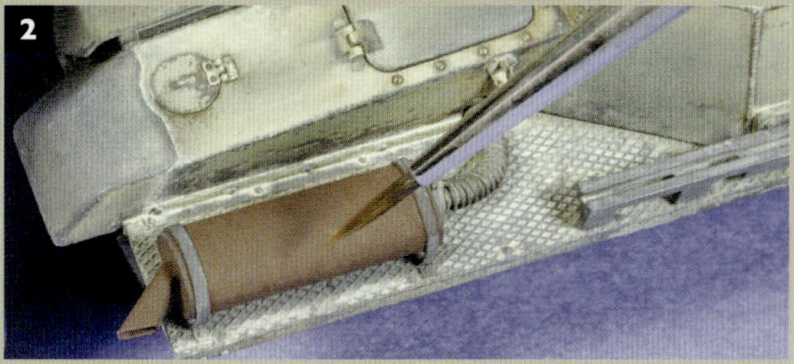

1. The exhaust in its original base coat.

2. As always when painting rusty exhausts, I started with the darkest color first. Rust Dark Shadow, the first color of the Lifecolor Rust and Dust set, is added.

3. This is followed by Rust Base color.

4. Next comes Rust Light Shadow 1.

5. Until this point, I tried to keep varying the general tone of the mufflers. Only when adding Rust Light Shadow 2, I started going back and forth between the different colors to try and get a more defined result. The trick here is to build the colors up gradually and keep the paint thin.

6 & 7. The mesh covers were rusted up with Raw Umber, Burnt Umber and Burnt Sienna oil paints.

8. Finally, some Mig Productions Black Smoke pigment (no. P023) was added to simulate soot.

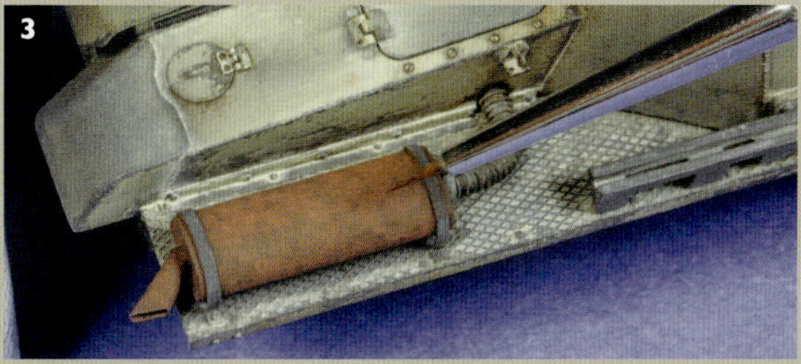

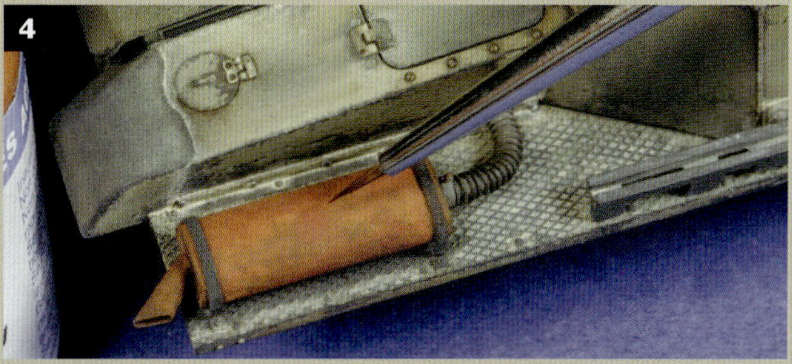

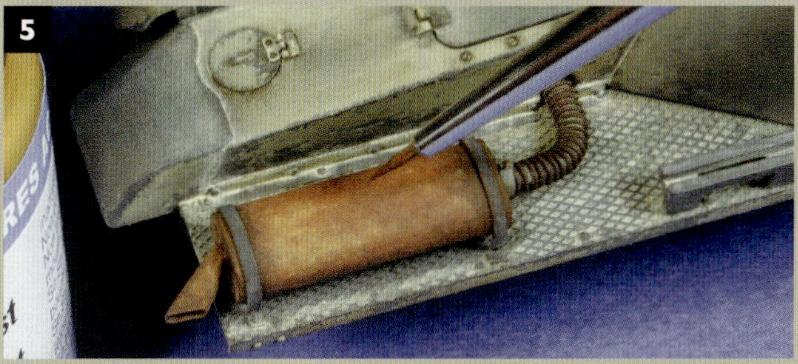

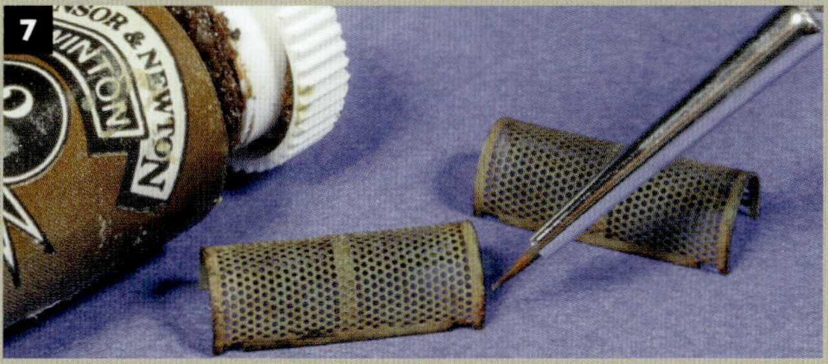

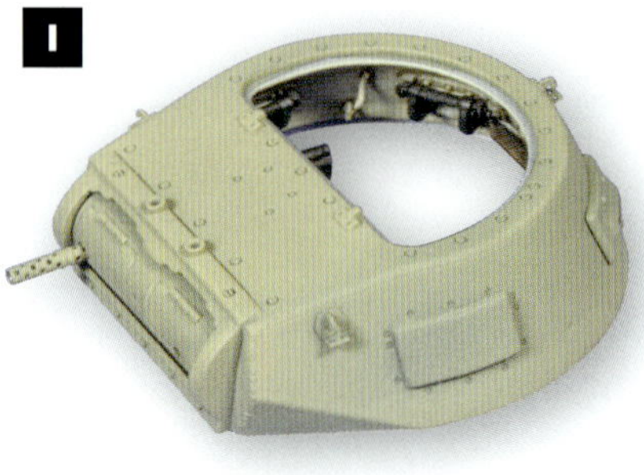

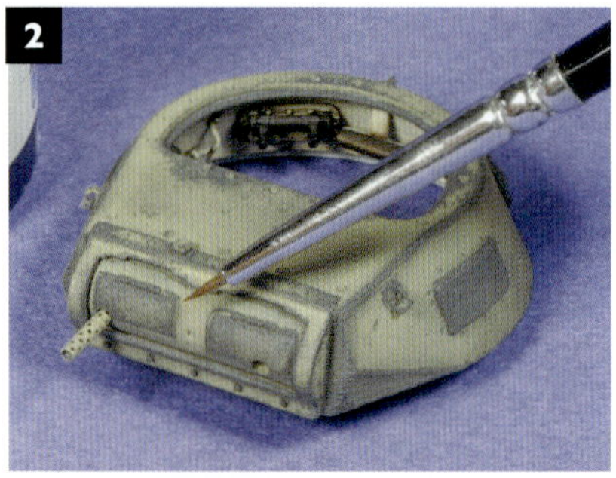

1. The turret with the basic paint on.

2. With a fine brush and Humbrol Matt Tank Grey (no. 67), chipped-paint effects and scratch marks were added.

3. With a wider brush, some careful dry-brushing was carried out, creating some softer effects of the base color regaining ground.

4. The turret after the dry-brushing and chipping stages with Humbrol Matt Tank Grey (no. 67).

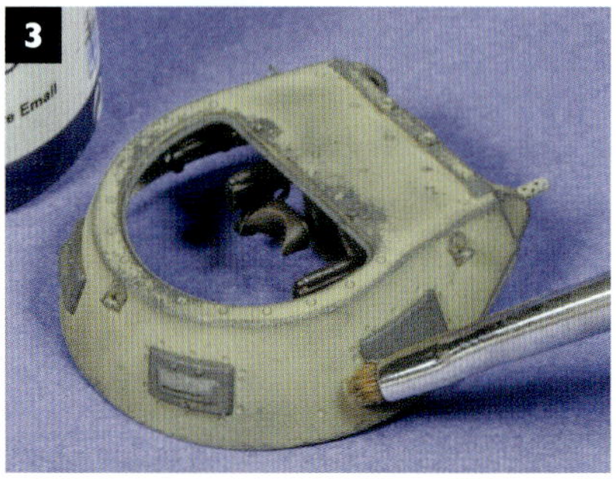

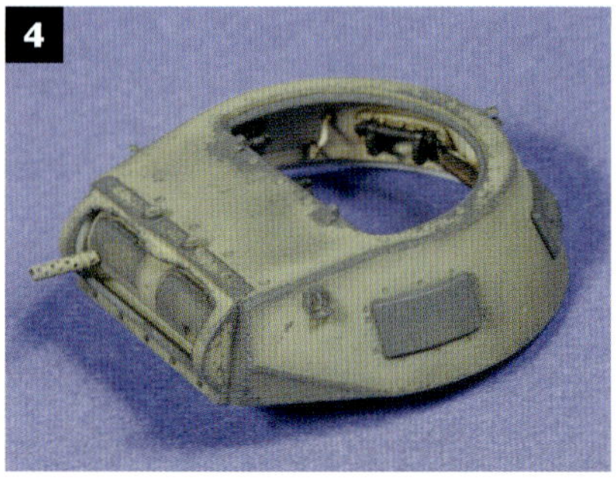

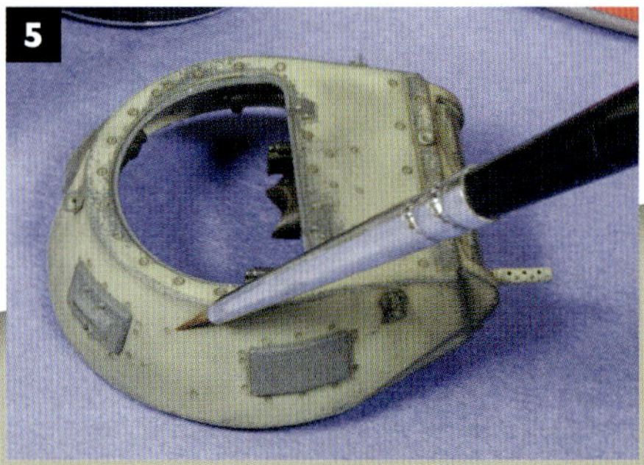

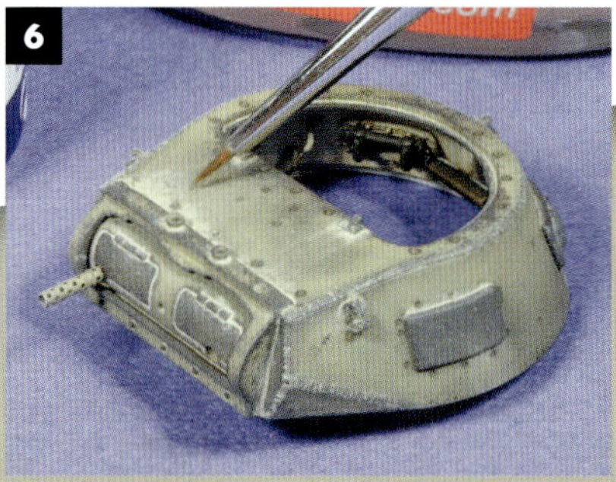

5. All bolts and details were then outlined with the Humbrol Matt Brown Bess (no. 170) and Matt Black (no. 33) mixture to create depth.

6. Dust was added with washes and filters using Humbrol Matt Dark Yellow (no. 94).

7. The turret after adding dust with washes and filters using Humbrol Matt Dark Yellow (no. 94).

8. Localized and controlled filters with Raw Umber oil paint are added to vary the Yellow base color.

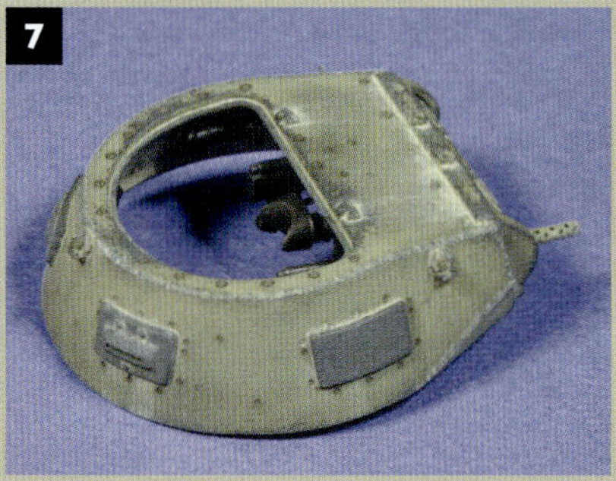

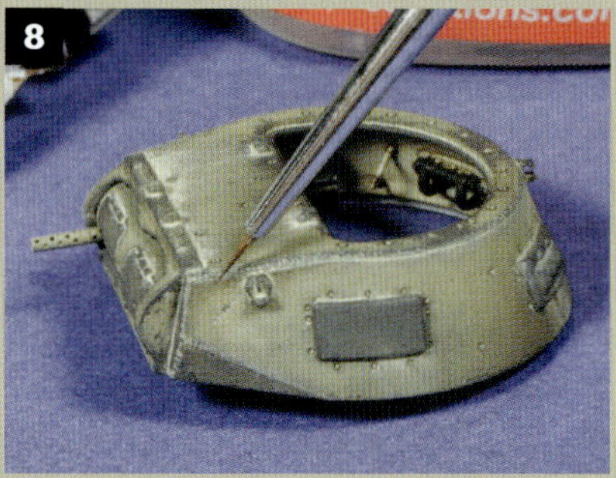

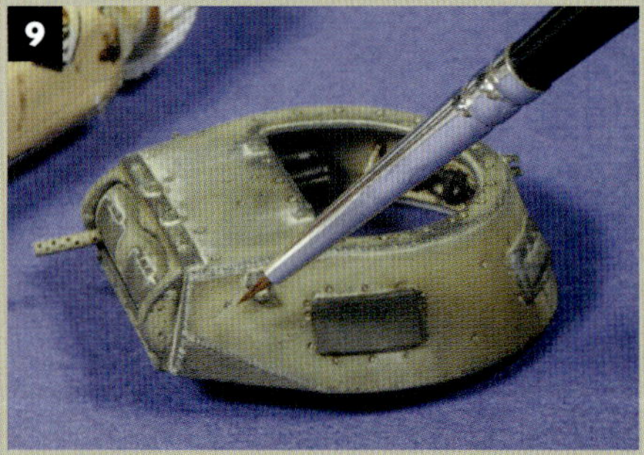

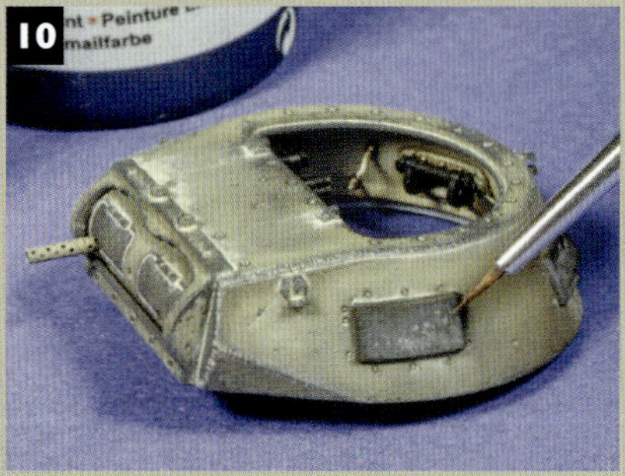

9. Naples Yellow oil paint was used to add highlights to the chipping and edges, thus creating a 3D effect.

10. Fading yellow camouflage color on the vision ports was simulated with a combination of adding Lifecolor Sandgrau (no. UA202) and again chipping it with Humbrol Matt Tank Grey (no. 67).

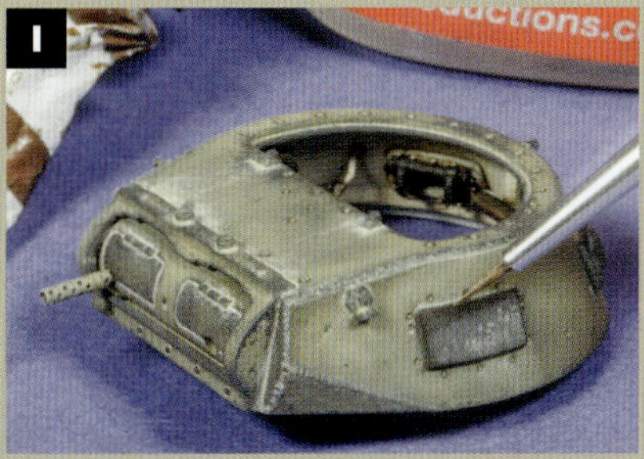

1. More weathering effects were added with Raw Umber oil paint.

2. The turret with most of the weathering done.

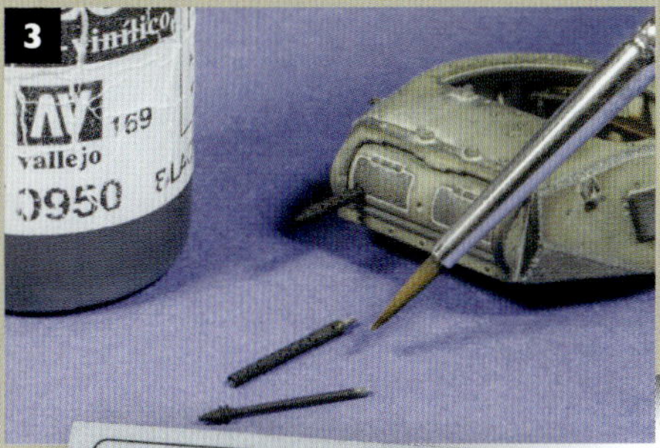

3. The machine-gun barrels were base-coated with Vallejo Black (no. 950).

4. They were then lightly dry-brushed with Vallejo SS Cam. Black Brown (no. 822).

Markings

Only a few markings were needed on this model. As usual, I went for dry transfers as they are easy to add, don't have a carrier film and are easy to remove in case this should be necessary.

The typical DAK vehicles' palm tree symbol was taken from an Archer sheet, while the numbers were taken from an old VP offering. Once added by gently rubbing them on the model with a pencil, the bright white color was toned down by subtly dry-brushing them with some Raw Umber oil paint.

Above. An old Verlinden Productions dry transfer sheet was used to source the numbers on the turret.

5. The numbers have been added. As usual, they stand out too much as they are too bright.

6. To blend them with the rest of the model, they were gently dry-brushed with some Raw Umber oil paint.

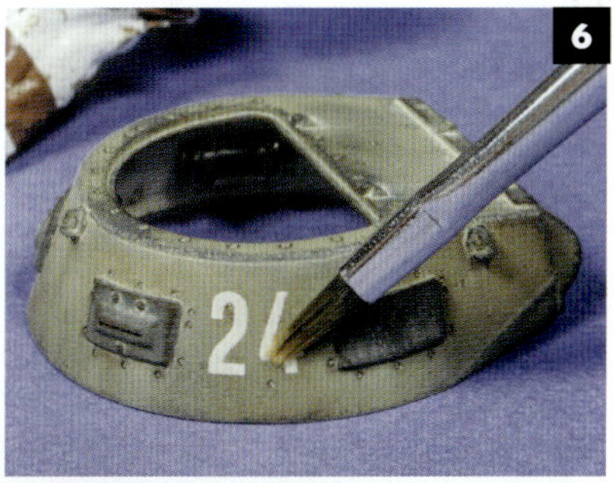

7. The turret with the numbers added and weathered. Finally, using a lead pencil, some edges were highlighted to simulate bare metal.

1

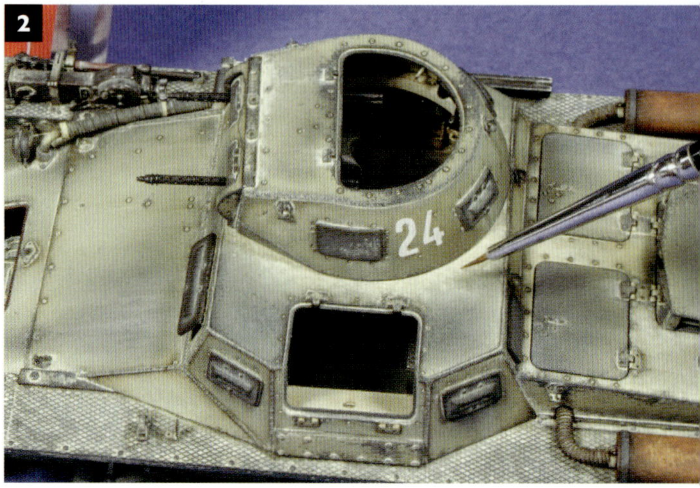

2

3

1. Some final dusting was done once the turret was added.

2. For variation, some Matt White was mixed into the Dark Yellow.

3. The transmission was greased up with some Lamp Black oil paint.

4. In turn, Raw Umber was used to add some final weathering on the transmission.

5 & 6. A lead pencil was used to buff up edges and other areas to create the illusion of metal.

7. Lifecolor Tropical Tan 2 was then used for chipping to represent bare wood.

4

5

6

7

TRACKS AND WHEELS

After base-coating the tracks with a mixture of Tamiya Flat Black (no. XF-1) and Red Brown (no. XF-64), they received several washes with Humbrol Matt Brown Yellow (no. 94) to give them the same dusty appearance as the rest of the model. Although Modelkasten tracks are great, they are fragile during the painting and final assembly stages as the pins that are used to put them together are quite short and can break off very easily – especially when paint builds up when adding the washes. The best option to repair them when this happens is to drill out the plastic pin and insert a copper one instead. It's quite easy to do, but can become frustrating if it needs doing a bit too often. Next, the color of the tracks themselves was brought back by dry-brushing them with Vallejo Cam. Black Brown (no. 822). As a final touch, all running surfaces, inside and out, were metalized by scribing them with a lead pencil.

The wheels and suspension were painted in the same way as the rest of the model. A mixture of Vallejo Black (no. 950) and Flat Flesh (no. 955) was used to base-coat the rubber tires. Putting the wheels on a toothpick makes it easy to spin them round, and, using a medium-sized brush, it then doesn't take long to paint all the rubber parts. As with the rest of the model, the wheels then received further weathering with various oil paints to add dirt and grease. After dusting with Humbrol Matt Brown Yellow (no. 94), the suspension had some of the lost details retouched with the gray base color. Also, the running surfaces of the rubber tires were made to look dust free by painting them a second time with the Vallejo mixture. Finally, a lead pencil was used to add some bare metal touches in selected places.

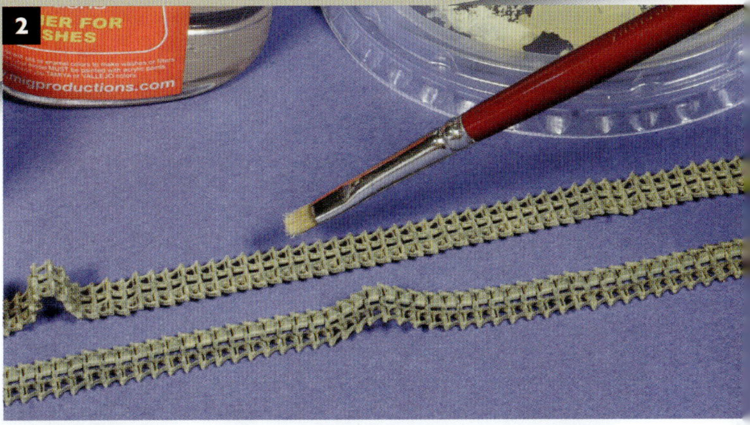

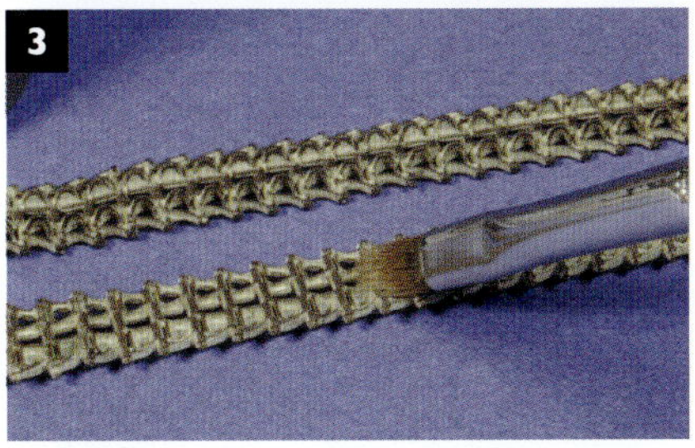

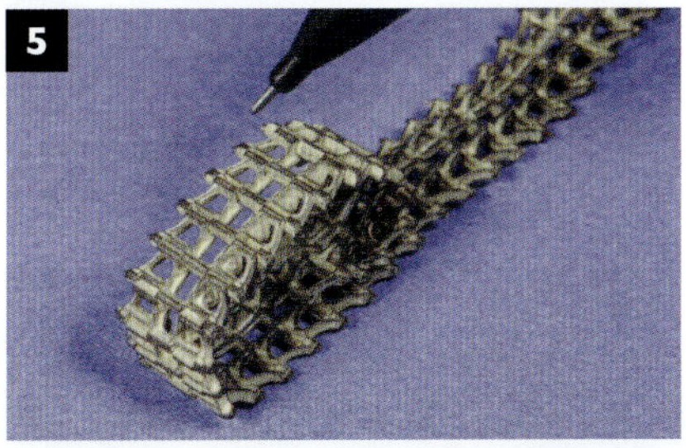

1. The tracks were airbrushed with Tamiya Flat Black (no. XF-1) mixed with some Red Brown (no. XF-64).

2. To reproduce the same dust as on the rest of the model, the tracks then received a heavy wash with Humbrol Matt Brown Yellow (no. 94).

3. Vallejo German Camouflage Black Brown (no. 822) was dry-brushed on all surfaces to bring out the metal structure again.

4. Lead pencils in various sizes were used to burnish up the inner running surfaces of the tracks.

5. The outside edges of the running surfaces got the same treatment.

1. The wheels received the same treatment as the rest of the model. Here, a fine brush and Humbrol Matt Tank Grey (no. 67) were used to add chip marks and scratches to the yellow camouflage color.

2. Next, all rubber parts were base-coated with a mixture of Vallejo Black (no. 950) and Flat Flesh (no. 955). The suspension arms were left unglued to gain access to the wheels and facilitate the painting.

3. Various oil paint colors (Raw Umber, Burnt Umber, Burnt Sienna and Sepia) were used to add washes and filters imitating grease, dirt and rust.

4. Pinpoint washing with a fine brush and Humbrol Matt Brown Yellow (no. 94) resulted in a dusty look.

5. Any detail lost or blurred because of the dusting was brought back with the gray base color.

1. Sometimes it's easy to use a different kind of paint for the same purpose.

2. After the dusting, the running surfaces of the wheels are painted with the Vallejo Black and Flat Flesh mixture again to make them dust free.

3. Edges received a metal sheen by rubbing them with a lead pencil.

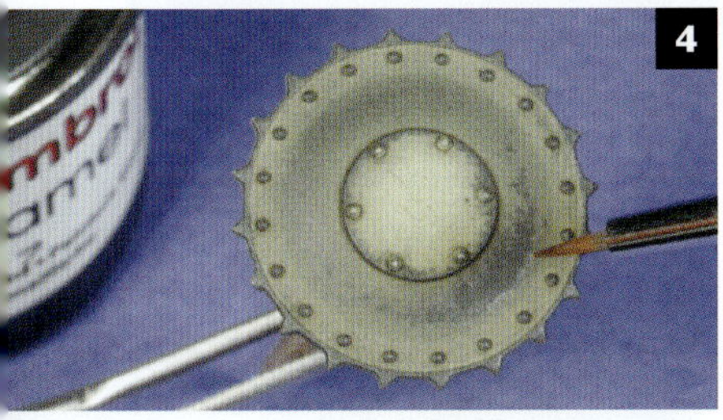

4. One of the drive sprockets getting the chipped-paint treatment.

5. Filters and washes with various oil paints (Raw Umber, Burnt Umber, Burnt Sienna and Sepia) were used to add grease, dirt and rust.

6. Dust was recreated by careful pinpoint washing with Humbrol Matt Brown Yellow (no. 94).

7. More rust tones were added with oil paints.

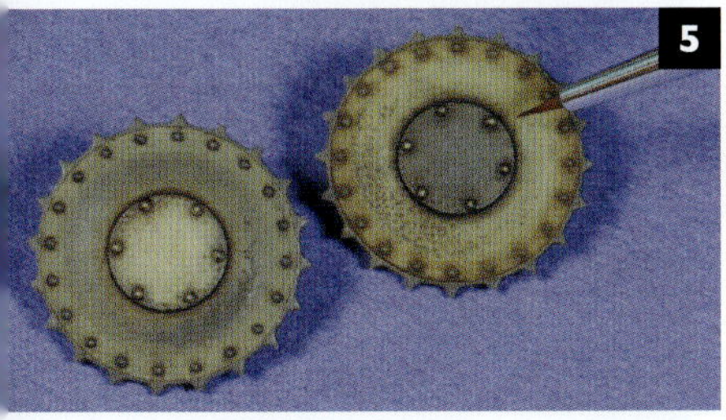

ACCESSORIES

All tools were painted with Vallejo colors and weathered with oils and/or Humbrol paints. They were added to the model after painting.

Archer produces a dry-transfer sheet with three different types of German fire-extinguisher placards. As I couldn't find any reference material as to which placard I should use for the fire extinguisher provided in the kit, I contacted Mr Vondracek at Archer Transfers via e-mail. He told me that there is no reference available as to exactly which placard would be "correct" for this type of extinguisher, but that any of the placards on the sheet can be used for any period during Word War II. After I added the placard of my choice, its brightness was toned down by adding a dusty filter with Humbrol Matt Brown Yellow (no. 94).

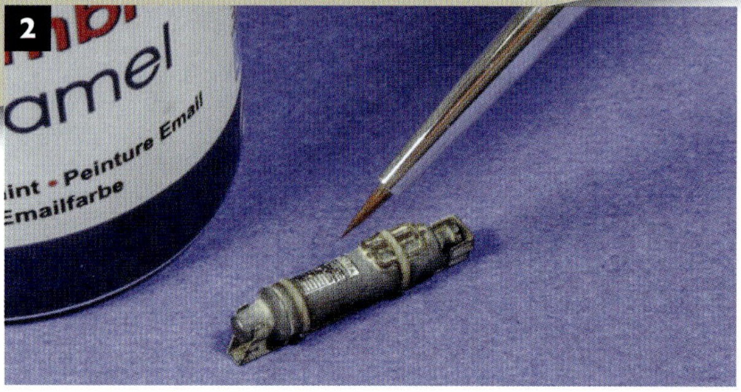

1. Archer produces a set of dry transfers to embellish fire extinguishers. Three options are given.

2. To tone down the brightness of the transfer, I added a dusty filter with Humbrol Matt Brown Yellow (no. 94).

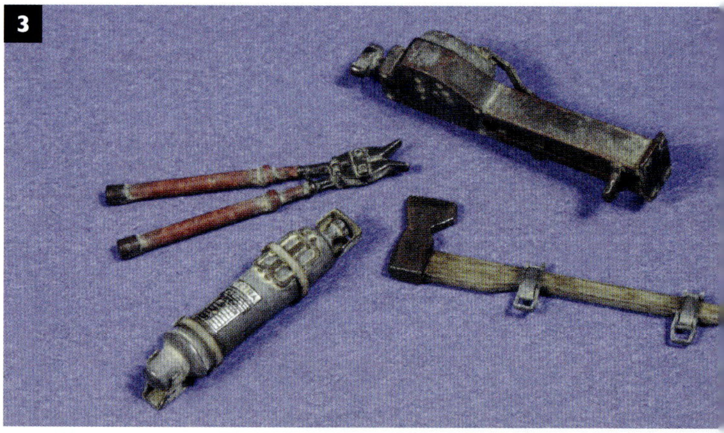

3. Some of the equipment carried on the Panzer I. The movable 1/48 tool clamps were added to the axe and then the whole assembly was mounted on the fenders.

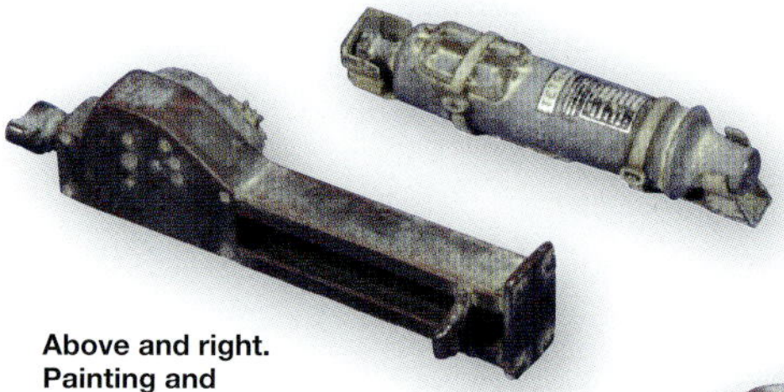

Above and right. Painting and weathering the jack was done with Vallejo paints, while Humbrol paint was used for the dust.

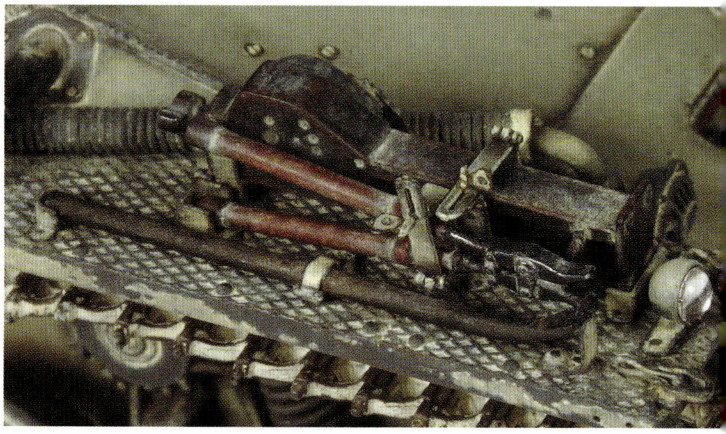

Left and above. The front fenders in close-up. The tools and equipment are fun to paint and add color and interest to a model.

Above. The inside of the hatches remains in the original outside gray color and adds a nice contrast to the sand-colored camouflage.

Above. A side view of the finished model. Note the different shades of gray on different features like the side of the fenders, inside hatches, fire extinguisher, etc. Varying the tones makes the model more interesting.

Right. A side view of the turret. The leather padding on the turret hatch was painted with Vallejo colors.

Below. Note colorful touches like the wire-cutters, the jack and the rim inside the transmission access hatch. The red primer rim in the transmission access hatch adds a bit of color. Note the route taken by the crew to mount the vehicle has faded the sand-colored camouflage; tiny scratch and scuff marks can be observed.

Above. Note the various shades of gray peering through the sand-colored base coat and the various details standing out.

Dirt, rust and dust give the model a worn look.

All lights received M.V. Products Realistic Light lenses.

Although a Panzer I A is a comparatively small model in 1/35 scale, it did keep me busy for quite a while as the inclusion of an interior added a lot of fun, especially in the painting stages. Because of the interior, adding a figure "in" the model was not an option as this would obscure just about everything there is to be seen through the relatively small hatches. Therefore, putting the model on a small vignette with one or two figures is still an option I have in mind.

If you haven't done a DAK model yet, or haven't done one for a while, I can recommend doing so as painting and weathering it can be a lot of fun!

A variation of paint fading and chipping can be found on the rear deck.

102

102

102

102

T-34/76 "ChTZ"

Russia, summer 1943

As it had been a long time since I had done a single green-colored vehicle, a T-34 would be the perfect subject to get my hands on. I had built a few T-34s in the past, but not yet the version that looked most appealing to me, which is the one with the turret with rounded edges produced at the Chelyabinsk Tractor Works in Tankograd, thus also known as the "ChTZ" version.

The only kit to date featuring this particular turret is made by Tamiya. Although the Tamiya kits are of age, they are still pretty good and can be brought up to today's standards with a bit of detailing. Not having the complete kit at hand, constructing this model would involve a bit of kit bashing. It would be possible to use a Dragon hull and a Tamiya turret, but as I didn't have a Dragon kit either, I simply opted to use what I had in stock of Tamiya kits. This meant that I used the hull of a T-34/85 kit, which, apart from the square front fenders, is identical to the other Tamiya hulls. Moreover, that kit also has the same type of road wheels as the "ChTZ" kit. When it comes to wheels, however, you can use various types of them, even on a single T-34, as this was a very common feature. The turret itself was given to me a number of years ago by my modeling buddy Gino Poppe (thanks, mate!)

For the basic detailing of the kit, I again delved into what I had in stock. Years ago, I had bought several On the Mark photo-etched sets made especially for the Tamiya T-34 kits. These sets are relatively small compared to today's detail sets, but they include the most prominent features, like the grilles for the hull and the rear hatch.

1/35

Tamiya

Items used:

The simple solution would be to use a complete Russian T-34/76 tank, "ChTZ" version, 1943 production kit (no. 149). As I didn't have one at my disposal, I combined the following Tamiya kits, after-market sets and materials:

- **Tamiya hull of T-34/85 Russian Medium Tank (no. 138)**
- **Tamiya turret of Russian T-34/76 tank, "ChTZ" version, 1943 production (no. 149)**
- **Tamiya gun breech of T-34/76 Russian Tank 1942 Production Model (no. 49)**
- **Aber Russian 76,2 mm F-34 tank Barrel for T-34/76 model 1941-43 (no. 35L-34)**
- **Archer Soviet Turret Numbers (no. AR35148)**
- **Modelkasten T-34.M41 (SK-35)**
- **On the Mark Models T-34 Soviet Tank (no. TMP-3503)**
- **Tristar Russian Tank Crew (no. 012)**
- **K & S Quality sheet metal (no. 258)**
- **Magic Sculp**
- **Spare parts box (chain)**
- **Aluminum and thin metal foil, plastic card, strip and rod, copper wire, brass tube and a Punch & Die set**

Construction

HULL

The fact that the Tamiya kits are of age can be witnessed by the presence of location holes for an electrical motor to drive the model. These holes will need to be filled with plastic card and putty. The Modelkasten tracks that I wanted to use for the model also included some parts to make the idler wheels movable, so that the track tension would be adjustable. This involved removal of the outer rim molded on the hull with a pair of cutters. Also, the idler wheel axles themselves needed some trimming.

Using the T-34/85 hull with the incorrect square front fenders presented no problems at all, as I had wanted to remove the front and rear fenders anyway. First, a pair of cutters was used to remove the bulk of the fenders. Then, using a file and some sanding paper, the remainder was cleaned up. Initially, I wanted to replace the side fenders with some homemade items, but in the end I just left them in place. Adding some small damage and thinning the front and rear edges would do just as well.

The next job on the hull would be to add some texture. This was done by tapping the entire surface with a brush dipped in liquid cement. The cement makes the plastic soft and gives an irregular pattern to the hull. Depending on the amount of liquid cement used, and on the amount of applications on the same area, more variation can be achieved – but be careful not to overdo it. Also make sure you don't apply it on soft metal parts like the fenders, etc. Further random pitting of the surface was achieved by using a small round-head drill bit in a slow-turning motor tool. This was used only sparingly.

Most of the weld seams present on the kit are not correctly textured: the texture usually runs in the wrong direction. To correct this, I again used liquid cement to soften the plastic and then engraved the weld seams in the right direction. Some missing weld seams were added with Magic Sculp.

A prominent feature on any T-34 is the grille in the rear hatch. Replacing the molded kit item changes the overall look of the model dramatically. The On the Mark photo-etch set provides an excellent alternative. Removing the molded grille and replacing it with photo-etch parts is not as difficult as it may seem. First, I removed the location pins on the rear. Then, to remove the molded grille, a series of holes were drilled close together, just inside the rim. Next, all these holes were connected by moving the drill around. This loosens the entire molded grille and it can be taken out. Using a file, the remaining edges were cleaned up. Also, you should remove the molded frame until about half its width. The reason for this is that when you put on the photo-etched rim, you will have a thin edge under which you can glue the mesh. Also, all plastic edges were beveled from underneath. The remainder of the molded rim was then sanded smooth. Next, the outer photo-etch frame was glued on and then all cross sections were added. To determine the correct size of the mesh, I used a piece of paper that was cut to fit the frame properly. Then, the paper template was traced onto the mesh, which was subsequently cut to size. Finally, the mesh was added.

The grilles for the hull side and top are also provided in the On the Mark set and require a somewhat different approach. They consist of two halves, five cross sections and three bars each. To make a strong assembly, these really need to be soldered. First, a bar, not cut to length yet, was inserted through the cross sections. These were then put together with one of the halves temporarily

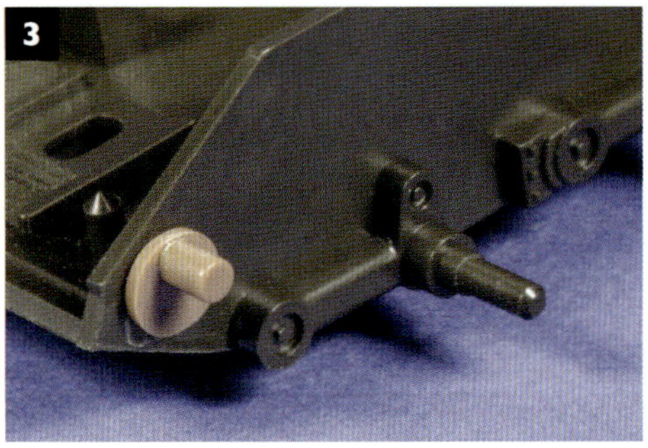

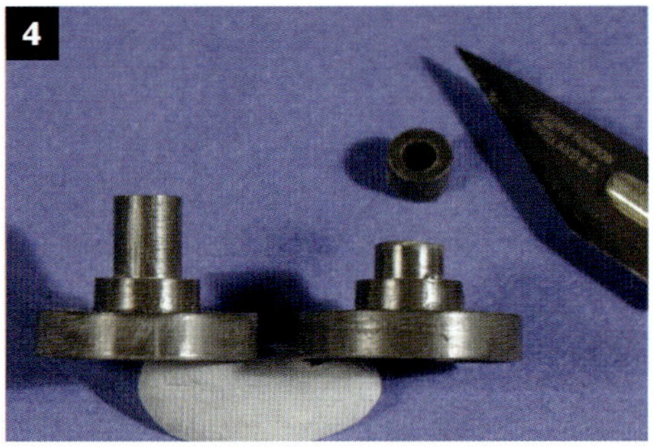

1. All locations holes for the electrical motor to drive the model, remnants of a past era, were filled with plastic card and putty, and missing detail was added.

2. To use the Modelkasten parts for the idler wheels, the molded rim on the hull needs to be removed.

3. The Modelkasten part in place.

4. The axle on the idler wheels needs to be shortened.

mounted on a small base with some Blu Tack. The base, in this case a piece of marble, is used to be able to handle the construction during soldering. One by one, the cross sections were then soldered in place. Next, after removal of the temporarily added bar, three bars were cut to the appropriate size and inserted through the cross sections. Then, finally the other half was added and both halves were soldered together. As with the grille in the rear hatch, the molded grilles on top of the hull also needed to be removed. The same procedure was used as before.

Before closing the two hull halves, the interior was brush-painted black with Vallejo paint. This way, there will be no reflection from the plastic through the grilles and other openings like the hatches. Also, I added some black cardboard paper to prevent a see-through effect, as that would reveal the lack of an interior. Some plastic card was used to close the gap underneath the fenders. To refine the side fenders, I first scraped them on the inside with a scalpel to thin the edge. Then the outside was sanded down as well.

The molded tie downs on the side of the hull were removed and replaced with copper wire items. To achieve a uniform look for them, they were all shaped by pushing the copper wire over an appropriate arm of a Hold & Fold device. The most tedious job on this model was then adding all the tiny weld seams to all those tie downs.

Being relatively small, the On the Mark detail set unfortunately doesn't include the two stowage bins situated on the fenders. As I wanted to add a little damage to both of them, I decided to make them from scratch using thin brass sheet. To get the correct dimensions, I measured the kit items and made scale drawings, which I then traced onto the brass sheet. After cutting them out with a pair of scissors, they were shaped just like an etched item and soldered for strength. To emboss the lid of the bin on the left fender, I again made a paper template and used a toothpick to do the actual engraving. The rest of the detailing was carried out with plastic strip and rod, copper wire and thin brass sheet. Photo-etched chains were taken from the spares box. To add some more character, the lid on the right stowage bin was left off.

Because I wanted to open the driver's hatch, the inside needed a bit of detailing. Molded details, like the handle and locking system, were removed and replaced. To add further interest, the periscope covers received some casting numbers made with Magic Sculp. A casting letter was also added to the machine-gun housing, while a brass tube found in the spares box replaced the barrel of the machine gun. The clips to hold the towing cables in place are missing at the rear, while the molded ones on the front were cut off and replaced with refined scratch-built items. Again, to add a bit of character, one of them received some damage. Adding small touches like this can give your model a more worn look. For the same reason, I cut off a few bolts on the rear hull plate, indicating they had been removed or lost at some point. Also, a damaged lamp would further suggest this way of thinking. I started thinning the edge of the lamp by carefully twisting a large round-head drill bit by hand. At a certain point, however, the large drill bit becomes too small to further thin the edge in this way. So then a smaller round-head drill bit in a motor tool was used to give it the final appearance. Be careful not to make the edge too thin. Also, the exhausts were thinned to bring them to scale.

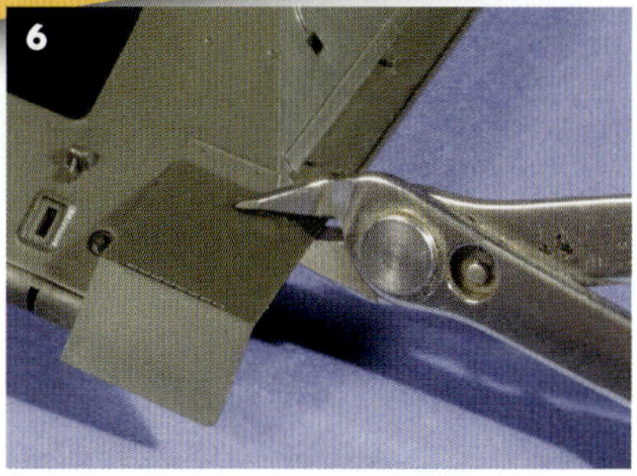

5. I used the upper hull of a T-34/85 model, which has the square and thus wrong type front fenders for the T-34/76 versions.

6. This, however, did not pose a problem, as I had planned to remove the fenders anyway. First, the bulk of the fenders was cut with a pair of cutters.

7. Then, using a file, the remaining rim was sanded smooth.

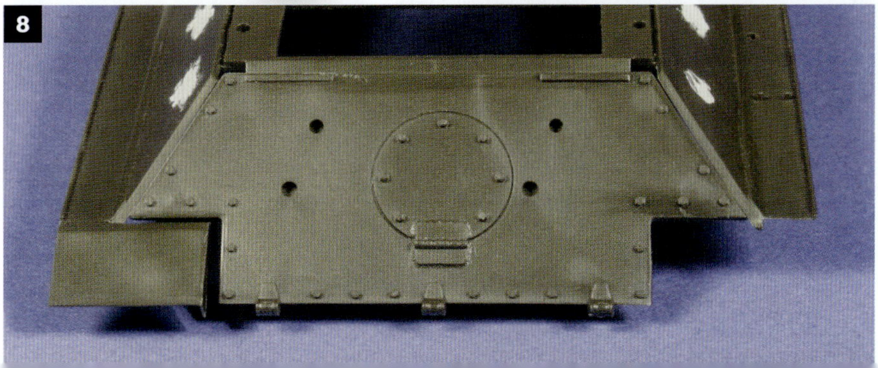

8. At the rear, the fenders were also removed. The edge of the side fender was thinned to scale.

1–3. The original kit welds are molded in the wrong direction. Using a conical drill bit, the welds were cribbed in the other direction. Also, the large molded weld around the machine-gun housing needs to be corrected. Other missing parts of the weld were added with Magic Sculp, including at the front of the hull.

4. Other missing weld seams were also added with Magic Sculp and textured with the tip of a rounded blade.

5 & 6. The molded clips to hold the tow cables in place were cut off and replaced for better detail.

7

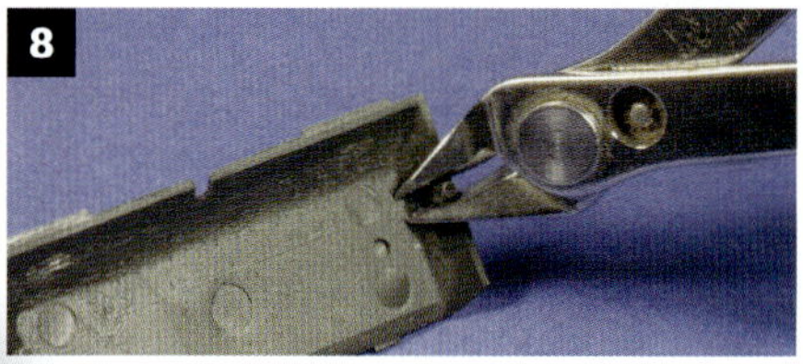

7 & 8. The original rear engine hatch with molded grill. First, the location pins are removed.

9. Then, using an electric drill, a series of small holes are made just inside the rim, allowing the molded grill to be removed.

10. Using a file, the remaining rim is then cleaned up and the molded strip is removed until about half its width.

11 12

11. The photo-etch outer frame is glued in place, and the cross sections are added.

12. To determine the size of the mesh, a piece of paper is cut and tested until the fit is perfect.

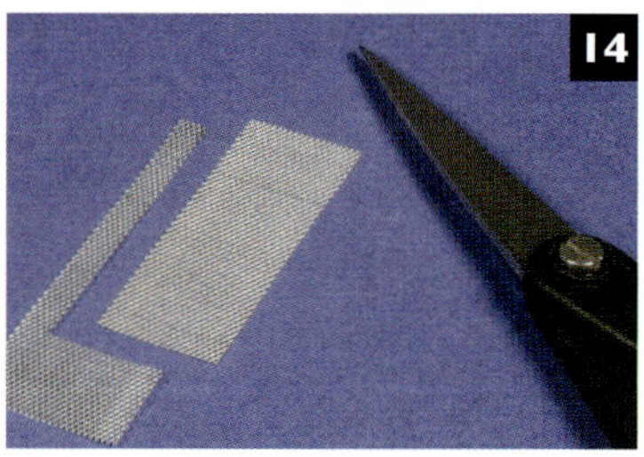

13. The paper template is then traced onto the mesh...

14. ...and cut out with a pair of scissors.

15. The mesh is then added in the grill.

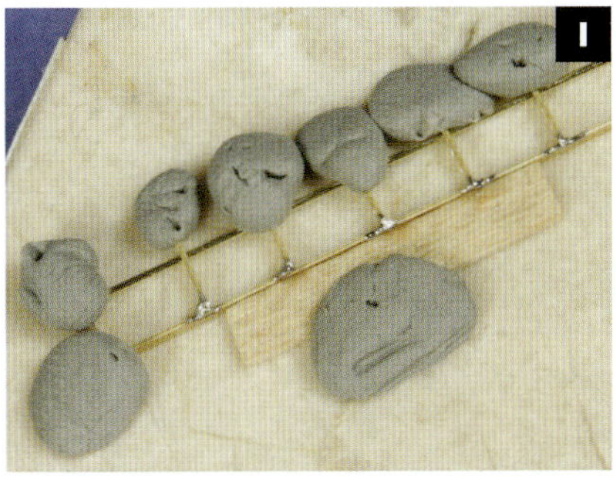

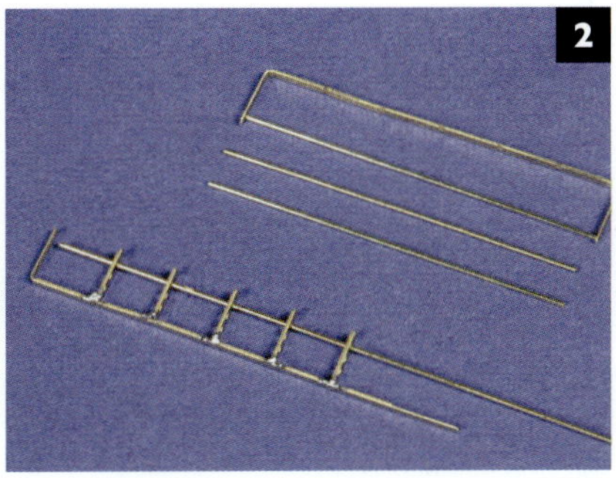

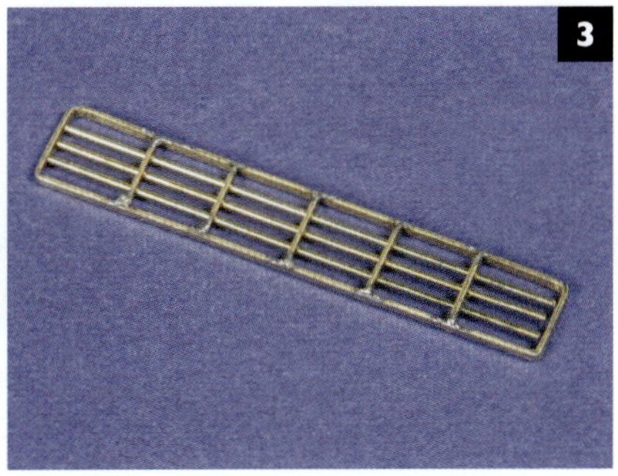

1. The grilles for the side and top of the hull consist of two halves and five cross sections that take three bars. First, the bottom half is partly shaped, while a bar is temporarily run through the cross sections. These parts are then temporarily mounted on a piece of marble and held in place with some Blu Tack while being soldered. Mounting the pieces on a small base aids the handling of the construction while soldering.

2. The bottom half has had the cross sections soldered in place and still holds the temporarily added bar. The top half has been shaped and three bars have been cut to length. The two halves of the grille have been soldered together with the bars in place.

3. The finished result. When turned round, the grille looks nice and clean as there are no traces of solder.

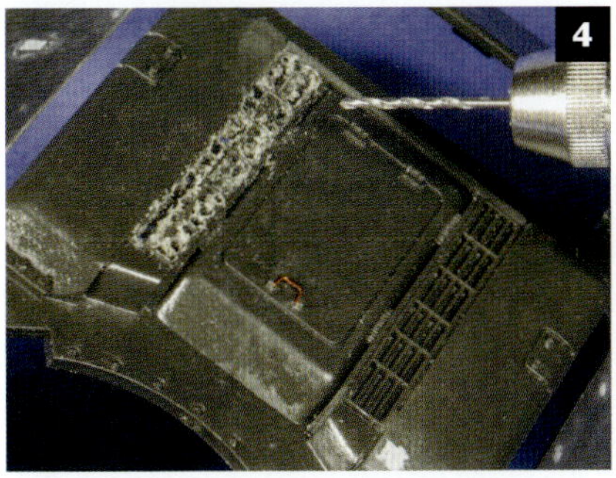

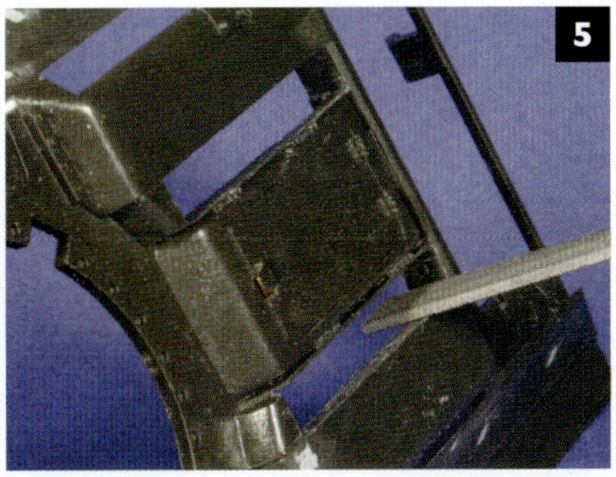

4. The same procedure is used as with the molded grille in the rear hatch. Using a drill, a series of holes is made to remove the grilles.

5. The remaining edge is cleaned up with a file.

6. The new grilles in place.

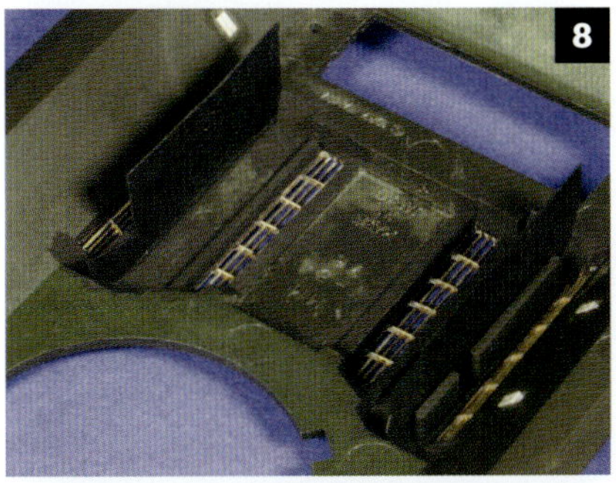

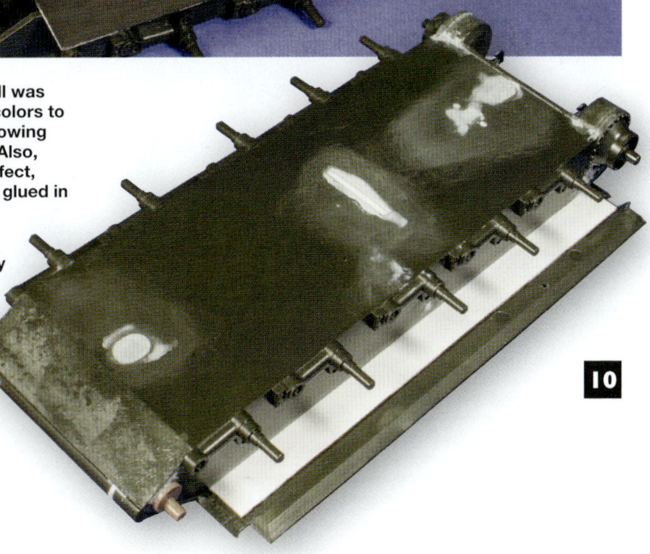

7 & 8. The interior of the hull was painted Black with Vallejo colors to prevent any bare plastic showing through the open hatches. Also, to prevent a see-through effect, some black cardboard was glued in strategic places.

9. The outer edge of the side fenders was thinned by scribing it with a scalpel from the inside, and by sanding it on the outside.

10. Typical for the older Tamiya kits is the aperture in the bottom of the upper hull next to the fenders. Some plastic card takes care of that.

1. To make new tie downs for the side of the hull, I used copper wire, a pair of pliers and a Hold & Fold.

2. The new tie downs in place on the hull. Small weld seams were added with Magic Sculp.

3. To make the storage boxes for the side fenders, the original kit parts were measured up and a simple scale drawing was made and then traced onto a piece of brass sheet.

4. After cutting it out with a pair of scissors, the brass box was folded to shape and then soldered together for strength. A toothpick was used to do the actual scribing.

5 & 6. The finished stowage box, with details added.

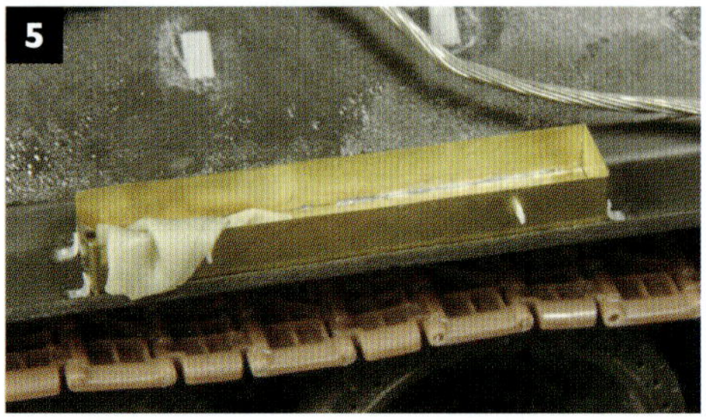

8–10. For scale thickness, the edge of the lamp needs to be thinned. First, a big round-head drill bit was carefully twisted around inside the lamp. I then used a small round-headed drill bit in a motor tool and carefully moved it around the inner edge.

7. The inside of the driver's hatch had some molded features removed and replaced with scratch-built items.

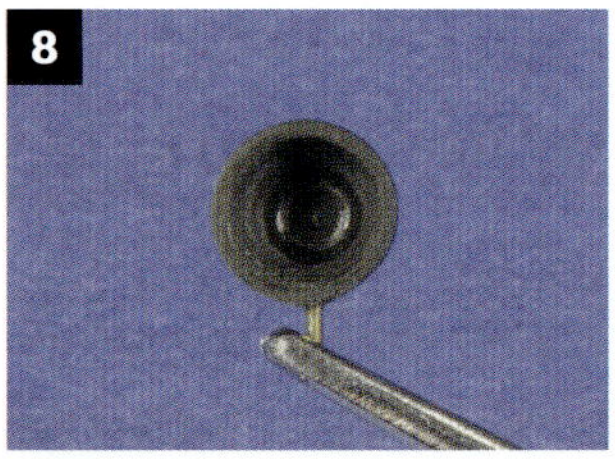

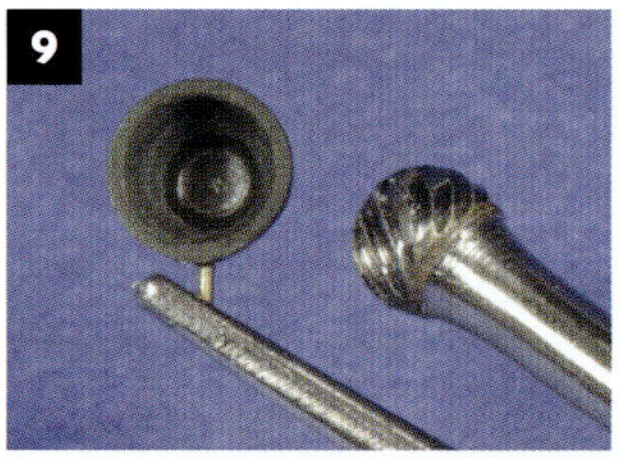

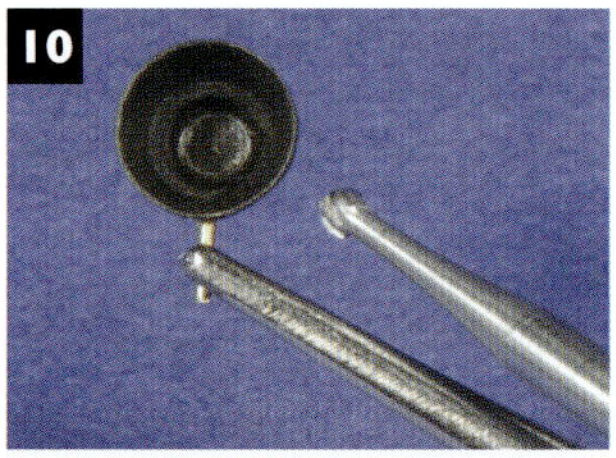

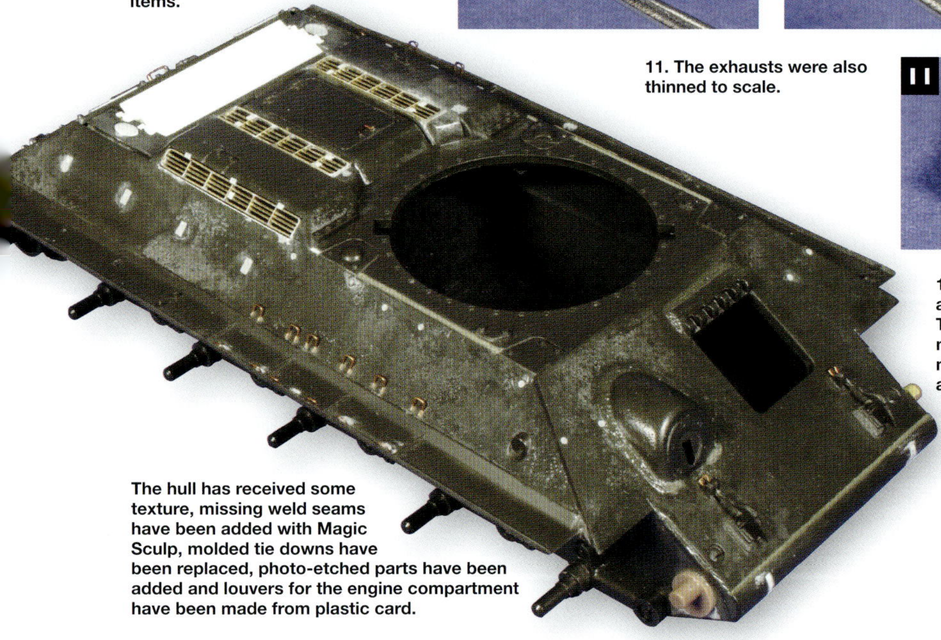

The hull has received some texture, missing weld seams have been added with Magic Sculp, molded tie downs have been replaced, photo-etched parts have been added and louvers for the engine compartment have been made from plastic card.

11. The exhausts were also thinned to scale.

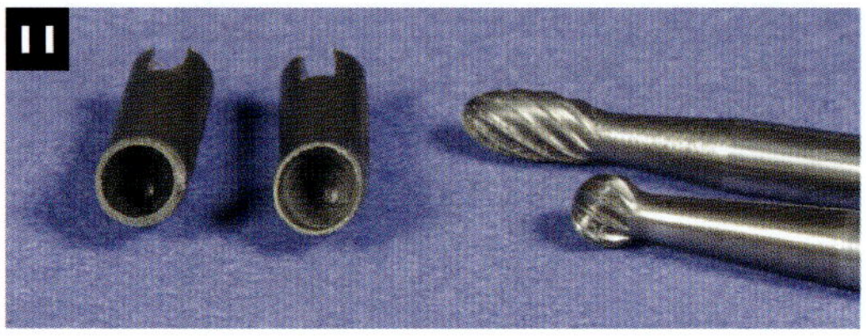

12. To recreate the texture of steel plates, I tapped the appropriate areas with a brush dipped in liquid cement. This softens the plastic and creates irregularities. Just make sure you practice first. Don't apply it to soft metal features like the fenders, etc. and above all, don't overdo it.

TURRET

Because I wanted to open up both turret hatches, the inside edges were thinned with a file for scale thickness. One hatch would take a crew figure, leaving the other one open. So as not to end up with a completely empty turret, I decided to add a partial interior in the form of a gun breach. This is an easy way to add a little bit of interest to an otherwise empty black hole. The gun breach was taken from a Tamiya T-34/76 1942 kit and received some basic detail with plastic card and Magic Sculp. It was painted entirely with Vallejo paints before installation. A pencil was used to simulate bare metal. Just like the hull, the rest of the interior of the turret was painted black before closing. The most prominent missing feature on the outside of the turret, the mechanism to lock the hatches in the open position, was recreated with some plastic strip. Also, a copper wire spring was added to the rear of the hatches.

Some missing torch cut marks on the gun housing were added by engraving them with a triangular file.

The casting texture on the turret is simply fantastic. It doesn't need any touching up whatsoever. Alas, that cannot be said of the gun mantlet, which lacks any texture. To create the casting texture, I used the same technique as before on the hull by dipping a brush in liquid cement and then tapping it on the surface. To get a rougher effect than on the hull, I also used a stiffer brush.

The only thing that was left to do was to add all the handles to the turret and hull that seem to be so typical. To achieve uniformity, I decided to make new ones from scratch. With a Punch & Die set, a series of holes was punched in a piece of plastic card. This was then cut into strips, which were shaped and sanded to make the bases for the handles. Pieces of rod were cut to length and inserted. Again, Magic Sculp was used for the weld seems.

1
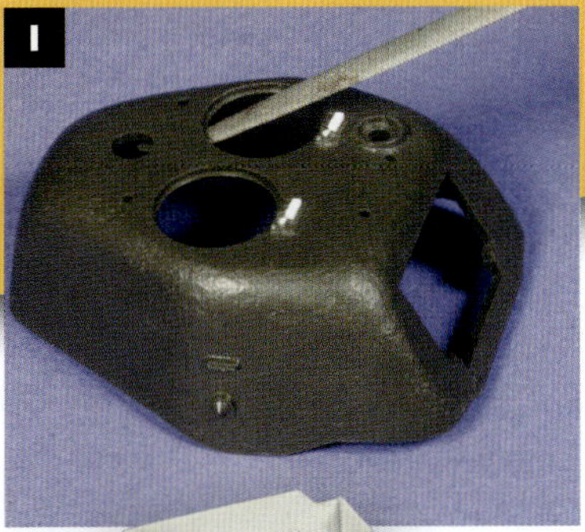

2

1. The inside edge of the turret hatches was thinned to scale thickness with a file.

2. Like the hull, the interior of the turret was painted black to avoid bare plastic showing through the open turret hatches. A few passes with Vallejo Black is all that is needed.

3
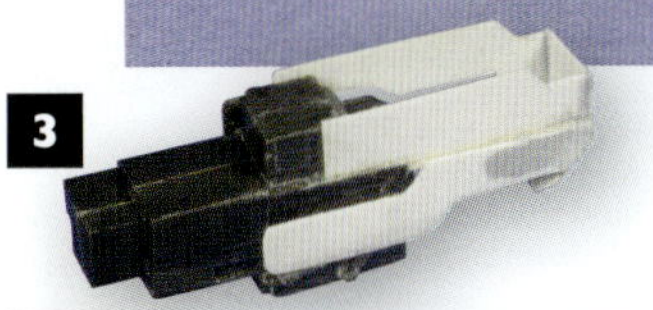

3. The gun breach, taken from a 1942 model kit, received some minor detailing.

4

4. A basecoat of Vallejo Air Interior Green (no. 10) was hand-painted on.

5

5. Some basic weathering was then added also using Vallejo colors. Bare metal effects were created with a pencil.

6
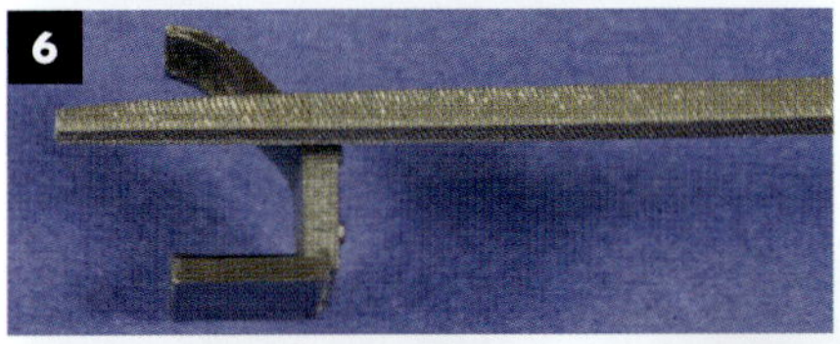

6. A triangular file was used to simulate torch cut marks.

7. Again, a file was used to thin the edge of a kit part – this time, the plate over the gun mantlet.

7
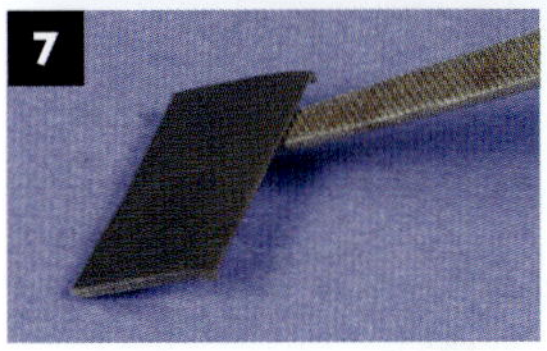

8

9

10

8. The gun mantlet lacks any form of texture.

9. As with the hull, I worked the surface with a brush dipped in liquid cement.

10. As I needed a heavier effect than on the hull, I used a stiffer brush.

1 & 2. On the turret, missing weld seams were created with Magic Sculp.

3. To make the bases for the handles, plastic card was pierced with a Punch & Die set and cut into strips. The ends were then shaped with sanding paper.

4. Plastic rod was inserted through the bases and Magic Sculp was used to make the welds on the hull.

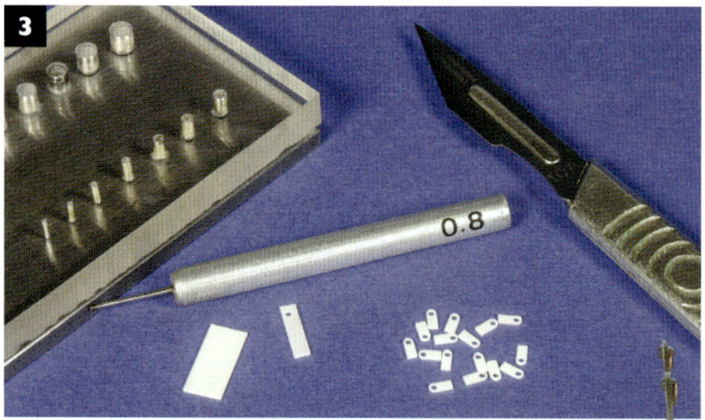

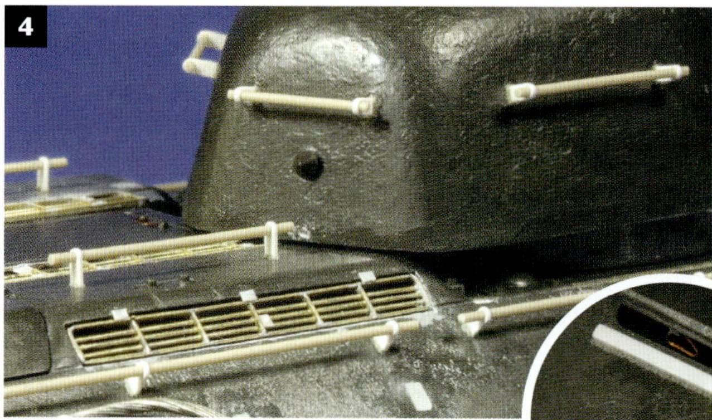

Right. A step in front of the driver's hatch and the mount for the clip to hold the towing cable were made from plastic strip.

Above. Note the slightly bent side fender. The holder for the saw comes in the On the Mark photo-etch set, while the box was made from scratch using brass sheet, copper wire, plastic strip and rod.

Left. Weld seams were made with Magic Sculp. The mechanism to hold the hatches in the open position is missing from the kit and was made from plastic strip.

Brass sheet and plastic strip were used to scratch-build the box on the rear right fender. A piece of cloth was sculpted with Magic Sculp.

Left. The rear lower hull. The clips to hold the towing cable in place are missing altogether and were scratch-built from plastic strip, rod and copper wire. Missing weld seams were made with Magic Sculp.

Right. Using Magic Sculp, casting letters were also added to the periscope covers on the driver's hatch.

Right. The louvers under the engine hatch were fabricated from plastic card.

Left. Some bolts were removed from the motor access hatch. Small touches like this can add some character to a model. The weld seams on the exhaust were later moved to the top.

Painting

BASE COATING

Not wanting the color of the T-34 to be too dark, I settled on using Humbrol Matt Army Green (no. 102). Although I usually do some preshading, this time I only airbrushed the base color. All subsequent changing of the base color would be done by brush.

Dry-brushing is a technique that hardly seems to be used these days. However, it's still a very good tool to weather your model, if handled correctly. For the first color variations, I used a new, unstirred jar of the base color and Humbrol Desert Yellow (no. 93). It is important that the paint is not stirred, otherwise you will not get a good result.

Little by little, and this is the key factor, more Desert Yellow was added to the base color and all surfaces of the model were dry-brushed. The reason why many a model may have been ruined in the past by dry-brushing is because too much of the brighter color is added too soon. This really needs to be done step by step. Rushing this process will only result in a kitschy looking model.

With the initial dry-brushing finished, I added a coat of Model Master Semi-Gloss varnish.

VARIATION AND DEPTH

Not entirely happy with the shade of green yet, I started adding filters on all surfaces. Mostly, I used pure Humbrol Grass Green (no. 80), but I also used some US Light Green (no. 117) and a combination of both. This resulted in a nice and bright green tone.

Next up, I started outlining all the details to add depth to the model. For this, a combination of Humbrol Brown Bess (no. 170) and Matt Black (no. 33) was used. When outlining, I always keep a clean slightly larger moist brush at hand, which I use to blend the paint with and to clean up any unwanted effects. A second dry-brush run is then called for to refresh the base paint and add more color variation. This time I used Army Green, Grass Green and Desert Yellow.

CHIPPED PAINT

The key to convincing paint chipping is trying to keep it "in scale." Finding the right balance between realism and some artistic license to make the model look good is not always easy. Variation in the chipping is therefore very important. This stage shouldn't be rushed, as it will for a large part determine the final look of your model.

To simulate the effect of worn-off paint, I first used the same Brown Bess, Matt Black mix that I applied for outlining the details. Needless to say, the paint was less diluted this time. To create a 3D effect, I then added some highlight chipping to some of the dark paint chips. It's important that the highlights are not too wide or too similar in appearance. A combination of the base color, Army Green and Naples Yellow oil paint was used. Also, a mixture of Grass Green and Desert Yellow was applied to recreate scuff marks that didn't go through the paintwork.

MORE VARIATION

Locally applied filters of Grass Green and US Light Green help to further enrich the monotone color of the model, while various brown tints, like Raw Umber and Burnt Umber oil paint, and a combination of Humbrol Brown Bess and Leather (no. 62) were used to simulate rusty areas. These same oil colors and also Vandyke Brown formed the oil and dirt streaks running down the side of the model.

Painting and weathering a model is not a straightforward procedure. There is a certain sequence of steps, but I constantly go back and forth between the different stages of painting to get the balance I'm looking for. So, to further vary the paint chipping, I then used Raw Umber oil paint straight from the tube.

1. The model was airbrushed with Humbrol Matt Army Green (no. 102).

2. Next, it was dry-brushed with different mixtures of the base color (using a fresh jar) and Humbrol Matt Desert Yellow (no. 93) to achieve tonal variation.

1. Then the model was varnished with Model Master Semi Gloss Clear. Matt models usually look a bit dull, while a satin sheen helps create the impression of a vehicle made of metal and steel.

2. Not entirely happy with the tone of the green so far, I started adding filters with Humbrol Matt Grass Green (no. 80) and Matt US Light Green (no. 117).

3. The next step was to create some depth, and for this, I outlined all details with a Humbrol Brown Bess (170) and Matt Black (no. 33) mix. I always keep a moist, slightly larger brush at hand to blend the outlining and to clean up any unwanted effects.

4. After the initial outlining, I always go for a second dry-brush run to freshen up the highlights and blend the paintwork some more. This time, I also included Matt Grass Green in the mixture.

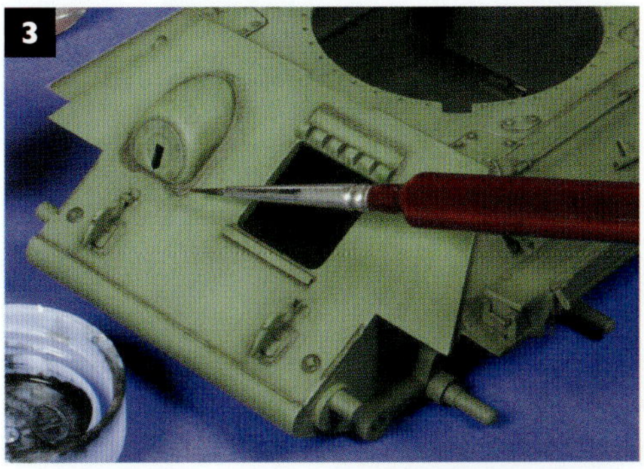

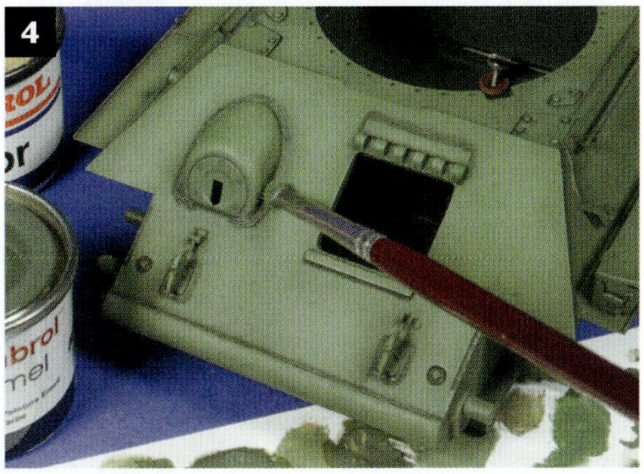

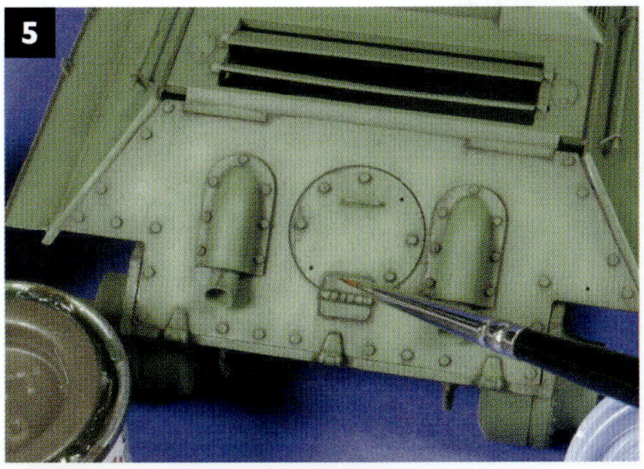

5. The Brown Bess and Matt Black mix used for outlining the details is also employed for adding some first chipped-paint effects and scratches. This time, however, less thinner is used. Depending on the mix of the Brown and Black, you can make darker or lighter chip marks. Variety works best.

6. Again, the same mix was used to create oil and grease spills.

7–9. To create a slight 3D effect, some highlight chipping was carried out by accentuating some of the Brown Bess–Black chips with a lightened version of the base color.

Here, I used Humbrol Matt Army Green in combination with Naples Yellow oil paint. Try to keep the highlights subtle and random.

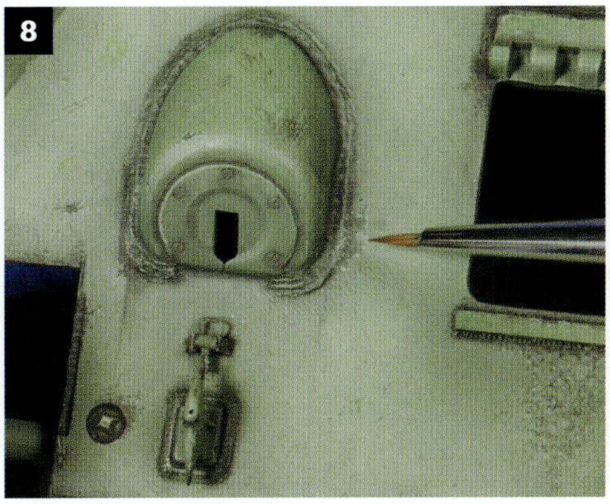

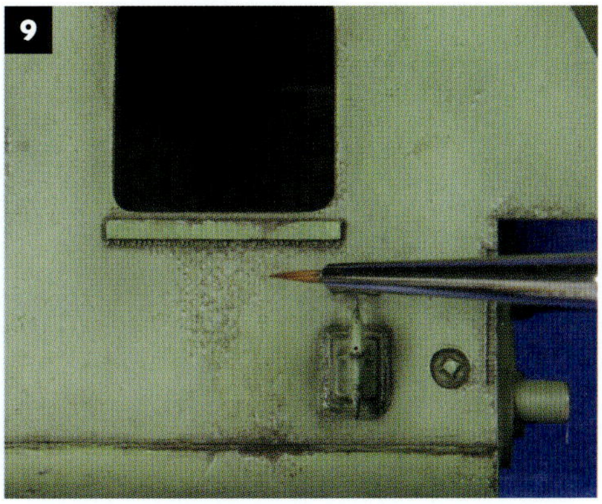

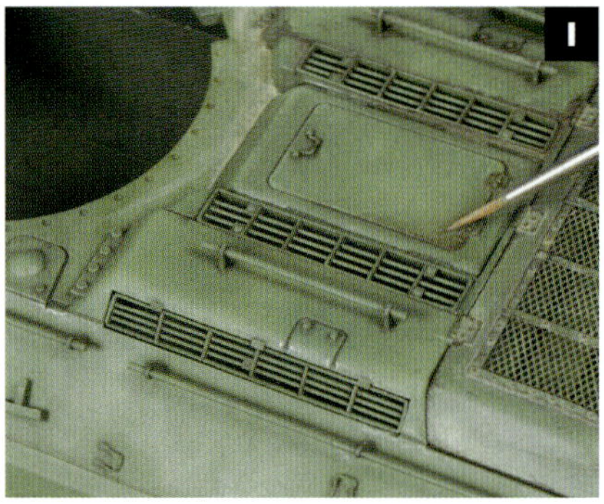

1. Various rust effects were created in different ways. Here, a Raw Umber oil-paint wash is added.

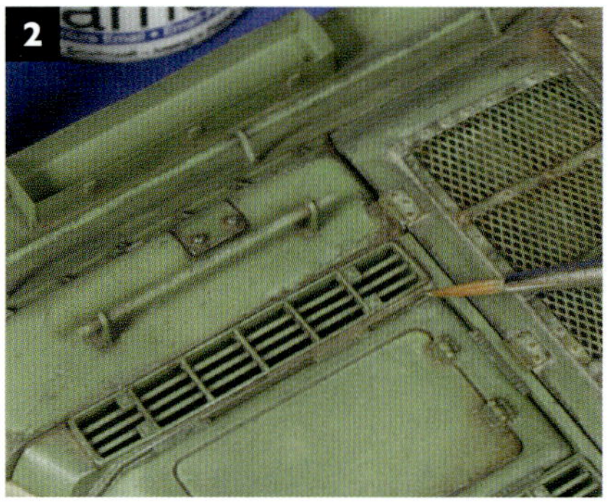

2. Other rust effects were made with a combination of Humbrol Matt Leather (no. 62) and Brown Bess (no. 170).

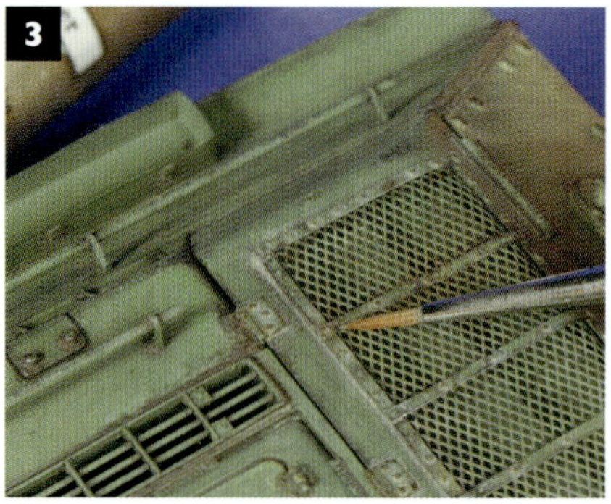

3. Some were done with washes of Burnt Umber oil paint.

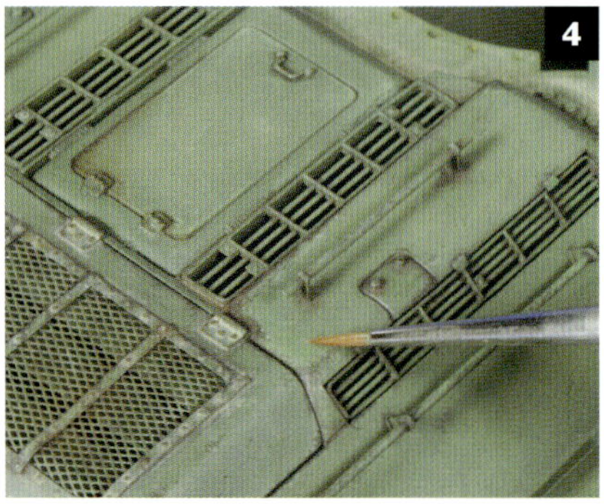

4. To get more tonal variation in the green base color, subtle local filters were added in different shades of green. Here, Matt Grass Green was used.

5. Other details were picked out in Matt US Light Green.

6. To make scratches and scuff marks that didn't go all the way through the paintwork, I used a mixture of Matt Grass Green and Matt Desert Yellow.

7. Grass Green was also used to add a fresher look to the inside of the right side stowage box.

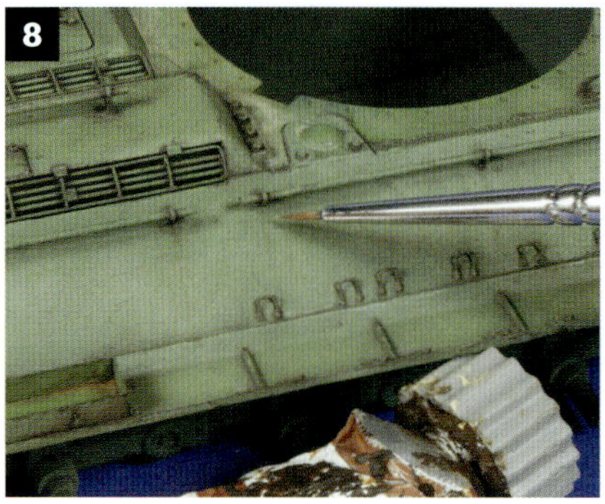

8–11. Dirt and rust streaks were simulated with various colors of oil paints.

12. Raw Umber oil paint was also used to add more variety to the chipped-paint effects.

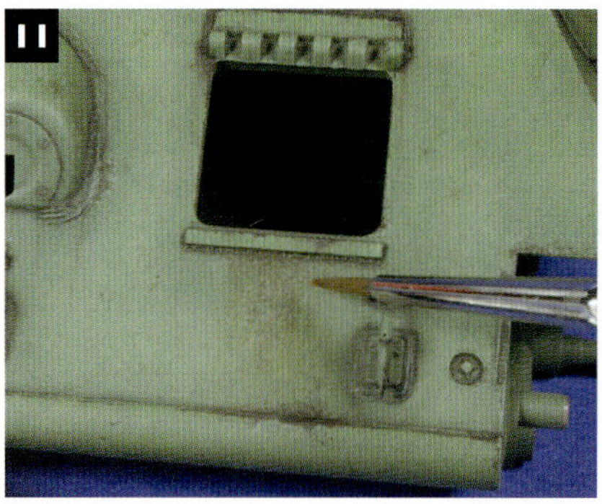

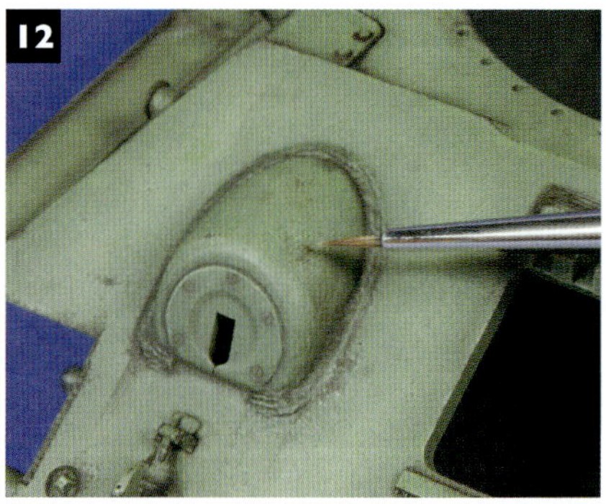

GREASE AND STEEL

Adding the right look to different elements of the model enhances the feel of reality. As dust needs to be matt, oil spills need to look greasy. Therefore, I mixed some Vallejo Air Satin varnish with Gloss varnish and ran it over the oil spills. The result is a convincing greasy look.

Careful chipping with dark brown colors is one way to give a plastic model the "feel of steel." To take it a step further, you can even add small touches of bare steel. The color of bare steel can be easily simulated with a graphite pencil. Depending on the area I'm working on, I use different pencils. For the most part, though, I use a simple filling pencil to touch up some edges that are prone to being buffed up by the crew or other weathering elements.

EXHAUSTS

Painting exhausts is always a fun moment, because it adds a dash of color and thus brings more life to a model.

For a base color, I started with Humbrol Brown Bess. In the next step, I mixed it with some Leather and then stippled it on, leaving the base color visible in some areas. This immediately creates a first weathering effect. To further the effect, I then used a combination of Leather and Pale Yellow (no. 81) and, as before, stippled on the paint. Some tiny rust spots were added again using the same technique, but this time with Burnt Umber oil paint. Finally, some soot was simulated with Mig Productions Black Smoke (no. 23). A bit of pigment was also added to the hull itself to represent soot deposits.

DUSTING UP

One of the main reasons why I wanted to do this model was the opportunity to bring it to life with a well-balanced layer of dust.

Dust is another one of those things that can make or break a model. So, the way to apply it needs to be chosen carefully. A very popular medium is pigments. However, as I had a particular finish in mind, I felt that pigments were not the right medium for this model as they are harder to control and in particular wouldn't give the finesse I was looking for. That's why I decided to use oil paints. On the one hand, they can be diluted and used as filters to gradually build up the layer of dust, while on the other, they can be painted exactly where you want them with great finesse and strong intensity. A bonus is that the paint can be worked for quite a while before it sets, which means there is sufficient time to correct any errors. Diluting the paint also results in a matt finish, which is essential to recreate a convincing layer of dust.

The colors used were a combination of Raw Umber with Naples Yellow and sometimes a bit of Yellow Ochre.

There was one area where I did want to use pigments, though. On the hull sides under the fenders I wanted to recreate a build up of dirt and dry mud. Pigments are perfect to add that particular structure.

To give the pigments a good base to adhere to, I again mixed Raw Umber and Naples Yellow, but didn't dilute it as before. The thick oil paint was dabbed on the surface and then covered with pigment powders. In this case, I tried to get as close to the oil paint color mix as possible and used a combination of Mig Productions Beach Sand (no. 30) and Gulf War Sand (no. 37). To make sure the color was similar in tone, I then added filters over the pigments with a diluted Raw Umber and Naples Yellow mix.

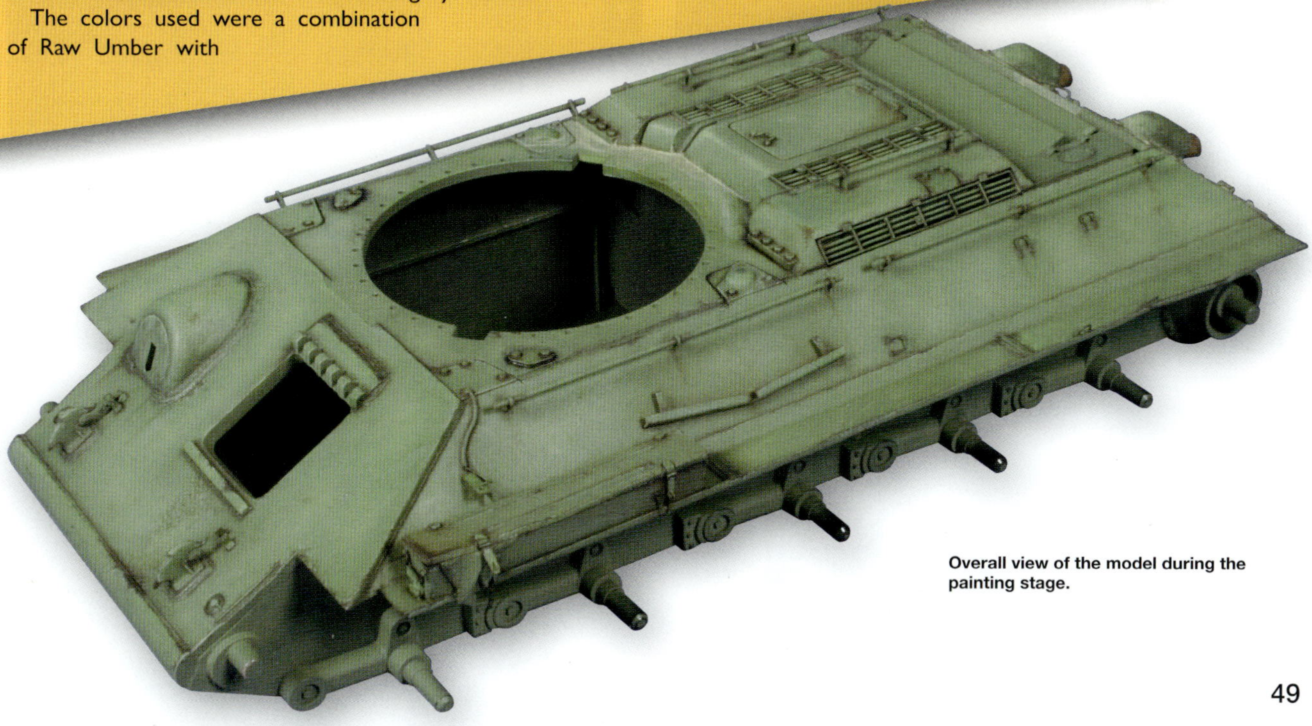

Overall view of the model during the painting stage.

1. Oil and grease spills need to look a bit glossy. Here, the spill still looks a bit too matt.

2. With a mixture of Vallejo Air Gloss (no. 58) and Satin (no. 60) varnish, the spills were made to look wet and greasy.

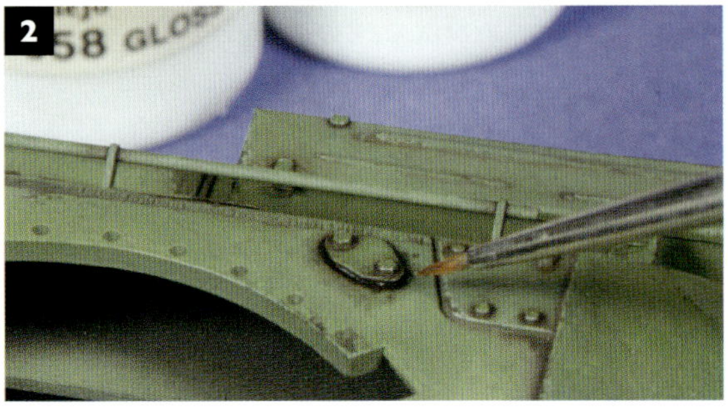

3. The left stowage bin so far with chipping, rust marks and subtle variation in the base color.

4. To produce a rusty looking exhaust, I first start with a Humbrol Brown Bess (no. 170) base coat.

5. Next, some Matt Leather (no. 62) is mixed with the Brown Bess and stippled on over the base coat. This creates a first tonal difference.

6. Then some Matt Pale Yellow (no. 81) is mixed with the Matt Leather and the procedure is repeated creating more tonal variation.

7. For final coloring, it is randomly stippled with some Burnt Umber oil paint.

8. To finish off, a bit of Mig Productions Black Smoke (no. 23) is used to simulate soot in the exhaust pipe…

9. …and soot deposits on the rear hull.

To create the dust, I used a combination of thinned oil paints. Raw Umber mixed with Naples Yellow, and sometimes adding a bit of Yellow Ochre for variation, gives a nice dusty tint. Oil paints can be much easier to control than pigments when carrying out minute painting. Adding small effects like lumps of dirt thrown up on the vehicle, which have subsequently run off, can be nicely reproduced in this way.

1 & 2. More minute paint chipping was carried out with Raw Umber used straight from the tube.

3 & 4. Highlighting the odd edge here and there with a pencil creates a bare-metal effect and gives more luster to the model.

Above. Overall views of the model during the painting stage. The entire model has now received some dusting. It's important to get a good balance and not coat everything with dust.

1. The right front corner of the hull. A small rusty patch can add some character and color.

2. The rear deck with a variation of shades in the green base color and rust effects.

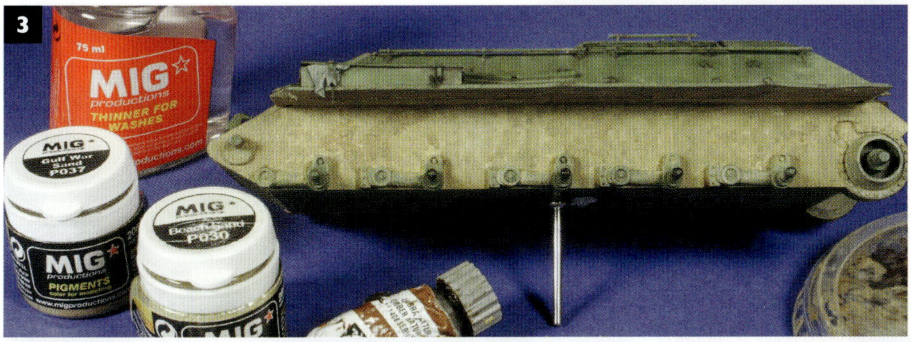

3. The hull sides under the fenders were given some texturing with Mig Productions pigment powders. First, a coat of undiluted oil paint was added onto which a mixture of Beach Sand (no. 30) and Gulf War Sand (no. 37) was dabbed. Then, to keep the color the same shade as the dust color on the rest of the vehicle, the pigments were filtered with the Raw Umber and Naples Yellow mixture.

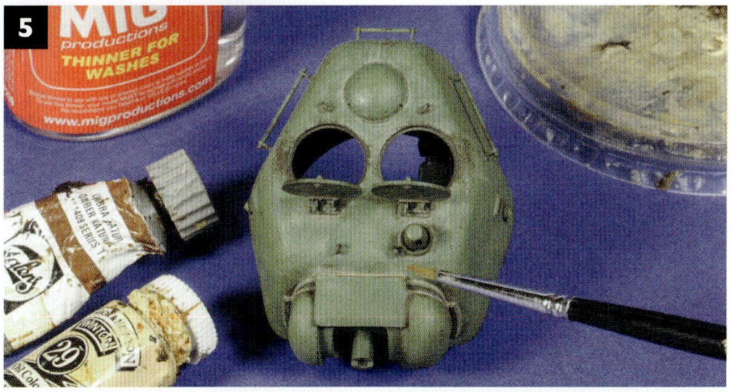

4. As on the hull, highlight chipping was carried out with a mixture of the base color Humbrol Matt Army Green (no. 102) and Naples Yellow oil paint.

6. Run-off dust streaks were simulated with the same mix.

5. Dusting the turret with a Naples Yellow and Raw Umber oil-paint filter.

7. Some edges and details were picked out with a pencil to give them a metallic sheen.

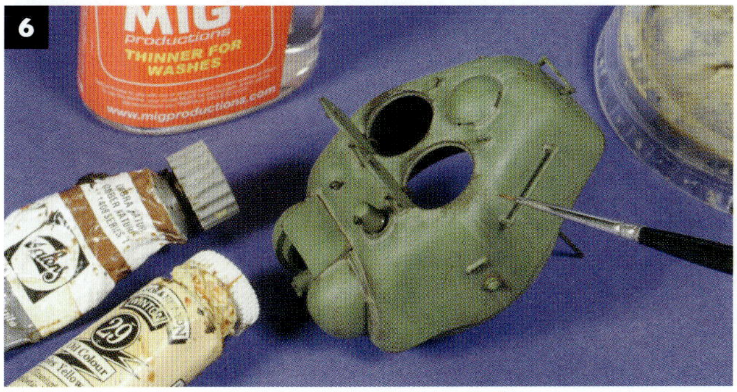

TURRET NUMBERS

I hardly ever use the wet decals included in the kit. The only time when I do use them is when the film can be cut off completely, leaving only the image itself. This happens when using, for example, license plates or divisional markings, etc. that are square or triangular or have straight lines that make it easy to remove the film. For turret numbers, I usually decide on dry transfers. These are easy to apply and if added incorrectly they can always be removed by carefully dabbing them off with a piece of tape – and your model will still be intact.

As they can be added in such an easy way, I usually add them in the finishing stages of a model. This also means that they have not been weathered with the rest of the paintwork. When the dry transfers have been put on, they will stick out like a sore thumb. The white tone is always much too bright. But it's fairly easy to blend them in. An easy way to break the white is to gently dry-brush the ciphers with some Raw Umber oil paint. Then, some more careful chipping, in this case also with Raw Umber, makes the blending process complete.

WHEELS AND TRACKS

The wheels were painted and weathered in pretty much the same way as the rest of the model by receiving filters, dusting, chipping, etc. The rubber of the wheels was painted with a Vallejo Black (no. 950) and Basic Skin Tone (no. 815) mix.

I use a lot of Vallejo to paint base coats and details. The advantage is it brush paints very well, and it dries instantly, so that you don't have to wait to proceed with the next step, which in this case was adding the dust filters. These were added mostly around the bolts and in the rims, and also in the contours of the rubber. When dry, the running surfaces where touched up with pure black. The running surfaces of the drive sprocket and idler wheels in turn were given a bare-metal look with a soft graphite pencil.

The tracks were airbrushed with Tamiya Red Brown (XF-64) and Flat Black (XF-1). To make the dirt on the tracks conform to the dust on the rest of the model, this time I also used the same Raw Umber and Naples Yellow oil paint mix instead of pigments. The entire surface was washed with a wide, flat brush. Next, the running surfaces were dry-brushed with a mixture of Brown Bess and Black to bring back the steel effect. On the inside, I then used a soft pencil to polish up the running surfaces. With the aid of a ruler, I made sure the edges ran perfectly straight – a small but significant detail. Surplus graphite was then carefully removed with a cotton stick. The edges of the running surfaces on the outside were polished up with a Silver Karismacolor pencil.

1

2

3

4
5

6
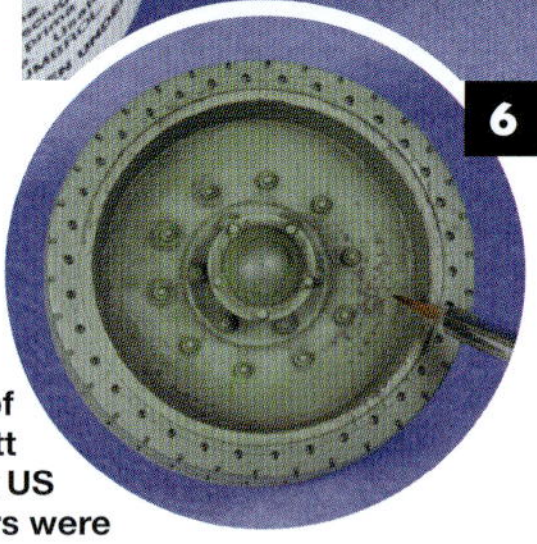

7

1. A set of Archer dry transfers was used for the turret numbers. They are easy to use and don't have any film that needs to be removed, or requires gloss varnishing of the turret to avoid silvering. The ciphers are cut from the sheet and added to the turret by gently rubbing them with a pencil.

2. To tone down the bright color of the numbers, they were dry-brushed with some Raw Umber oil paint. Here, you can clearly see the difference between the dry-brushed and non-dry-brushed ciphers.

3. Further weathering of the numbers was carried out with a fine brush and Raw Umber oil paint.

4. The wheels were airbrushed in Humbrol Matt Army Green (no. 102) with the rest of the model.

5. To gain color variation, some of the wheels were filtered with Matt Grass Green (no. 80) and/or Matt US Light Green (no. 117), while others were left in the original base color.

6. A variety of chipped-paint effects was added with the Humbrol Brown Bess (no. 170) and Matt Black (no. 33) mixture, as can be seen here, and with Raw Umber oil paint.

7. The rubber tires were hand-painted with a mixture of Vallejo Black (no. 950) and Basic Skintone (no. 815). Adding the Skintone results in a nice, warm gray.

ACCESSORIES, TEXTURES AND FINISHING TOUCHES

Adding some accessories with different textures is another way to help bring more life and color to a model, as it will break up the monotone look of the steel. The accessories I selected for this model were some pieces of cloth, spare tracks, a shovel, a chain and a towing cable. They would add different colors all around the model. For the rags, I used Magic Sculp, while the shovel was made from scratch using thin metal foil for the blade and a piece of rod for the handle. Making the blade from metal foil will result in a more to scale thickness. I modeled the blade on the shovel included in early Tiger I kits and, being different, it makes a nice change from the usual type of shovel. The crew probably picked it up somewhere, maybe when inspecting a knocked-out Tiger. For the towing cable, I used a length of twisted metal wire and the ends of a towing cable supplied in the kit. To fix the cable to the model, I made straps from thin metal foil and buckles from copper wire.

Final touches included adding the reflective interior to the lamp. The glass itself was omitted, suggesting it had been broken at some point. Painting the interior of a lamp somehow never looks convincing, so I resorted to using aluminum foil. Using a template, I cut a round disk, which was then carefully pushed into the lamp with the end of a brush.

The final touch was adding some straw, to suggest this had been used at some stage to camouflage the vehicle. As the straw was not properly fixed, it would have been blown off while driving. The places where the straw is still present will therefore be behind the bins and on the hull behind the turret, where it is more likely to stay or accumulate. The straw itself is made from a natural product which can be bought from some model shops. It's rolled up into a ball and individual strands can be plucked. Some wood glue was used to fix it to the model.

8 & 9. Dusting was done with washes of Raw Umber and Naples Yellow oil paint. All crevices received the dust wash.

10. The running surfaces were then made dust free by painting them with Vallejo Black.

11. Close up of a finished wheel.

12. The running surfaces of the drive sprockets and idler wheels were rubbed with a soft graphite pencil to give them a bare-metal look.

13. The tracks were base-coated with a mixture of Tamiya Red Brown (no. XF-64) and Flat Black (no. XF-1).

14 & 15. To achieve uniformity in the dust color with the rest of the model, the tracks received the same Raw Umber and Naples Yellow oil-paint mix on both sides.

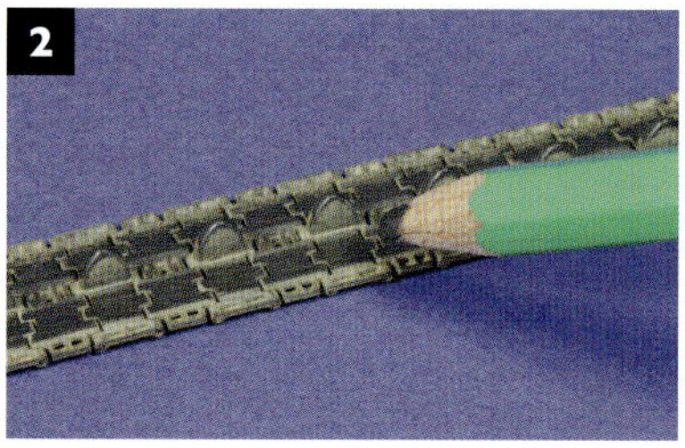

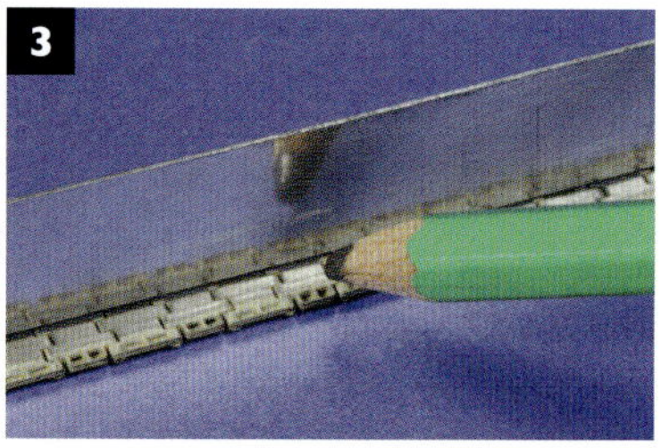

1. All running surfaces, inside and out, were then dry-brushed with a Brown Bess (no. 170) and Black (no. 33) mixture, leaving the dust untouched in the deeper areas.

2. The inside running surfaces were then buffed up with a soft graphite pencil.

3. To get a straight line, I used a ruler. It's important that the running surfaces are marked by a straight line, as they wouldn't look realistic otherwise.

4. Using a cotton swab, loose graphite was removed. If not, it might be picked up by the rubber wheels later, which would look unrealistic.

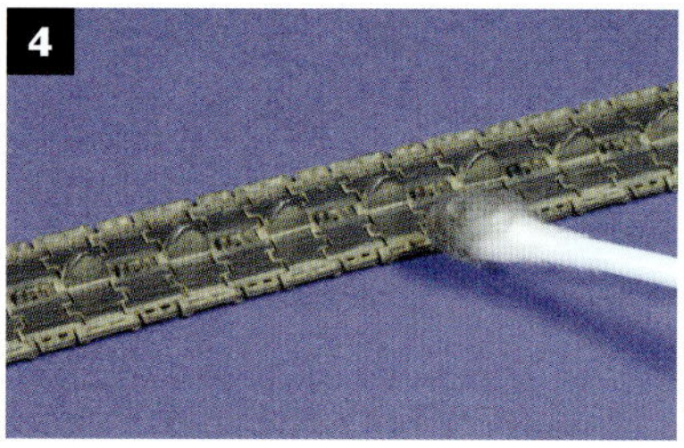

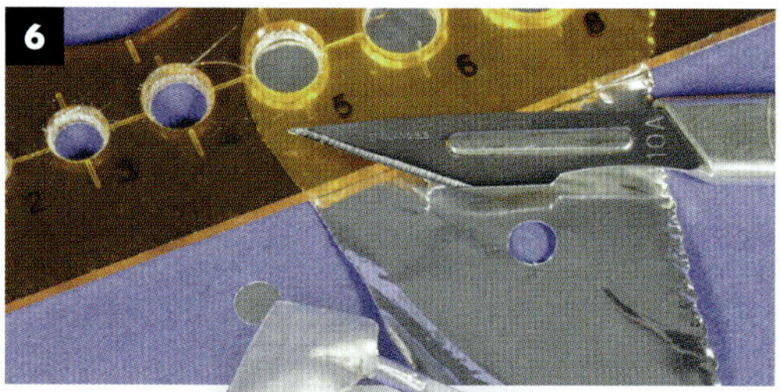

5. The edges of the outer running surfaces were metalized with a Silver Karismacolor pencil.

6. To make the inside of the lamp reflective, I used ordinary aluminum foil. Using a template and a scalpel, I carefully cut a round disk.

7 & 8. The round disk was then inserted in the lamp with the aid of a brush handle.

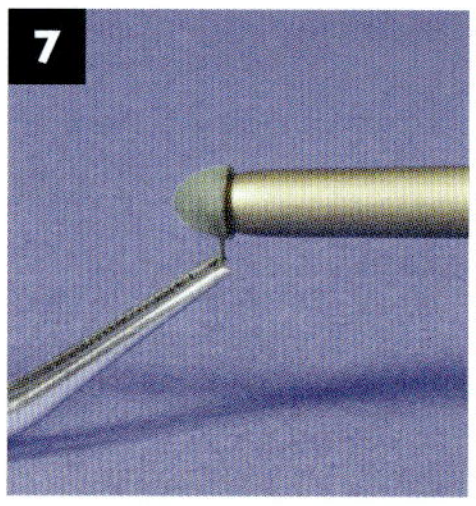

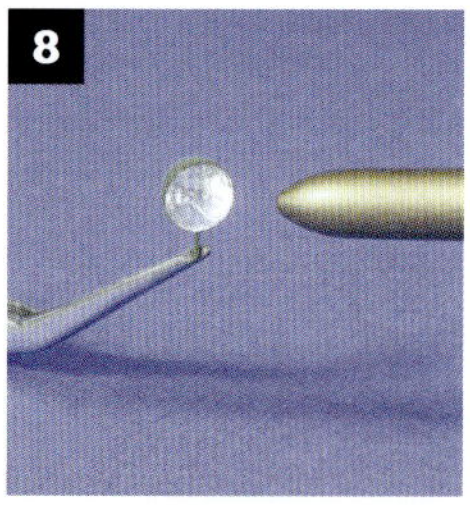

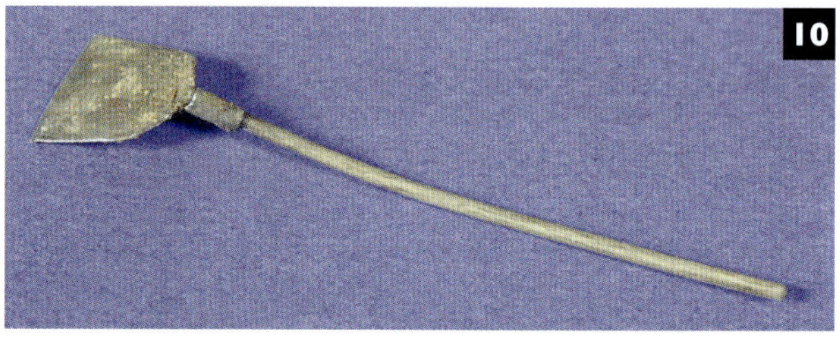

9. The large shovel of a Tamiya Tiger I kit was reproduced using thin metal foil and plastic rod.

10. The finished shovel. Accessories need to be treated as little kits in themselves, and must be painted to the same standard as the rest of the model. It's the little details that make a model great.

11. The finished shovel on the model.

12. Some leftover tracks from the Modelkasten set were used for spare tracks. To add interest, one of the tracks received a pin.

13. The unpainted tracks on the model.

14. The finished tracks.

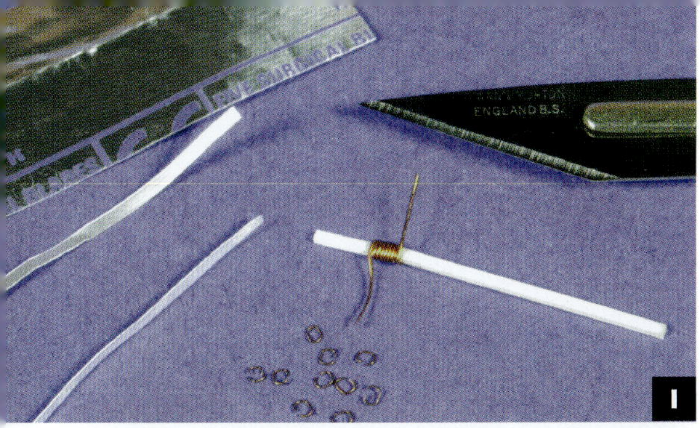

1. An easy way to make buckles for straps is by winding thin copper wire around a piece of square plastic strip. When cut, you have a series of square shapes that can be turned into buckles. The straps themselves can be made by cutting thin metal foil, like, for example, the wrapping of Swann Morton blades, into strips.

2. A strap and buckle made from thin foil and copper wire.

3 & 4. The painted strap and buckle.

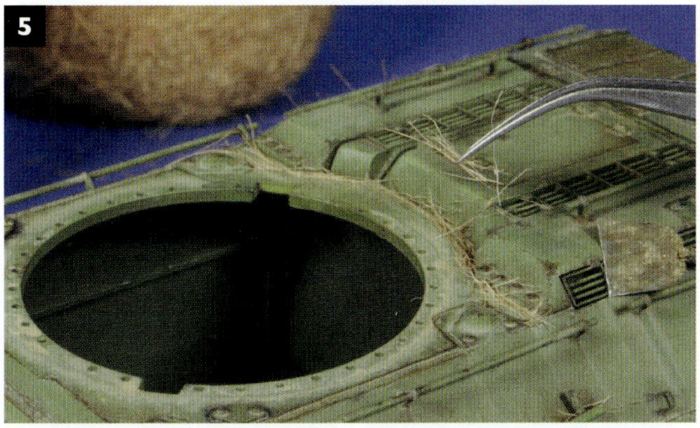

5–8. A feature sometimes seen on vehicles is dried straw or grass, probably as a remainder of some sort of camouflage. To recreate the straw, I used a natural product that resembles individual strands of straw very well. With some wood glue, the straw was fixed on the model in places where it was more likely to accumulate.

Figure

CREW

One of Tristar's Russian Tank Crew figures was chosen to occupy an open turret hatch. It was used almost straight from the box, as the sculpting, especially the facial expression, is very nice. Some details were refined by undercutting them with a scalpel and doing some engraving with a scribing tool. This was mostly done around the collar and on the hands. Also, the flaps of the cap were thinned on the inside, bringing them down to scale thickness. The position of the head was changed, which involved some reworking of the neck with Magic Sculp. The only real change I made was adding part of the legs. The figure is not supplied with legs, so I added them partly with Magic Sculp, as they would be visible through the second open hatch in the turret. The arms were left off until the hands and the front of the uniform were painted. That way, it was much easier to paint these areas.

For painting the figure, I used Vallejo acrylics. As always, I started with painting the hands and face first and used Brown Sand (no. 876) as a base coat. For highlighting, the base color was gradually mixed with Basic Skintone (no. 815) and applied in the appropriate areas. Burnt Cadmium Red (no. 814) was added for shading. Deep shades were made by mixing a little SS Camouflage Black Brown (no. 822) with the Burnt Cadmium Red. A bit of stubble was recreated with a mixture of Black (no. 950) and Basic Skintone. The strands of hair on the forehead were painted with English Uniform (no. 921).

Leather Brown (no. 871) was used for base-coating the cap and belt. Shading was done with a mixture of black and some SS Camouflage Black Brown, while highlighting was done by adding some Orange Brown (no. 981) to the Leather Brown base coat.

The overalls were base-coated with Khaki (no. 988). Some Buff (no. 976) was added for highlighting, and Leather Brown for shading. Russian Uniform WWII (no. 924) was used for the collar of his tunic. It was highlighted by adding some buff and shaded by adding some black.

The final addition was a strap on the cap made from thin metal foil. The table below lists the colors I used:

	Base	Highlight	Shadow
Skin	Brown Sand (no. 876)	Brown Sand (no. 876) + Basic Skintone (no. 815)	Brown Sand (no. 876) + Burnt Cadmium Red (no. 814) Deep shadows: Burnt Cadmium Red + SS Camouflage Black Brown (no. 822)
Stubble on the upper lip: Black (no. 950) + Basic Skintone (no. 815)			
Hair on the forehead: English Uniform (no. 921)			
Leather cap and belt	Leather Brown (no. 871)	Leather Brown (no. 871) + Orange Brown (no. 981)	Black (no. 950) + SS Camouflage Black Brown (no. 822)
Overalls	Khaki (no. 988)	Khaki (no. 988) + Buff (no. 976)	Khaki (no. 988) + Leather Brown (no. 871)
Tunic collar	Russian Uniform WWII (no. 924)	Russian Uniform WWII (no. 924) + Buff (no. 976)	Russian Uniform WWII (no. 924) + Black (no. 950)

1

2

3

1. Apart from refining some details, the only changes made to the Tristar figure were changing the position of the head, and sculpting part of the legs with Magic Sculp. The sculpted parts can only be seen from the rear through the second open hatch, so the front needn't be detailed at all.

2. More attention was paid to the rear of the legs.

3. The arms were left off for easy access until the front part of the uniform was painted.

4

4. While still separate, the hands and inside part of the arms were also painted.

5 & 6. View of the finished figure. Vallejo paints were used throughout. A strap made from thin foil was added to the helmet.

5

6

The facial expression on the Tristar figure is very nice and needed no replacement with an aftermarket head. Note the excellent texture on the turret: this is how it comes in the kit.

Although the Tamiya T-34 kits have been around for a long time, they can still be turned into nice reproductions of this very popular Russian vehicle. All it takes are some basic improvements, which should be within every modeler's grasp. So don't always immediately discard the older kits when new releases are put out on the market.

The access route for the driver shows signs of wear and tear. Note the gun breach inside the turret. Although only minimal, these details do add further interest to the model.

Some straw is still caught behind the right, lidless stowage box, which is filled with some cloth and chain. The towing cable is kept in place with a leather strap made from thin metal foil.

The white turret numbers, spade, rusty spare tracks and the cloth hanging from the metal box add color and character to the monotone green color of the vehicle. Various shades of green have been used to break up the base color.

Thrown-up lumps of earth and dust are simulated using oil paint. Note the casting letters on the driver's visors and machine-gun housing.

Note the polished running surfaces on the inside of the tracks.

Lots of subtle variation in the green color breaks up the monotony of the overall base color. The rusty spare tracks add a touch of color.

Panzerkampfwagen VIII Maus

Germany, 1946

Sometimes it can be fun, interesting and even instructive to build a model in a different scale to what you are normally used to. This forces you to adapt your painting skills and step out of your comfort zone. If you go down in scale, you have to work in a more subtle way. This can sometimes be a good exercise, because you may benefit from the experience when you go back to larger-scale models. It is fun to study a model up close, detecting more details and finessing as you go along. Therefore it's important to try and work "in scale." This is a relative idea, though, because a lot, if not most, of what we do in the way of (let's say) "chipping" is over-scale. That said, it does add a certain sense of realism to a model, provided it is done in a balanced and attractive way. Creating a perfect copy of a real vehicle is impossible. Therefore, we use different painting techniques to try to create the idea – the illusion – that a model looks realistic, even if reality is something different entirely.

The PzKpfw VIII, nicknamed "Maus," is the largest fully enclosed AFV ever built. Only two hulls and one turret were completed. Both vehicles were captured by the Soviets, although the second prototype, which carried the turret, was destroyed by German forces. The Soviets refitted the turret to the remaining hull and shipped it back to Russia for further testing. The remaining "Maus" is now on display at the Kubinka Tank Museum.

Items used:

- **Easy Model 1/72 German "Maus" tank No. 36203**
- **Plastic strip**
- **Magic Sculp.**

1/72

Easy Model

Construction

Being the largest tank ever built, a model of the Maus has an impressive size in 1/35 scale. Scaled down to 1/72, it becomes much easier to handle, yet it is still large enough to be an enjoyable painting exercise, which is exactly what I was looking for when I bought the already assembled Easy Model (No. 36203) offering. The China-based company offers four different models of the Maus, each in a different color or camouflage, with two of them carrying an external tank on the rear. I went for the simple overall red primer version, as this seemed the obvious choice for a repaint.

Having said that, I could not start repainting immediately, as I felt some details looked a little rough and could do with a little refining and extra detailing.

Starting with the headlights, they needed some putty on top where there was a flat spot from the sprue being cut off too close. In other areas, like on the hatches in the turret, sprue still needed to be removed. Both exhaust pipes were drilled out. Using a small drill first, a series of holes was drilled by hand in the area to be opened up. Then, using a scalpel, the remaining plastic between the holes was cut away. With the aid of a small round-head drill bit in a slow-turning motor tool (make sure you set the motor tool to low speed), the opening was further refined resulting in a more-to-scale thin rim. Also, both gun barrels were drilled out to scale thickness by using round-head and conical-shaped drill bits. No need to use a motor tool here: careful drilling by hand will suffice. Although the casting structure on the turret looked quite good, the sides of the hull looked anything but. To get the sides to look more realistic and similar to the rest of the casting structure present on the model, I first sanded the surfaces to remove the overly rough texture. Then, using a slow-turning motor tool and various shaped drill bits, I added new texturing. To get a feel for casting texture on vehicles, study some photographs of the real thing before commencing work on your model. Also, the smooth surface on the side of the gun mantle received extra attention. Molded seams were removed, while putty was used to fill some gaps as on the rear where the upper and lower hull meet. Missing all over the kit are the typical torch cut marks. These were simulated by engraving them with the edge of a triangular file – a farily fast and simple procedure with realistic results. The missing interlocking seams of the hull armor plates were also added using a slow-turning motor tool and the edge of a flat-topped drill bit. Missing weld seams on the front and rear where the lower and upper hull meet were sculpted using Magic Sculp. The over-scale heavy housing of the front periscope and rear Notek light were refined by sanding them down with a file and scalpel. Finishing off where I started, the headlights also received some extra detailing using plastic strip.

The Easy Model Maus comes assembled and painted. Four different options are available. I went for the red primer version, as this would be the most logical for a repaint.

Overall views of the model. It comes with some form of weathering in that it has had dark filters to add some depth.

1. Front close up. Note the difference in texturing on the front glacis plate and the side of the hull. The latter needs sanding down and retexturing.

2. The headlights have flat spots on top where they were cut from the sprue.

3. Texture on the turret looks quite good as opposed to the hull. The exhausts will need opening up.

4. Some parts still carry remains of sprue and will need to be cleaned up. Putty will be needed to fill up small gaps and inaccuracies.

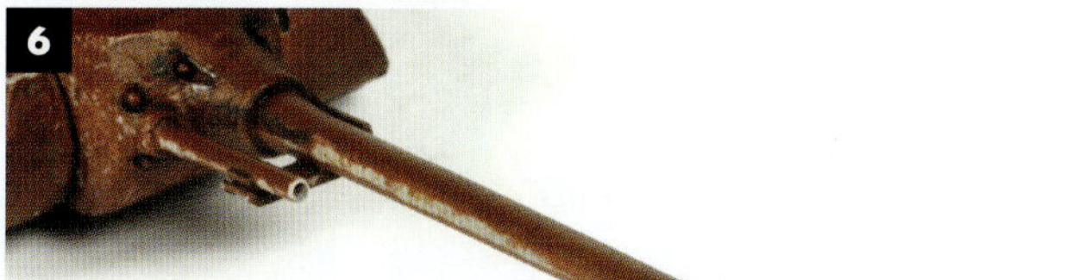

5. The barrels were drilled out for scale thickness as well. For the smaller barrel, I used a round-head drill bit.

6. A larger conical drill bit was used to thin the edge of the larger barrel. No motor tool was used for either barrel.

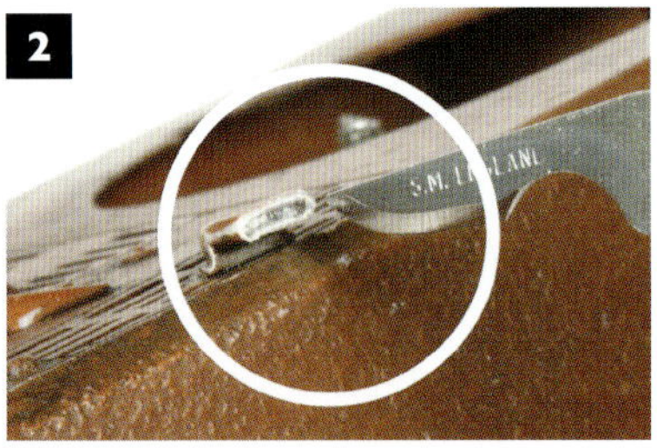

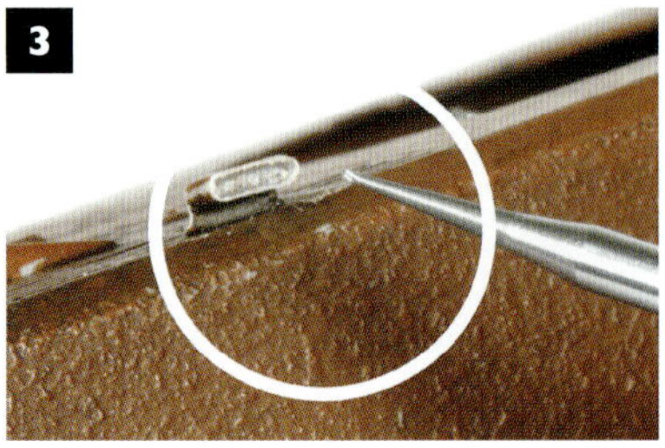

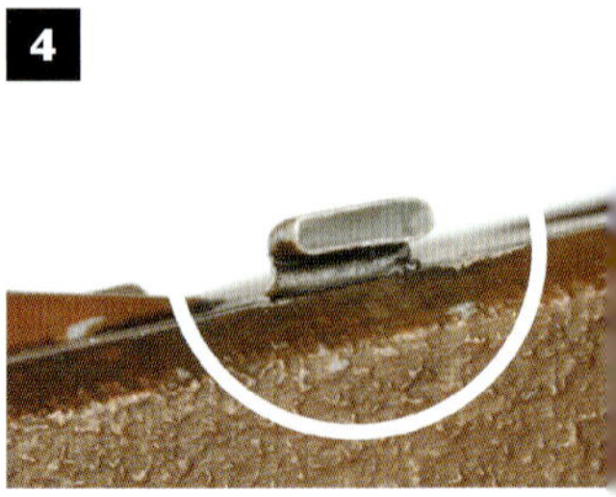

1. To open up the exhausts, a series of small holes was carefully drilled by hand.

2. Then the plastic between the holes was removed with a scalpel.

3. Using a small round-head drill bit, the opening was then increased further. Make sure you set the motor tool at slow speed. These parts are very fragile.

4. The opened-up exhaust. Note how thin the rim of the exhaust is.

5. On the rear where the lower and upper hulls meet, some putty will be required.

6. The sides of the hull were sanded down to remove the coarse texture and then reworked with various drill bits in a slow-turning motor tool. Drill bits used were either small round-head or flat-topped. Each gives a different result.

7. The side of the gun mantlet could use a little more texturing as well.

8. Torch cut marks were engraved with the sharp edge of a triangular file. Putty was used to fill the gap between upper and lower hull.

9. The interlocking seams of the hull armor plates were simulated with the side edge of a flat-topped drill bit. Shallow holes were opened up with a small drill.

10. A rather fast and simple method to simulate missing torch cut marks is to engrave them using the sharp edge of a triangular file. Here, the hull sides are being taken care of.

11. Missing weld seams on the front were added with Magic Sculp. The arrows indicate the weld seams made with Magic Sculp.

12. Also on the rear, Magic Sculp was used to add missing weld seams. The arrows indicate the weld seams made with Magic Sculp.

1. The Notek light housing on the rear was thinned to scale by sanding it down with a file. The sides were thinned with a scalpel.

2. The cover for the periscope on the front of the hull received the same sanding.

3. It also received the same cutting treatment as the Notek light housing to thin it down to scale.

4. The flat spots on top of the headlights were reworked with putty, while a small strip was added for extra detail (the arrow indicates the added detail). The drilled out exhausts look much more realistic. The sides of the hull were sanded and texturing was reworked. Note the torch cut marks on the upper sides of the hull still need to be added.

Overall views of the model ready for painting. The areas revealing gray plastic indicate where some work was done. Note that the torch cutting on the top hull sides still needs to be reworked.

Painting

AIRBRUSHING

With the refining and detailing work done, I restored the red primer with an overall coat of Vallejo Surface Primer German Red Brown Ral 8012. Both barrels were next airbrushed with Vallejo Model Air Black Grey (056), Dark Grey Blue (054) and German Grey (052) in consecutive layers starting with the darkest first. The lightest color, German Grey, was only misted on the tip of the main gun to generate interest in an otherwise monotone colored barrel. After masking both barrels, the rest of the model was given a brighter coat of red primer with Vallejo Model Air Fire Red (084). The reason for doing so was because I first intended to use the hairspray technique to do some chipping, but I later decided to go the traditional way and use paint and a fine-tipped brush instead. Working with vinyl acrylic paints such as these means you need to work fast, because once they are fully dry, they are very hard to chip.

As there were only ever two vehicles completed, the painting options are rather limited – unless of course you decide to take the "what if" route and design your own paper panzer camouflage, which is what I did. When doing a paper panzer, you can be as creative as you want, as there are no rights or wrongs. However, I decided to keep it simple and not go overboard with colors and patterns. Instead, I used an image of one of the other Easy Model kits, which featured an overall yellow turret on a yellow hull carrying green camouflage stripes, as inspiration (kit No. 36204).

For the yellow basecoat, I mixed two drops of Vallejo Model Air Dark Yellow (025) with four drops of Model Air White (001). Working in a small scale, it is always better to keep the model rather light in color. Dark base colors are, in general, not that attractive, while details will be harder to see.

Instead of using a wavy soft edge pattern camouflage, I decided to design a hard-edge splinter scheme. With 1/72-scale drawings and pencil and ruler, I got to work. Once I was happy with the design, I put the drawings in a plastic folder. Putting it in a plastic folder makes it easy to add masking tape on top, onto which the design can then be copied. The masking tape was then removed and transferred to a hard surface, which enabled me to cut out the masks. They were then transferred to the model. First, both sides were prepared while the rest of the model was masked off to prevent overspray. For the green, I mixed two drops of Vallejo Model Air Camouflage Light Green (006) with one drop of Model Air Pale Green (095). As always, I added one drop of Vallejo Airbrush Thinner (061) per three drops of paint to make everything flow smoothly.

Next, the rear and front were prepared for painting. Note that designing the sides on the scale drawings was relatively easy, as they are straight up with only a little slope at the top. The front and rear glacis plates, however, are positioned at an angle, so to get the dimensions of the masks correct in scale with the actual plates on the model, I measured the plates and made new, correct, full-size drawings of the plates onto which I designed the camouflage.

The hull top was left blank, while the camouflage on the front and sides was carried through to the sloped shields on top of the hull. To a person standing next to the vehicle, the camouflage would seem to run all over the hull.

1. After the model had been worked over, the red primer was restored with an overall coat of Vallejo Surface Primer German Red Brown Ral 8012.

2. Both barrels were next airbrushed with Vallejo Model Air Black Grey (056), Dark Grey Blue (054) and German Grey (052) in consecutive layers. The lightest color was only misted on the tip.

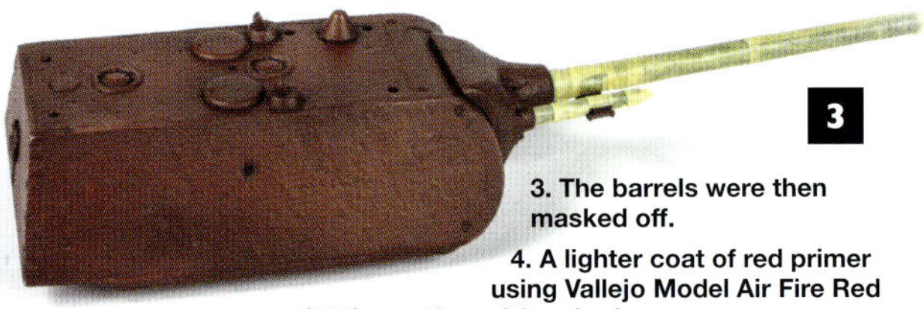

3. The barrels were then masked off.

4. A lighter coat of red primer using Vallejo Model Air Fire Red (084) was then airbrushed on.

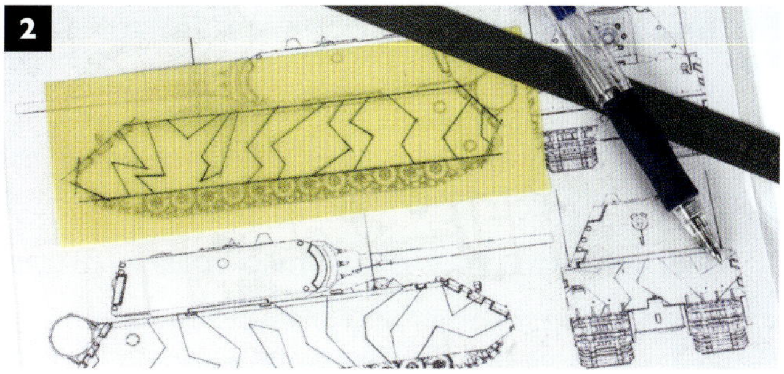

1. The base color was mixed with two drops of Vallejo Model Air Dark Yellow (025) and four drops of White (001).

2. Scale drawings were used to design a hard-edged, splinter-pattern camouflage for the hull. When finished, the drawings were put in a plastic folder. Masking tape can then be put on top to copy the pattern.

3. Next, the masking tape is put on a hard surface and the pattern is cut out.

4. It can then be transferred to the model. The rest of the model is masked to prevent overspray. The camouflage color was mixed with two drops of Vallejo Model Air Camouflage Light Green (006) and one drop of Pale Green (095).

5. The front received its appropriate masking patterns. Note how the camouflage is carried through to the screens on top of the hull.

The hull with the masking tape removed, revealing the camouflage.

BRUSH PAINTING AND WEATHERING

With the airbrushing done and the masking tape removed, it was time to do some touching up. The inside of the lower hull received a fresh coat of red primer, while small inaccuracies where green paint had seeped under the masking tape were touched up with the yellow base color. Panzer Aces Highlight German (Black) (337) was used to base-paint the tracks. The running surfaces of the wheels were initially painted Model Color Black (950).

PIN WASHES, DRY-BRUSHING AND HIGHLIGHTING

The next step after finishing the base painting is creating some depth with a first run of pin washes. Thinned Vandyke Brown oil paint was carefully run around all details and into nooks and crannies. Any unwanted effects were cleaned up with a wider brush moist with odorless white spirit. Although it creates an instant shadow effect, it takes more than one run of pin washes to create the depth I'm looking for. Gradually building up the effect always looks best. After the first pin wash follows a first dry-brushing with the yellow base and green camouflage color. I do this to blend unattractive-looking remains of the first pin wash and to refresh the sharpness of the details. Although acrylic colors are more difficult to use for dry-brushing (because of their thin consistency), it is not impossible to do so.

Here are some pointers for those who are not familiar with the dry-brushing technique, which is usually carried out using enamel paints, as they are not as thin as acrylic paints.

1. Take some of the paint gathered at the bottom of an unstirred jar of paint. It's important not to stir the paint for dry-brushing.
2. Place the paint on a piece of card and let it settle for a few moments so that the oil gets soaked up by the card.
3. Use a clean, dry brush (preferably wide; size depends on the area you are working on) and dip it in the paint.
4. Wipe the brush on a piece of kitchen paper or a cloth to remove most of the paint.
5. Gently move the brush over the model and you'll see a subtle effect of paint appearing. Gradually building up the effect results in a much more realistic finish. Don't rush it!

With acrylic colors, I mix them in a palette, using the same mixing ratio for the colors as before, without diluting them. After picking up the paint with a wide, flat brush, I remove most of it by gently stroking the brush on a paper towel. When the paint on the brush is dry enough, I take it to the model and start dry-brushing. You'll notice that details will get highlighted again and pin washes are blended, resulting in a softer finish – but because I want more depth and sharper details, the whole process is repeated. Even in later stages, details get picked out and highlighted and more local shadows

The model ready for weathering.

are created where necessary. There is no strict rule to follow of what comes first and then next, as it is more a case of going back and forth between the different stages until the desired result is reached.

In this case, before the second outlining, I also added small variations in the yellow base color on the turret by using the speckling technique. This involves adding small speckles of paint to a surface by flicking the paint from a brush onto the model. It can be used to create subtle variations in the base color, or to add rust, dirt, etc.

To do this, I added four more drops of Model Air White (001) to the base mix to create a lighter color. Then, using a wide, flat brush, the paint was picked up. Sometimes you need to change the consistency of the paint by adding some water. So, before speckling the model, I first test the result on a piece of paper. I stroke the brush against a toothpick, directing the splatters onto the paper. If the splatters are too large, then the paint is too thin. If they are too small or too close together, the paint is too thick. Only when I've found the right consistency do I take the brush to the model. Specks of paint that don't belong can be removed before the paint dries with a brush moist with water. If the paint has already dried, you can use a little Vallejo Airbrush Thinner (061) instead. Using the thinner may leave glossy spots, which in turn can easily be removed by gently brushing them with some water.

Apart from the speckling, I also painted on dots and scratches using the same color and a fine-tipped brush. At the same time, some details were picked out and highlighted.

Because the hull was painted in two colors, I didn't use the speckling technique, as this would involve too much masking. Instead, I again hand-painted dots, scratches and highlights with a brush. For the green camouflage color, I added two drops of Dark Yellow and four drops of White to the two drops of Camouflage Light Green (006) and one drop of Pale Green (095) base color. In other words, the camouflage green base color was thus lightened by adding the yellow base color.

There now followed a second pin wash, followed by another subtle round of dry-brushing and picking out details.

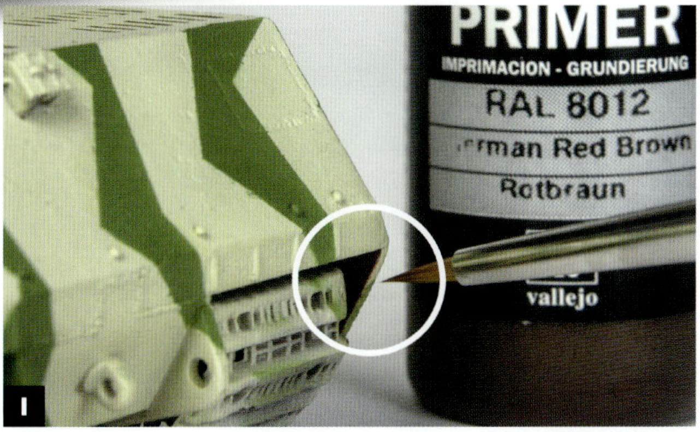

1. Some areas need a little touching up. Here the red primer on the inside of the lower hull is getting some attention.

2. Here and there, the camouflage color seeped under the masking tape and needed a little touching up with the base color.

3. The tracks were base-coated with Panzer Aces Highlight German (Black) (337).

4. Shadow areas and running surfaces of the wheels were painted Model Color Black (950).

1. All details, nooks and crannies were pin washed with Vandyke Brown oil paint. This is only "Round 1."

2. The turret receiving its initial pin wash.

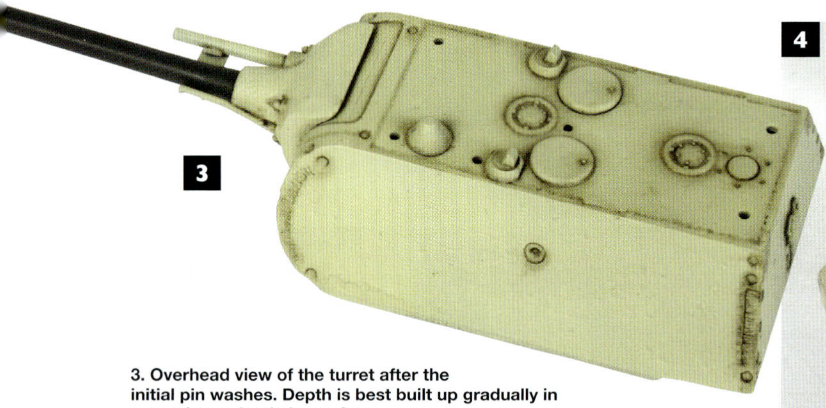

3. Overhead view of the turret after the initial pin washes. Depth is best built up gradually in several rounds of pin washes.

4. After the first pin wash, or outlining session, has taken place, I give the model a quick dry-brushing to blend unattractive remains of the washes and refresh the details. The same color mix was used as for airbrushing.

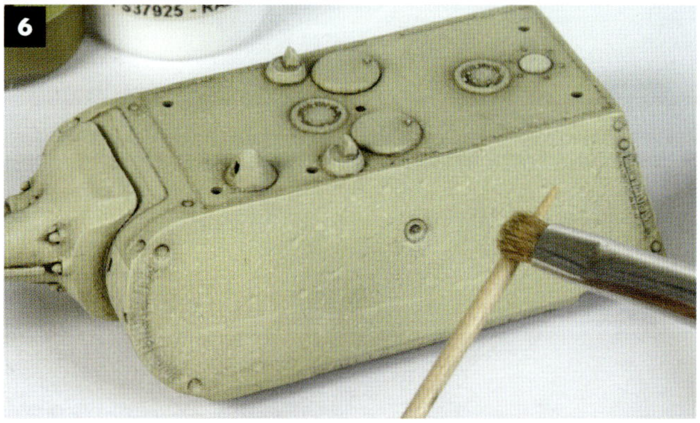

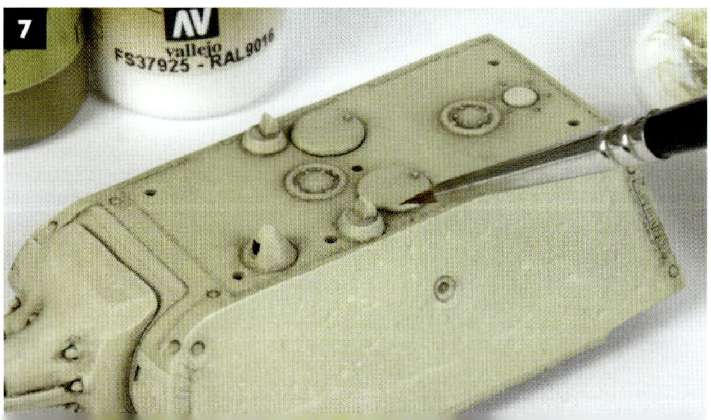

5. The green camouflage receives the same treatment.

6. Using the speckling technique, I added small variations in the yellow base color on the turret. The paint – I used a lighter version of the base color by adding four more drops of white – is picked up on a wide, flat brush and flicked onto the model by stroking the brush against a toothpick. Some testing to find the right consistency is called for.

7. Using a fine-tipped brush, more dots, scratches and highlights were added.

1. Because of the camouflage areas, I refrained from using the speckling technique on the hull.

2 & 3. To create a lighter shade of the green camouflage, I simply added the yellow base color to it.

4. A second pin wash is carried out to create more depth and add crisper details. Details stand more proud and more depth is present after the second pin wash or outlining.

5. After the second outlining, again details are touched up and lifted out with a fine-tipped brush.

6. On the turret too, details were touched up and picked out with a fine-tipped brush.

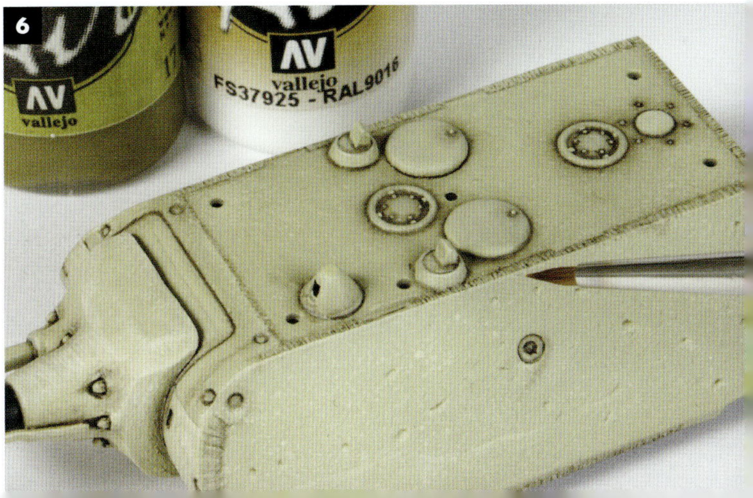

CHIPPING

As mentioned already in the introduction, chipping can add a sense of realism to a model in the way that it creates a feeling of use and age. It can make a model more or less attractive depending on how well the result turns out. One thing to always bear in mind is that you should try to keep the chipping roughly in scale. I say "roughly" as most chipping done on models is actually over scale. Have a look at real paint chips on objects in your surrounding; then try to visualize them in the scale of your model … Right!

Working on a 1/72-scale model therefore doesn't make things any easier, as actual in-scale chipping would hardly, or in most cases not at all, be noticeable. So a certain amount of artistic license is called for. If the chipping is done in a balanced and attractive way (if the composition works), then we can get away with it. But, don't forget, less is more – or, to put it bluntly, too little doesn't look as bad as too much.

Late war, paper panzer and red primer are three concepts that seem to go together well. So, from the outset I had in mind to chip the model, revealing the red primer instead of the usual dark brown color simulating metal beneath the primer. The red primer, yellow and green seemed quite an attractive combination. For the primer, I settled on Vallejo Model Color Cavalry Brown (982). It is advisable to build up the chipping gradually and logically. Remember, don't get carried away: you can always add more later.

HULL

From this stage on, I decided to finish the hull first. Using Raw Umber oil paint, I now added oil and grease stains. A bit of Raw Umber in combination with Yellow Ochre was used in selected areas to vary the yellow base color. The paint can be applied thinned, as filters, or stippled almost dry and then blended with a dry brush. Both methods work well and were used in combination. A mixture of Burnt Umber and Yellow Ochre oil paint creates a nice tint for rust streaking, while Vandyke Brown in turn was used for heavy oil or grease spills. More subtle streaking was added with pure Raw Umber. The streaks were painted individually with a fine-tipped brush and then blended using another slightly moist fine-tipped brush.

To simulate rust on the exhaust pipes, I stippled the ends with a mixture of Burnt Umber and Cadmium Yellow oil paint. Initially I had used Burnt Umber to paint fuel spills, but as this color seemed too similar to the rusty exhausts and the spills were situated basically next to the exhausts, I added some more filters with Vandyke Brown oil paint to change the color of the spills and add more variation. They also received a coat of Mig Productions Wet Effects and Damp Earth mixture (P409). On the other hand, when the rusty oil paint stippling on the exhausts was fully dry, I added a coat of Tamiya Flat Clear (XF-86) because rust is matt.

The periscope was picked out in Model Color Black (950). A coat of gloss varnish can be added if so desired. Here, I again used Mig Productions Wet Effects and Damp Earth mixture (P409). In the same area, on the front glacis plate, a couple of recent impacts from enemy fire were simulated by first painting them with German Camouflage Black Brown (822), and then adding a metal effect with a Karismacolor Silver pencil. Later, the centers of the impacts were again touched up with German Camouflage Black Brown.

1. The color chosen for the red primer chipping is Vallejo Model Color Cavalry Brown (982).

2. The red primer chipping is gradually added using a brush.

3. Oil and grease marks were recreated using Raw Umber oil paint.

1. To vary the base color, I used a mixture of Raw Umber and Yellow Ochre oil paint and used it in selected areas by applying it in the way of filters or by stippling it with an almost dry brush and then blending it.

2. Overhead view of the hull at this stage. Note how every new layer of paint gives the model more character.

3. At first I painted some fuel spills using Burnt Umber oil paint.

4. Rust streaking was done with a mixture of Yellow Ochre and Burnt Umber oil paint.

5. Heavy oil spills were simulated using Vandyke Brown oil paint.

6. Subtle general streaking was done with Raw Umber oil paint. Streaks were painted individually and blended using a fine-tipped brush.

1. The exhausts were given a rust treatment by stippling them with a mixture of Burnt Umber and Cadmium Yellow oil paint.

2. To make the fuel spills stand out more, they were given extra filters with Vandyke Brown oil paint.

3.Further filters were added with Vandyke Brown oil paint and Mig Productions Wet Effects and Damp Earth mixture (P409).

4. When fully dry, the rust on the exhausts was coated with Tamiya Flat Clear (XF-86) to give it the typical matt appearance.

5. The periscope was painted with Model Color Black (950).

6. A coat of Mig Productions Wet Effects and Damp Earth mixture (P409) was added to simulate the glass.

7. A couple of heavy impacts on the front glacis plate were undercoated with Model Color German Camouflage Black Brown (822).

8. Then a Karismacolor Silver pencil was used to add bare metal.

9. After this, the centers where again touched up with German Camouflage Black Brown (822).

RUNNING GEAR AND TRACKS

I now moved to the running gear and tracks. Also here, I used Cavalry Brown (982) to simulate red primer chipping and paint the odd red primer wheel. Although it is debatable if red primer wheels were ever used, it does add a touch of color and interest and, as mentioned before, with an imaginary subject there is no right or wrong: anything goes!

The tracks were given local filters with Lifecolor Rust Dark Shadow (UA 701) and Rust Base Color (UA 702) to add variation. Next, a series of dust filters was added using AK Interactive Summer Kursk Earth (080) and Rainmarks for NATO Tanks (074) enamel color washes. Then, when dry, the outer surfaces were dry-brushed using German Camouflage Black Brown (822), before receiving bare metal highlights with a Karismacolor Silver pencil. On the inside of the tracks, the areas touched by the rotating wheels were buffed up with a propelling pencil. Make sure to draw straight lines and only in the appropriate places, as nothing looks more unrealistic than buffed metal areas where the tracks remain untouched by the wheels. The running surfaces of the wheels themselves were brush painted in a bare-metal color with Model Air Steel (065). AK Interactive Dark Mud (023) and Summer Kursk Earth (080) were used to dirty up the lower areas of the hull and parts of the running gear. They were used in selected areas, sometimes overlapping one another.

TURRET

With the hull almost finished, I returned to the turret and applied the same steps as I did on the hull, save the dirtying up. The smaller of the two barrels received some chipped-paint effects with Model Air Black Grey (056), while for the main gray barrel I used Model Color German Camouflage Black Brown (822) as well as Flat Brown (984). Also, some stippling with a mixture of Naples Yellow and Titanium White oil paint was added. The tip of the barrel was given a metal edge by gently buffing it with a propelling pencil.

MARKINGS

Although neither of the two built hulls, nor the turret, seemed to have any markings, I nevertheless wanted to add some in the way of a single turret number, and thus decided on a large white digit. As I prefer to use dry transfers, I ended up choosing a cipher from Archer's Soviet Turret Numbers (AR 35148) transfers set. Although the markings were not intended for German vehicles, I liked the shape and felt it would look good once in place. Moreover, as this was a fictional Maus, and the only two that had actually ever been completed had been captured by the Soviets, a Soviet turret number would not seem such an odd choice. To make the story complete, it had to be number 3.

The numbers were carefully cut from the sheet, positioned on the turret and then gently rubbed down with a propelling pencil. After adding the numbers on both sides of to the turret they were toned down with some Raw Umber oil paint.

I also felt it would be nice to carry the number on the hull. Not having a smaller version of the Archer digit, I hand-painted one on the rear of the hull using Panzer Aces Stencil (313). This too received further weathering with Raw Umber oil paint.

FINISHING TOUCHES

Once everything else was done, I added some soot to both exhausts with Mig Productions Black Smoke pigments (P023). The reason I add this last is because I don't want to run the risk of touching the pigments afterwards while handling the model, as fingerprints made with black pigment can be hard to remove.

1

2

3

1. The running gear also received the red primer treatment with Model Color Cavalry Brown (982). A red primer wheel always adds a nice touch of color.

2. To vary the color of the tracks, they were filtered with Lifecolor Rust Dark Shadow (UA 701) and Rust Base Color (UA 702).

3. Dust and dirt were added by filtering with AK Interactive enamel color washes Kursk Summer Earth (080) and Rainmarks for NATO Tanks (074).

1. The outer running surfaces of the tracks were then dry-brushed with Model Color German Camouflage Black Brown (822).

2. Bare-metal highlights were added with a silver pencil.

3. On the inside, the guide teeth and surfaces polished by the rotation of the wheels were given a metal sheen with a propelling pencil.

4. The running surfaces of the wheels were in turn painted with Model Air Steel (065).

5 & 6. The lower hull and running gear received dust and dirt using AK Interactive Dark Mud (023) and Summer Kursk Earth (080). They were not mixed, but were sometimes used in consecutive layers.

7. The turret received the same treatment as the hull. Here, red primer chipping is on the way using Model Color Cavalry Brown (982).

8. To break up the monotone yellow base color, a mixture of Raw Umber and Yellow Ochre oil paint was applied in selected areas. It can be applied as filters, or stippled on almost dry and then blended with a wider dry brush.

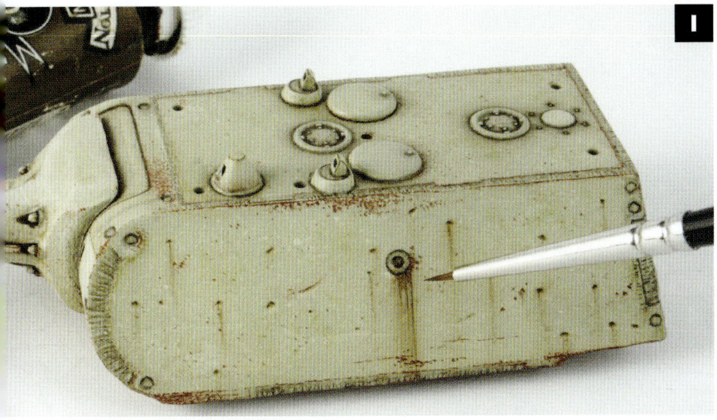

1. Rust streaks were simulated with Burnt Umber oil paint.

2. As with the hull, the periscopes were painted Model Color Black (950).

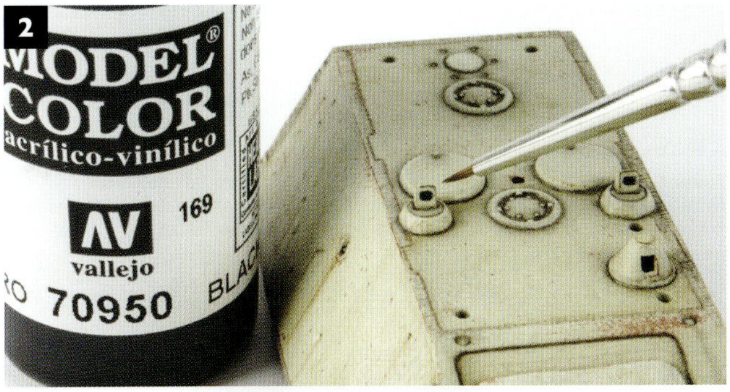

3. Again, a coat of Mig Productions Wet Effects and Damp Earth mixture (P409) was added to simulate the glass.

4. The smaller of the two barrels was left in its yellow overspray base color and received some gray chipping with Model Air Black Grey (056).

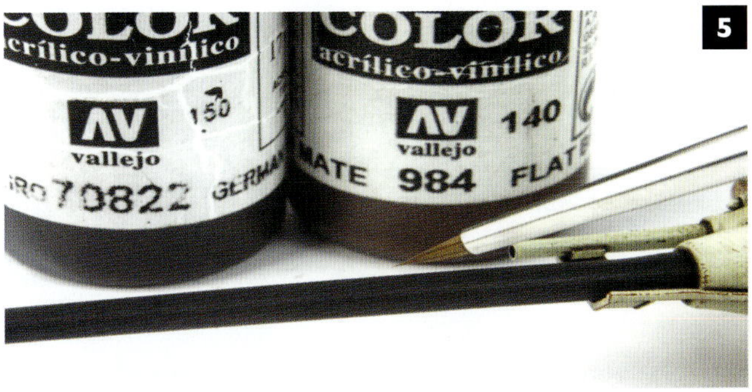

5. Model Color German Black Brown (822) and Flat Brown (984) were used to chip the main gun.

6. Some stippling with a mixture of Naples Yellow and Titanium White oil paint was also added.

7. The tip of the main gun was also given a little polish with a propelling pencil.

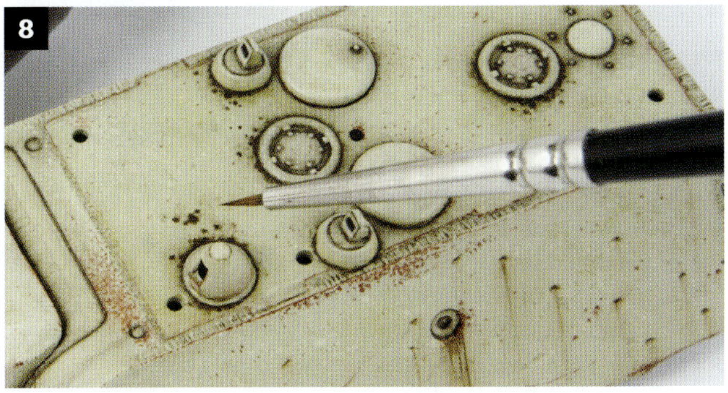

8. Oil and grease stains were simulated with Raw Umber oil paint.

1. For the turret number, I selected Archer dry transfer Soviet Turret Numbers (AR35148). Strictly speaking, they are for 1/35 scale, but the size was perfect for the large 1/72-scale sides of the Maus turret.

2. The number was cut from the sheet, positioned and then gently rubbed down with a propelling pencil.

3. Using some Raw Umber oil paint, the number was then toned down and weathered.

4. More dirt was added to the roof, again using Raw Umber oil paint.

5. Panzer Aces Stencil (313) was used to hand-paint a number on the rear of the hull.

6. As with the turret numbers, it was toned down and weathered using Raw Umber oil paint.

7. Finally, Mig Productions Black Smoke pigments (P023) were carefully used to add some soot residues from the exhaust.

The aim for doing this model was to have some fun with a simple painting exercise. Sometimes it can be fun to keep construction and detailing to a minimum and thus quickly get to the painting stages. Working in a scale that you are not accustomed to forces you to come out of your comfort zone, which will in turn improves your skills. When working smaller scale, it will oblige you to work in a more subtle way than what you are perhaps used Also, doing a "what if" model can be a lot of fun as there are no rights or wrongs – anything goes!

Side view of the finished model showing the overall yellow turret on a camouflaged hull. Note the soot from the exhausts.

Left and below. Close up of the area in front of the turret. Again, note the oil and grease marks under the turret, as well as the fuel spills.

Below. Thrown-up dirt can be seen on the lower areas of the hull. Rust streaking shows wear and tear. Note how red primer chipping is more prominent in some areas than in others: variation creates interest. The red primer chipping contrasts nicely with the yellow and green.

Left. Close up of hull and turret. Note the oil and grease spills under the turret. Various oil paints were used to create color variation, dirt, and oil and grease spills. Archer dry transfers were used for the turret numbers.

Note the absence of camouflage on top of the hull, except for the camouflage on the vertical shields.

SU-152

Eastern Front, winter 1943

Having enjoyed previous excursions to 1/48 scale, my interest was drawn by Bronco's new release of the SU-152 in quarter scale. A kit review showed perfectly molded mesh covers on the rear deck, a feature that usually needs replacing with an after-market update set. All that seemed to be needed here was a good paint job. Although I do enjoy detailing, this could be another quick build to get to the painting stages.

Based on the heavy KV tank chassis, the SU-152 was a self-propelled assault gun-howitzer, whose successes in destroying Tiger and Panther tanks earned it the nickname "Beast Killer." Production ran from January to December 1943, when it was replaced with the improved ISU-152.

- **Bronco 1/48 Russian Self-Propelled Gun SU-152 (April, 1943 Production) – ZB-48004**
- **Friulmodel KV-1/KV-2 tracks – ATL-4803**
- **Plastic strip, plastic rod, copper wire, Punch & Die set.**

1/48

Bronco

Construction

First inspection of the kit shows a detailed model that just needs some basic fine-tuning here and there. With well-shaped link and length tracks that are free from ejector-pin marks, and a small photo-etched fret, the kit seems quite complete.

To start off, the hull is prepared to take a handle which will facilitate holding the model during the painting stages later on, as well as drilling a couple of holes to mount the model on a base once it is finished. It is best to do this from the outset before any fragile details are added.

The hole for the handle is of course drilled in the center of the base, while the two holes to take the mounting pins are drilled diagonally, hiding them behind road wheels. As the floor of the hull is rather thin, some plastic strips are glued inside the hull to give the pins more body to grip to. A short metal tube will form the base for the handle, the latter being a holder for small drill bits. To keep the metal tube in place, a piece of copper wire is soldered to the top, giving it a square appearance. After the metal tube is inserted and glued in the hull, pieces of plastic strip are glued around the square top to prevent it from twisting while the model is being handled.

Commencing work on the suspension, it soon became apparent that there is a bit of leeway between the suspension arms and their location pins. This means you need to take care to align all arms if you want to display your model on a flat surface, as otherwise some of the wheels may not touch the floor. I proceeded by gluing the four corner arms first, making sure the model was sitting parallel to the floor. Then, all arms in between were added, always making sure they touched the floor and thus lined up. The axles for the wheels are all very short. As a result all wheels will need to be firmly glued in place. Another option would be to add longer axles made from plastic rod. I only did this for the drive sprockets, as that would make it easier to keep them in place during dry fitting. Using Blu Tack, the wheels were all temporarily fixed in place to determine the length of the tracks. Although the link and length tracks provided in the kit look very good and are easy to clean up (they are completely free of any ejector-pin marks), I still decided to replace them with Friulmodel metal items because I find workable tracks easier to paint.

Refining details to bring them to scale gets you a long way when building a model (almost) from the box. Sanding the rear guard is one of them.

Although no interior is provided, the gun breach is nicely detailed and could be viewed through the open hull hatches if you so desire. The gun housing and mantlet look a bit too smooth and can do with some texturing. First, they are stippled with liquid cement, causing the plastic to melt, giving them a rougher, more random appearance. Then, using a small round drill bit in a slow-turning motor tool, more pitting is added. Don't forget to study some photos of the real thing before you get to work. A second thin coat of liquid cement will take care of any plastic dust remains and sharp edges that need softening. To reproduce the typical torch cutting on the side of the mantlet, it is gently sanded with one of the sharp edges of a triangular file.

What struck me as odd in an otherwise very nicely detailed kit, is the unrealistic texturing of the upper hull. Not only is the pitting rather large in scale, it is also very evenly spaced and not at all random – quite the opposite of what it should look like. Using Tamiya putty, all existing texturing was filled and sanded. Again, using a small round drill bit in a slow-turning motor tool, random texturing was added

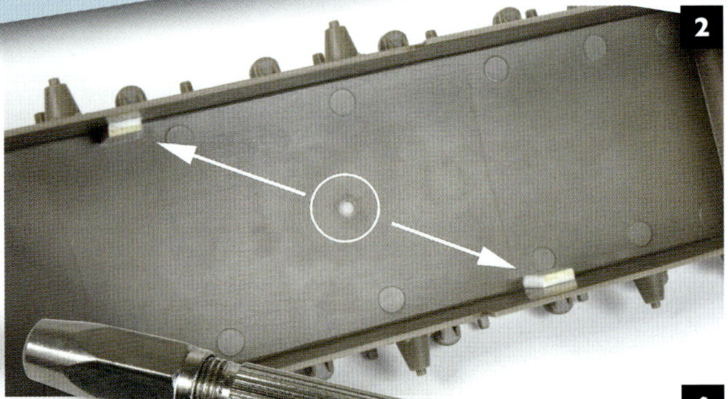

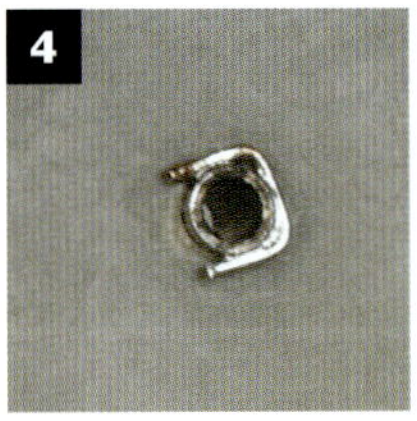

1. From the beginning, the hull is prepared to take a handle to facilitate holding the model during the painting stages. Two further holes to mount the model on a base are drilled as well.

2. On the inside, plastic strip is used to give the mounting pins more body to grip to.

3. Copper wire was soldered to the top of a piece of metal tubing.

4. This was then inserted and glued in the hole, and would later serve as a grip for the handle.

5. Plastic strip was glued around the square copper rim to prevent the tube from twisting.

6. A handle for small drill bits will be used to hold the model during the painting stages.

that was more to scale. A thin layer of liquid cement sealed the work. In fact, all surfaces received the liquid cement treatment giving them a "steel" appearance. Only thin metal surfaces, like the fenders, were exempt. Here and there, extra pitting was added using the motor tool.

Leaving off some of the fenders always adds character to a model, so I decided to leave off both front fenders, as well as the entire rear section of the left fender. The unwanted parts were cut off using a scalpel. Typical for molded fenders is that they are too thick in scale and need sanding down. Simply beveling the edge with a file does the job. The next series of actions are in accordance with that, as they are all done to refine molded details. Lift hooks were carefully drilled out, tie downs were hollowed out with the tip of a scalpel and tubular shapes were undercut to make them look round and less heavy.

With the rear deck mated to the lower hull, the seams near the top hull sides need to be obscured as the deck rests between, rather than on top of, them. The top sides, all the way to the front and rear, require torch cutting simulation. Molded detail was softened with liquid cement and after a few moments recreated with a scribing tool. Further detailing of the lower hull again consisted of refining molded detail on the front of the hull by scraping it with a scalpel. The overall fit of parts is very good. I only used two plastic strips to fill small gaps: one on the lower hull area where the mesh is situated, and one where the rear deck meets the upper hull compartment.

To get a neat, clean look, it is often better to remove the larger location pins present on (for example) the arms for holding the fenders. The location holes in the fender are again filled with plastic strip and sanded smooth. Although I could have reworked the kit part, I again used plastic strip to replace one of the arms of the missing left fender. As I wanted to portray a damaged headlight, leaving out the glass, the edge of the lamp needed to be brought to scale by thinning it. Using a larger round drill bit in a slow-turning motor tool (the emphasis is on "slow"), the lamp was carefully hollowed out. The same was done with the exhausts, as they also looked too heavy. Along the same lines, where necessary, all onboard equipment and holders were drilled out and refined.

To add to the used look of the vehicle, I opted to add only one of the fuel cans strapped to the fenders. Also here, the molded handles were reworked as the middle parts were cut and replaced with thin plastic strip, making them hollow. The weld seam was worked over by softening it with liquid cement and then scribing it with the tip of a scalpel.

1

1. To make sure the model sits level, the four corner suspension arms are glued on first, then tested with the wheels on.

2. Then all suspension arms in between are added, always making sure they sit parallel.

3. Axles on the suspension arms are very short to say the least and wheels will need to be glued on firmly. Both axles for the drive sprockets were lengthened with plastic rod.

2

3

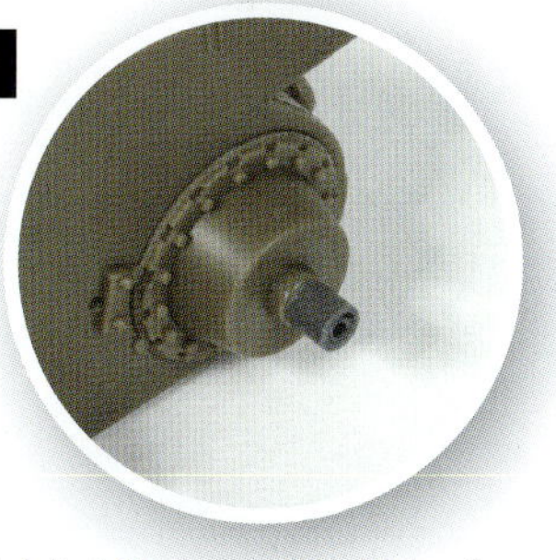

4

4. Photo-etch bolts supplied in the kit were glued in place with a little liquid cement.

5

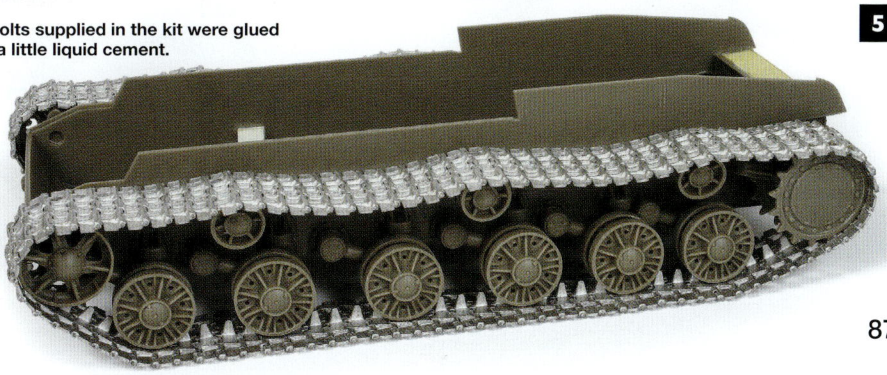

5. Although nicely detailed, the link and length tracks from the kit were replaced with metal items from Friulmodel.

1. Refining the kit often means sanding down parts to scale thickness.

2. The completed gun assembly ready to be installed in the hull.

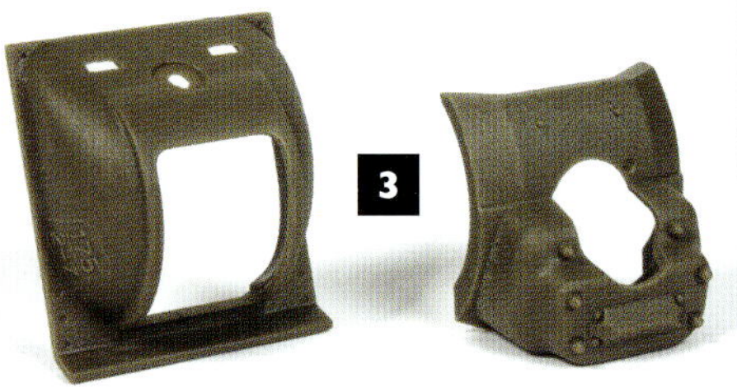

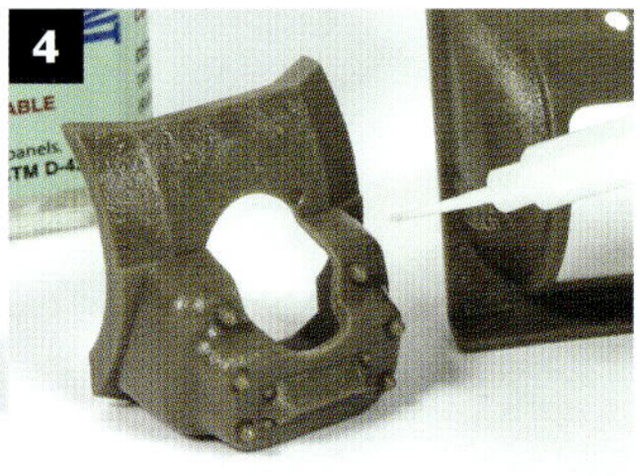

3. The texture on the gun housing and mantlet looks a bit too smooth.

4. Therefore, the surface is worked with some liquid cement, adding a more random and rough-cast effect.

5. More pitting was added with a small round drill bit in a slow-turning motor tool.

6. Torch cutting marks on the side of the mantlet were made by using the sharp edge of a triangular file.

7. The texture on the upper hull looks very unrealistic. The pitting is rather large and evenly spaced.

8. Tamiya putty was used to fill the pitting and create an even surface.

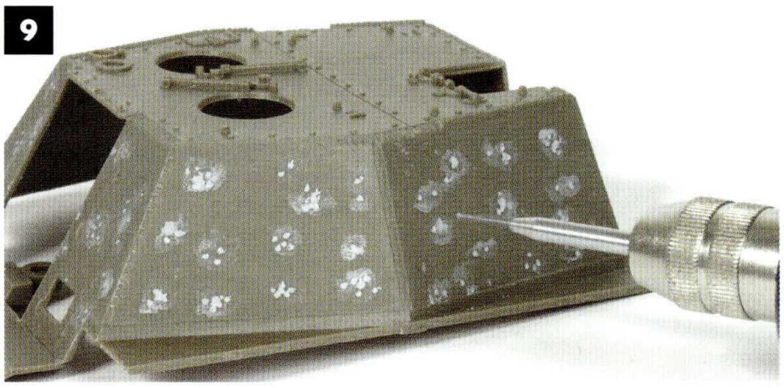

9. As on the gun housing and mantlet, the upper hull was then worked with the small round drill bit in a slow-turning motor tool to create a more realistic and in-scale effect.

10. To create a texture that looks more subtle, the whole model, saving thin metal parts such as fenders, was treated with the liquid cement.

11. Pitting was added on all the heavily armored parts of the model.

12. The liquid cement gives a realistic result.

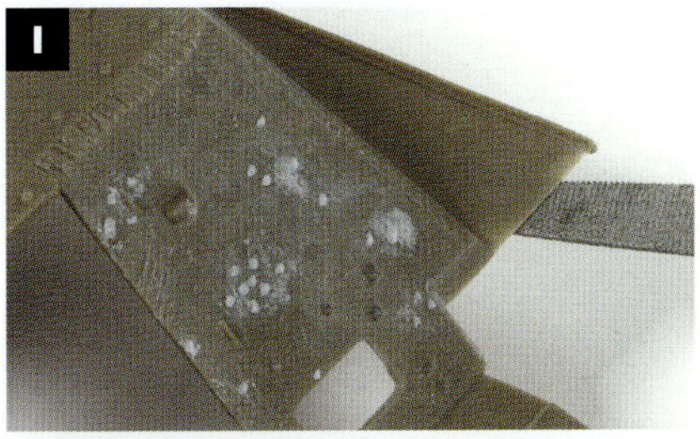

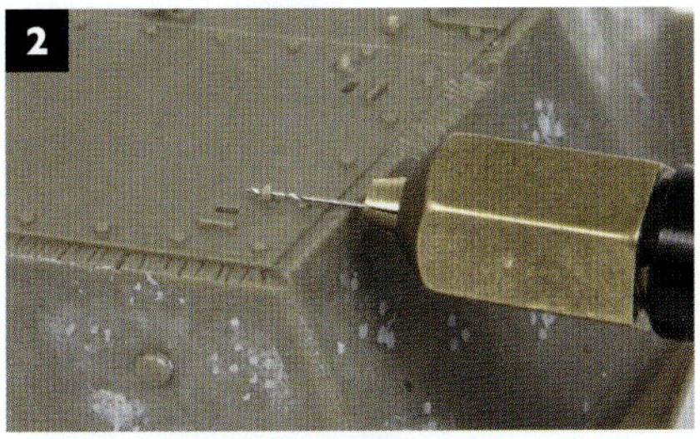

1. The fenders were thinned to scale thickness.

2. All lifting hooks were carefully drilled out for more realism.

3. The molded tie downs were hollowed out with a scalpel for the same effect.

4. Tubular moldings were undercut to reinforce the round shape and, as a result, make them look less heavy.

5. Detail on the front of the hull is brought to scale by scraping it with a scalpel.

6. The seam where the rear deck meets the hull sides needs to be obscured, as the deck is supposed to sit between the hull sides.

7. Putty, sanding and liquid cement make the seam disappear.

8. Plastic strip is used to close the odd gap.

9. Torch cut marks all over the length of the hull sides are engraved after softening the plastic with some liquid cement.

10. A second strip was used between the rear deck and upper hull.

11. Both front fenders, as well as the rear left, were cut off to add character to the model.

The upper and lower hull have been assembled.

Refining small details like this can make the model look much more crisp.

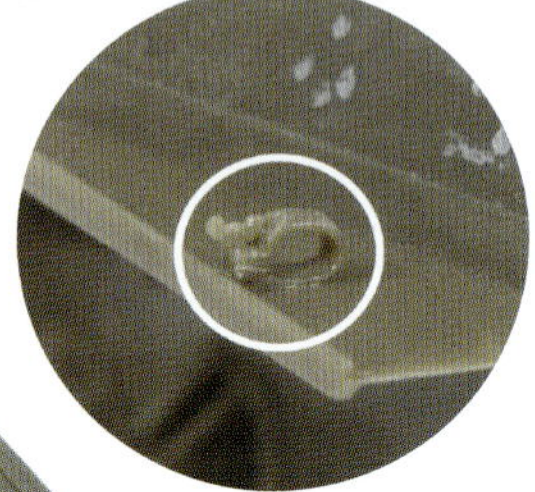

1. Location holes in the fender were filled with plastic strip.

2. The location pins were removed for a neater result.

3. Using a smaller round drill bit, the rim of the exhausts was brought to scale. Note the difference between the original and reworked part.

4. The holder for the headlight was sanded to scale.

5. Because I wanted to portray a damaged headlight, the rim needed to be thinned. A larger round drill bit in a slow-turning motor tool got the job done.

6. Using a small drill, the tool holder for the pickaxe was first drilled out. Then, a fine-tipped knife was used to hollow it out further.

7. Also, the ends of the gun cleaning rods were drilled out.

8. For the same purpose, molded handles on the fuel can were cut to remove the bulk from the middle. A small piece of strip was used as replacement, making it hollow.

9. The weld seam on the side was softened with liquid cement and then worked with a scalpel to give it better texture.

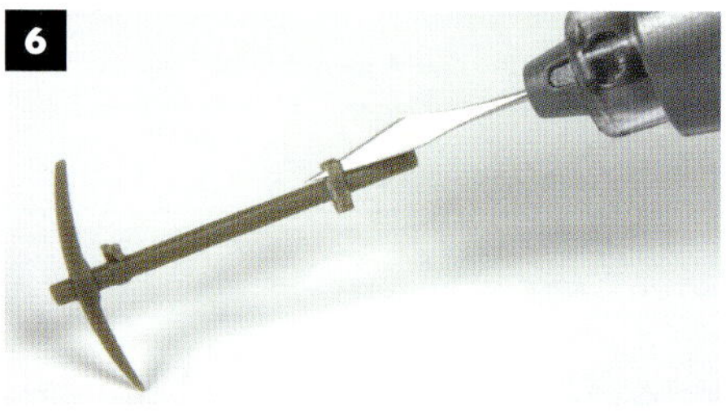

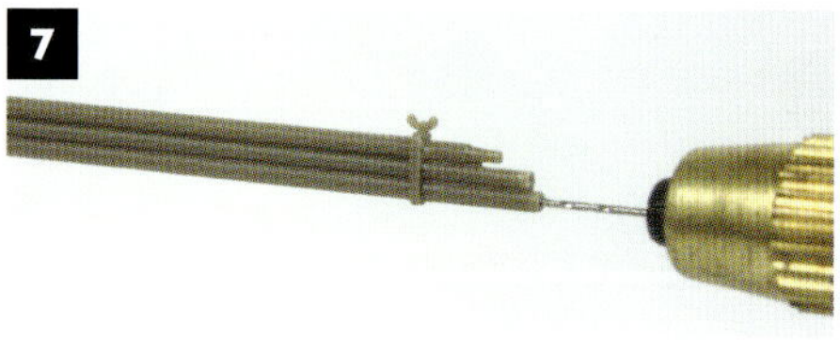

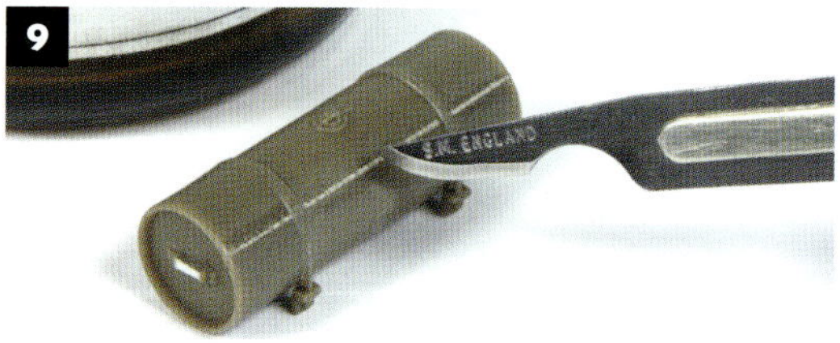

Overall views of the model, ready for painting. One of the supports of the missing fender was made from plastic strip.

Above. The spare track link is bolted down with some plastic strip and the wing nuts from the original kit part.

AIRBRUSHING

As I was going to use acrylic paints for airbrushing, the model first needed a good primer for the paint to adhere to. Although it is a Soviet model, I went for Vallejo's UK Bronze Green surface primer (607) instead of its Soviet 4 BO counterpart, as the latter looks very dark and very different from the color I was going to use as base color. Not that the darker primer color wouldn't have worked, but after a test I preferred the base color as it showed up over the Bronze Green primer. After putting on the primer, I masked all around the excellent molded mesh covers and airbrushed them with Vallejo Black surface primer (602) to create depth and shadow. Then, the mesh covers themselves were masked and left until all airbrush work was finished.

For the base color, I resorted to A. Mig 4 BO Russian Green (019), which is the color that would have been used for a Soviet vehicle of that era. To make the paint flow better, I added some Vallejo new formula airbrush thinner (061). The usual ratio is one drop of thinner for every three drops of paint, but you can thin according to your own discretion. The fuel can received a slightly different color basecoat, as I added a few drops of Vallejo Air Camouflage Light Green (006) to the A. Mig 4 BO Russian Green (019) for variation. After that, the model was sealed with Vallejo Air Gloss varnish (058), which was then mostly over-sprayed with Vallejo Air Satin varnish (060), save the round parts, like, for example, the barrel, the dome on the engine deck hatch and the fuel can; these were left glossy. The spare track, on the other hand, was airbrushed with Vallejo Air Matte varnish (059).

The painting instructions of the kit suggest two overall green vehicles, one overall whitewashed and one partly whitewashed vehicle. In my mind, there had never been any doubt about the paint scheme I was going to do: a faded whitewash. Not only is painting faded whitewash schemes a lot of fun, it also gives you plenty of choice on what the final result will look like, as there can be many gradations of the faded white covering of the vehicle. In this case, I was going for a whitewash that mainly concentrated on the front of the vehicle, with the rest mostly whitewash free. Incidentally, the partly whitewashed scheme suggested in the instructions also concentrates on the front of the vehicle.

There are several ways to go about recreating a whitewash. A popular way to get good results is the omnipresent hairspray technique. Having used this technique before, I wanted to revisit it. Readily available chipping products make the search for a good working hairspray product unnecessary. Having said that, you still have the option of mixing the regular and heavy chipping fluids to your own needs, as different mixes, put on in more or

1. Although dealing with a Soviet vehicle, the model was primed using Vallejo UK Bronze Green surface primer (607).

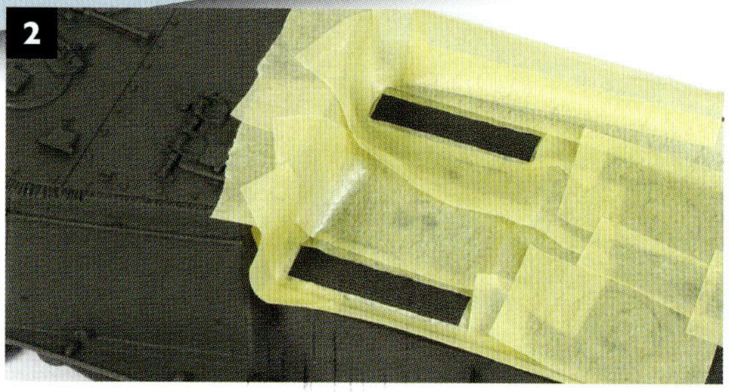

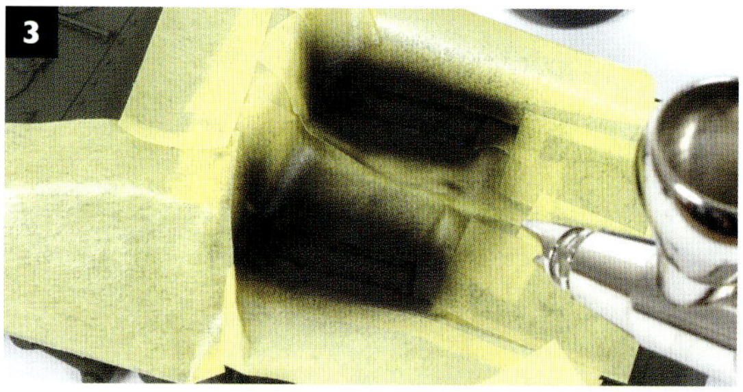

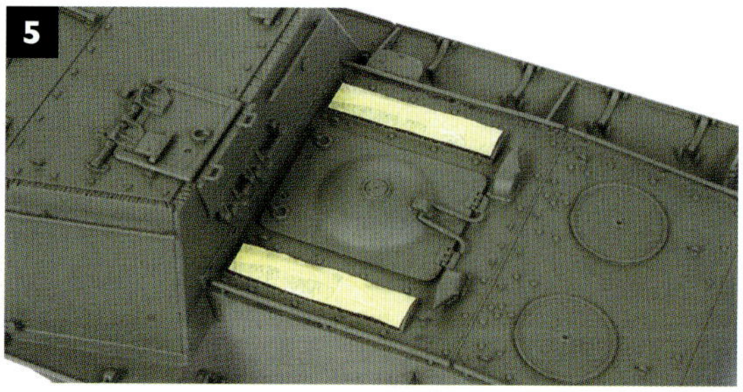

2. The molded mesh covers on the rear deck were first masked.

3. Then they were primed with Vallejo Black surface primer (602).

4. This will provide depth and shadow areas for later.

5. Masking tape was then used to protect the black areas from the next airbrushing stages.

fewer layers, give different results. After some tests, I went for two straight layers of AK Interactive Heavy Chipping acrylic fluid (089), as I wanted the paint to come off rather easily. The fluid was airbrushed on over the areas that would receive the whitewash later, while areas that were to remain green were not touched. Next on was a thin coat of Tamiya Flat White (XF-2) diluted with water. Using water to dilute the paint makes it easier to remove it later on. Also, using Tamiya paint means that you will be able to remove the paint even weeks after it has been airbrushed on. No need to hurry there.

When putting on the white, you should already have some idea about how the whitewash ought to look. You should roughly know which areas will be covered and which not. Covering everything with white, assuming you are going to take away the paint where it is not wanted afterwards anyway, might not give a satisfactory result. Using the paint in selected areas adds to the faded look, as this way you get soft borders of white, while an opaque layer will not. So, thinking about composition at this stage is important.

For removing the white paint, I use different-size brushes ranging from small round ones to larger flat ones. Also, a scribing tool can be a good choice should you want to draw scuff marks along the side of the vehicle, where the paint gets damaged when traveling through shrubs etc. Removing the paint is of course done by first gently moistening the area you want to work on with water, and then using a moist brush to work the surface. Depending on which and how much chipping fluid you use, the paint will come off more or less easily.

To disturb the paint on the large sides of the model, I mostly worked in a downward motion, as rain tends to run down removing the whitewash over time. For the most part, I just altered the edges of the white areas, only sometimes taking away some paint inside the larger surfaces. Remember, less is more. Don't get carried away when removing white paint. It is easier to take away some more paint later, than to get out the airbrush again to touch up the white in case too much has been removed. Once satisfied with the result so far I added a new coat of varnish to seal the whitewash for further weathering.

1

2

Left. Overall view of the model with the basecoat on.

3

1. A. Mig 4 BO Russian Green (019) was airbrushed on next to serve as a base color. A little thinning with Vallejo New Formula Airbrush Thinner (061) makes sure the paint flows well.

2. A coat of Vallejo Gloss varnish (58) sealed the basecoat. It was then followed with an overspray of Satin varnish (60), saving round parts like the gun barrel, dome on the rear deck hatch, etc.

3. To help create the faded whitewash, I next put on a couple of layers of AK Interactive Heavy Chipping fluid (089). Only the areas that were to receive a coat of white were treated.

1. Tamiya Flat White (XF-2) diluted with tap water was then misted on selected areas.

2–6. Overall views of the model after the whitewash has been airbrushed on.

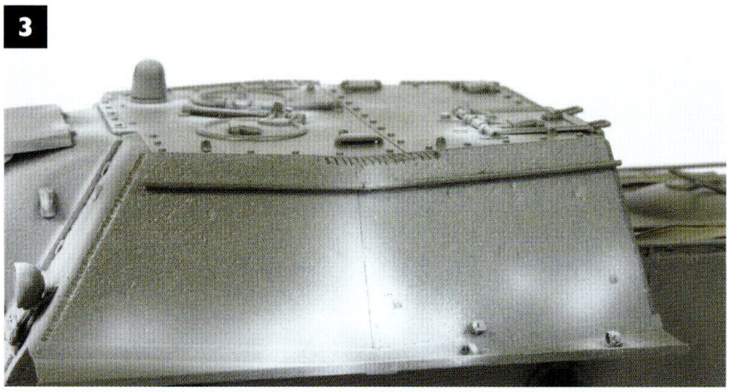

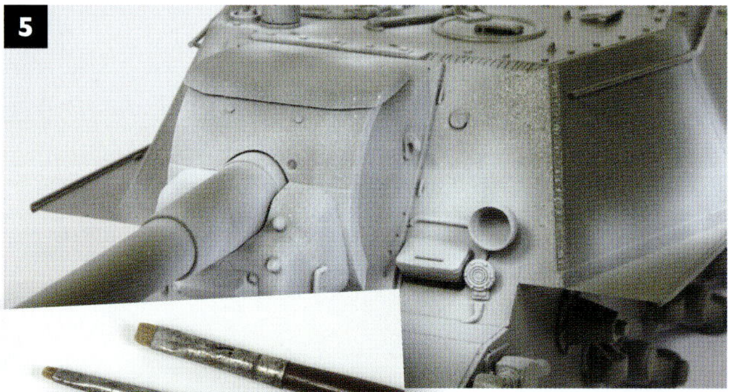

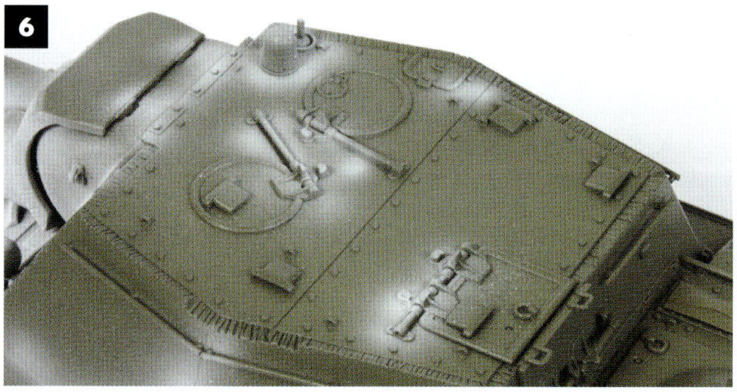

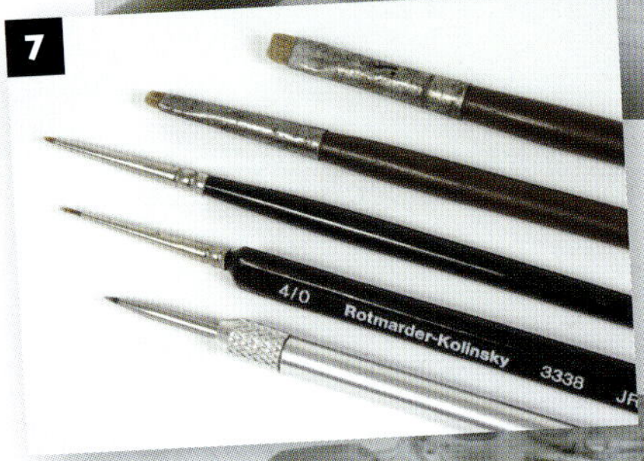

7. To remove parts of the whitewash, I use some smaller round fine-tipped brushes, wider flat brushes and even a scribing tool.

8. After wetting an area, a moist brush is put to work to remove parts of the whitewash. Here, on the hull sides, I'm working in a downward motion, mostly disturbing the edges of the white areas.

9. On horizontal areas, such as the roof, I mostly work in a front to rear motion, again mainly disturbing the edges of the white areas.

1. As rain tends to wash off the whitewash over time in a downward motion, it looks best if you go about distressing the paint in the same way.

2. I tend to stay away from the middle of the white areas and mainly concentrate on distressing the edges. A small, round, slightly blunt brush gives me a lot of control.

3. Only here and there are small disturbances made in the center of the white areas.

4. Working in a downward motion gives a more realistic result, as it suggests the whitewash has run off over time.

Left. Views of the model at this stage. Note how the whitewash has changed since the previous step. It now looks much more realistic.

5. When happy with the result so far, the whitewash was sealed with varnish to protect it from the next weathering stages.

GENERAL WEATHERING

Before actually starting the weathering process, I first dealt with the mesh covers on the rear deck. During the airbrushing stage, they received a black coat, creating depth and shadow. Now it was time to give them some color. Using the 4 BO Russian Green base color, I gently dry-brushed them, lifting out the mesh structure. The rest of the model was also carefully dry-brushed with the base color mixed with some A. Mig RAL 7028 Dunkelgelb aus '44 (011), to lift out some detail and create a first variety in the base color. To further add tonal differences in the overall green look of the model, I added local filters with Lifecolor RAL 6003 Olivegrün (UA 206) and picked out more details highlighting them with Lifecolor Olive Drab Green Tone (UA 427). With a first variety of base color present, the next step was to start the shading process. Vandyke Brown oil paint was thinned with odourless white spirit and run along all details and into all nooks and crannies, creating depth. After the first outlining session, I always give the model a quick dry-brush run with the base color to freshen up the overall look of the model and remove any unwanted remains of the outlining. As a next step, I started chipping with Lifecolor RAL 7008 GrauGrün/KhakiBraun (UA 212), concentrating mostly on edges, small details and well-worn places. Here and there, I added further highlights to the chipping by using the Lifecolor Olive Drab Green Tone (UA 427).

The process of highlighting and shading can go back and forth, adding several layers until the desired result is reached. There is no fast rule dictating how many layers you should add: it's up to you. In my case, it was time for a second outlining. Again, all details, nooks and crannies received the Vandyke Brown oil paint treatment. A second outlining will create more depth, more variation and will thus add more life to the model.

So far, apart from outlining, the faded whitewash received no further attention. The initial chipping using the hairspray technique can create great effects, but there is always room for some fine-tuning. Small detail chipping on the whitewash was carried out with a brush and the 4 BO green base color. Subsequent chipping was carried out on the rest of the model with a mixture of Vallejo Model Color German Camouflage Black Brown (822) and Chocolate Brown (872). I would usually opt for straight German Camouflage Black Brown for chipping, but here the color seemed a bit too dark and unnatural looking, hence the mixture with the lighter Chocolate Brown. As before, I concentrated on well-worn areas. Although I knew it would probably get lost during the final weathering stages, I still went ahead to create a visual reminder of where the missing fender was once located. To do this, I taped off the surrounding area and painted on the brown chipping mixture. Immediately after that, I used Vallejo Airbrush thinner (061) and a brush to distress the brown paint. The result is a faint reminder of where the fender used to sit.

Attention was now turned back to the whitewash. The gun mantlet could use some more variation in color, and therefore Vallejo Panzer Aces White (Ger. Winter Tkcr.) (344) was applied to create some interest. The same color can be used to add small remains of whitewash around details like bolts and such. In some areas, I opted to use Titanium White oil paint, as this can be worked for a longer time.

To paint the exhausts, I resorted to the trustworthy Lifecolor Dust and Rust set (CS-10). Starting with the darkest color first, I then proceeded until I was happy with the result. For a final darker tone on the base of the exhausts, I used Vallejo German Camouflage Black Brown (822). The insides were given a dark soot color with Lifecolor's Smoke (TSC 208). In the final stages, soot deposits will be reproduced on the rear deck using Mig Productions Black Smoke pigments (P023).

1. With a wide flat brush, the base color was carefully dry-brushed over the mesh covers, lifting out the detail.

2. Using a mixture of the 4 BO green base color (019) and RAL 7028 Dunkelgelb aus '44 (011), the entire model was dry-brushed to lift out details and add variety in the base color.

1

2

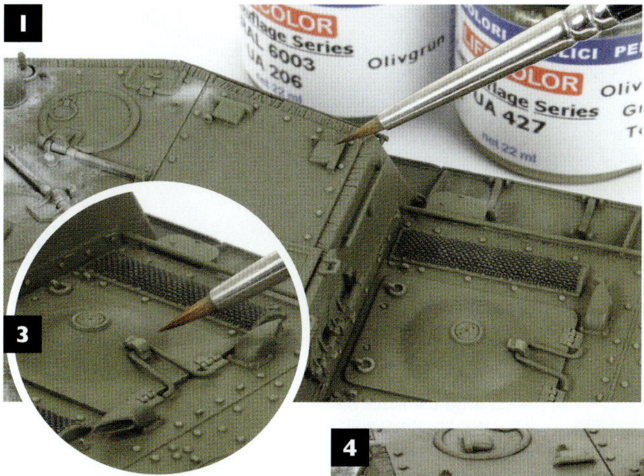

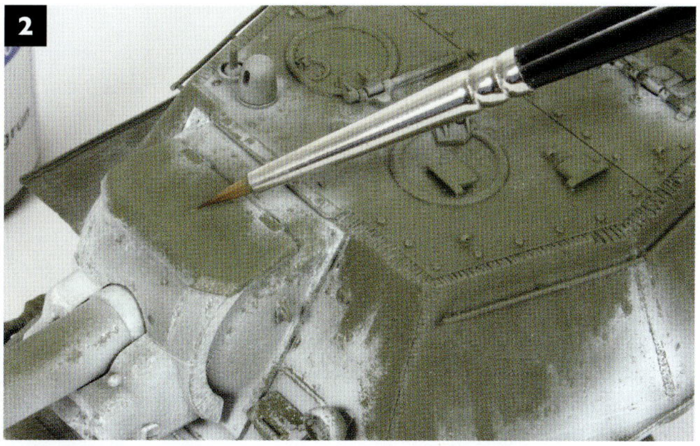

1. Local filters with Lifecolor RAL 6003 Olivegrün (UA 206) and Lifecolor Olive Drab Green Tone (UA 427) were applied to add further interest and bring out details.

2. Some larger panels were picked out with Olivegrün.

3. Smaller details where highlighted with Olive Drab Green Tone.

4 & 5. A fine-tipped brush and Vandyke Brown oil paint thinned with odorless white spirit were used to outline all details and fill all nooks and crannies to add depth.

Overall view of the model at this stage. More outlining will follow to enhance the effect.

1. Front view of the hull at this stage.

2. After the initial outlining, I always give the model a quick dry-brushing with the base color to revive colors and clean up any unwanted remains.

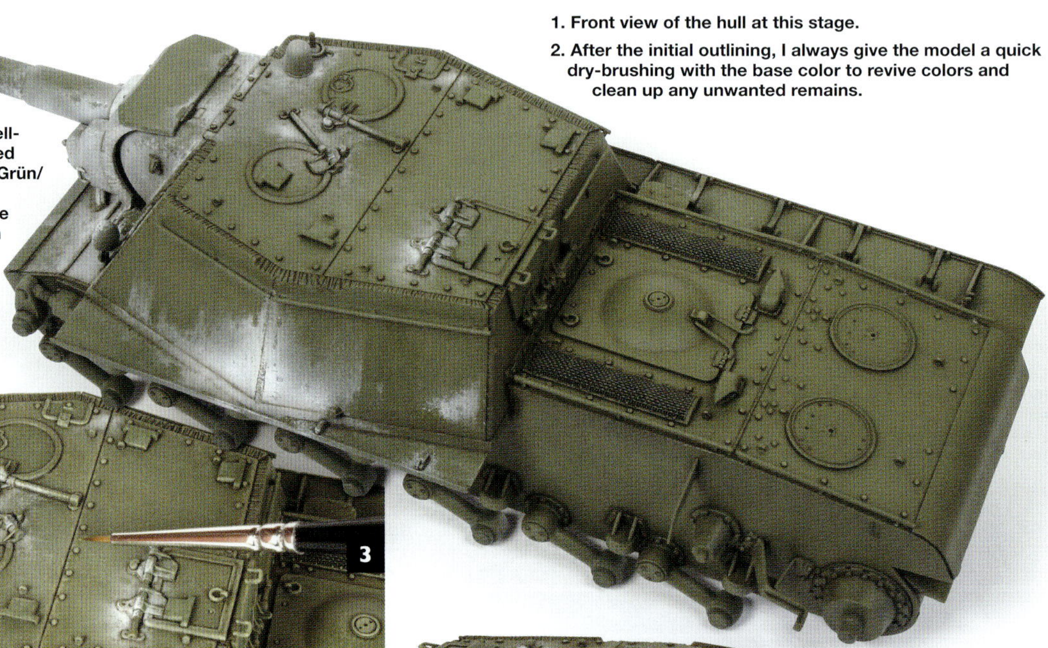

3. Edges, small details and well-worn places were then chipped with Lifecolor RAL 7008 GrauGrün/KhakiBraun (UA 212). Extra highlights in the chipping were added in selected places with Lifecolor Olive Drab Green Tone (UA 427).

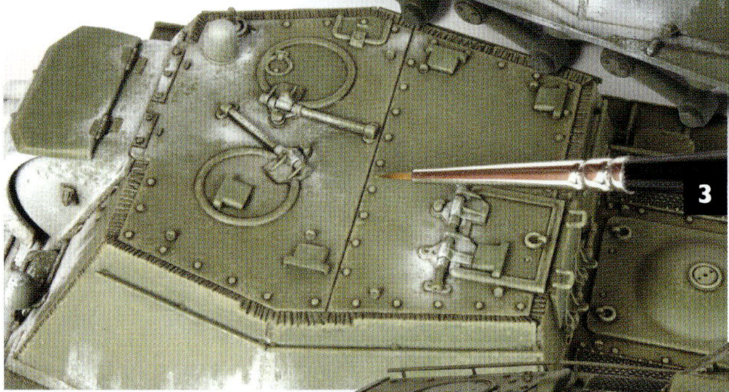

Above. Overall view of the model at this stage. Note how the overall color has changed as compared to the previous stage.

4. Note how details stand out due to highlighting.

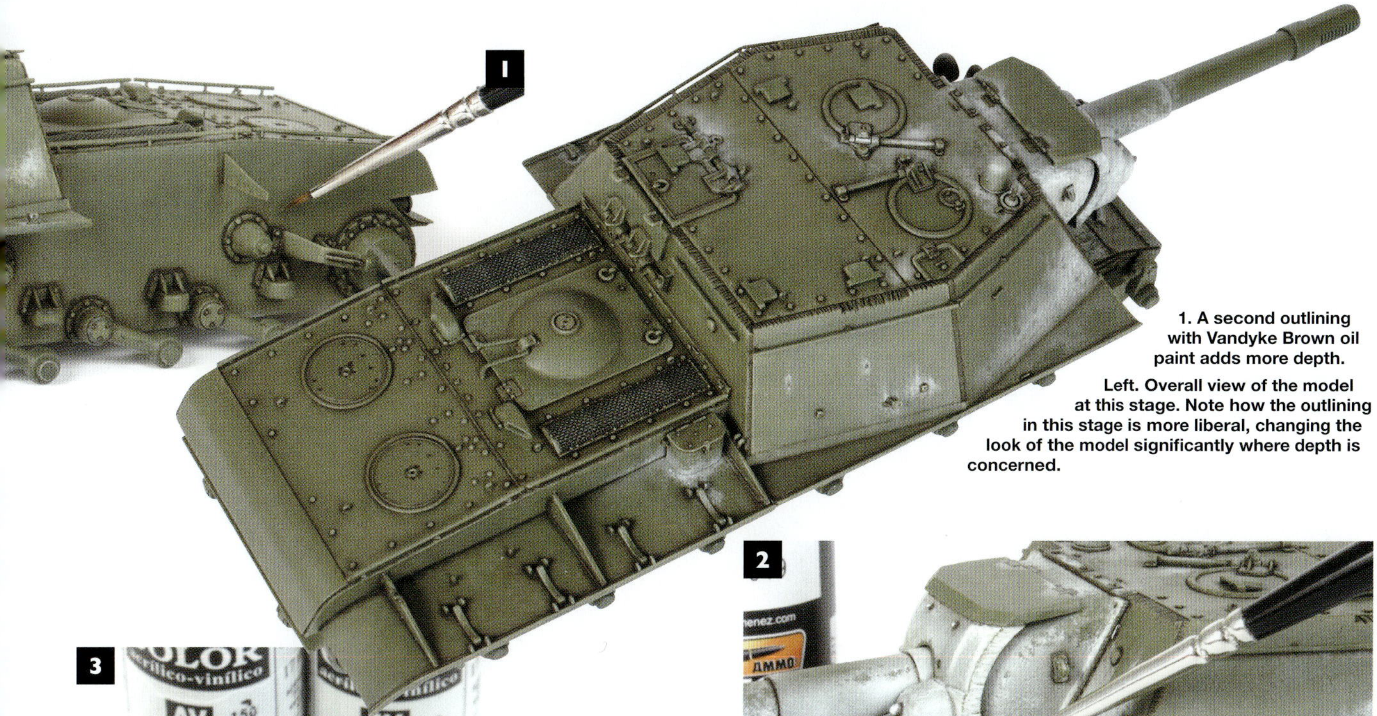

1. A second outlining with Vandyke Brown oil paint adds more depth.

Left. Overall view of the model at this stage. Note how the outlining in this stage is more liberal, changing the look of the model significantly where depth is concerned.

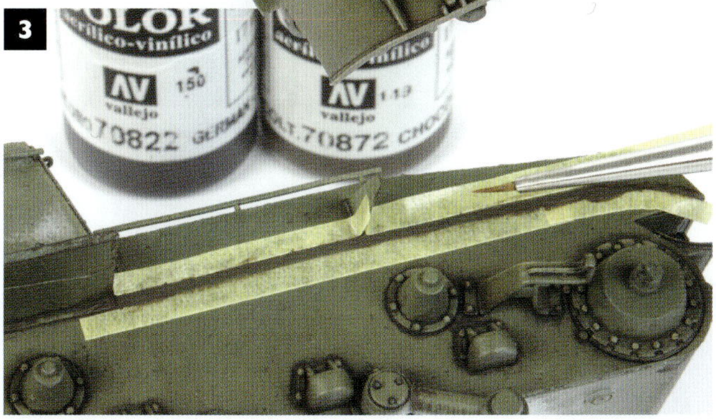

2. Detail chipping on the whitewash was carried out with a fine-tipped brush and the 4 BO green base color.

3. To act as a visual reminder of where the missing fender was once located, I taped off the surrounding area and painted on a mixture of Vallejo Model Color German Camouflage Black Brown (822) and Chocolate Brown (872).

4. Immediately after, I worked the painted area with Vallejo Airbrush Thinner (061), removing part of the paint.

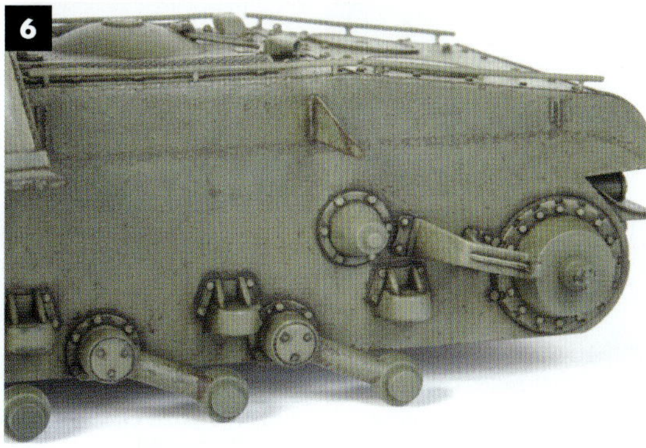

5. The rest of the model was also chipped with the brown mixture, mostly concentrating on well-worn places.

6. Note the faint trace of where the fender once used to sit.

1–4. To paint the exhausts, I turned to Lifecolor's Dust & Rust set. The colors were used from dark to light, sometimes going back and forth to reach the desired result.

5. For the lower, darker areas, I used Vallejo's German Camouflage Black Brown (822).

6. Simulating soot on the inside of the pipes was done with Lifecolor Smoke (TSC 208).

7. The lower hull received some rather heavy chipping in places.

8. More variety in the whitewash was created with Vallejo Panzer Aces White (Ger. Winter Tkcr.) (344).

9. The same color was used to add small remains of the whitewash around details.

10. Previously added white areas can be improved or changed.

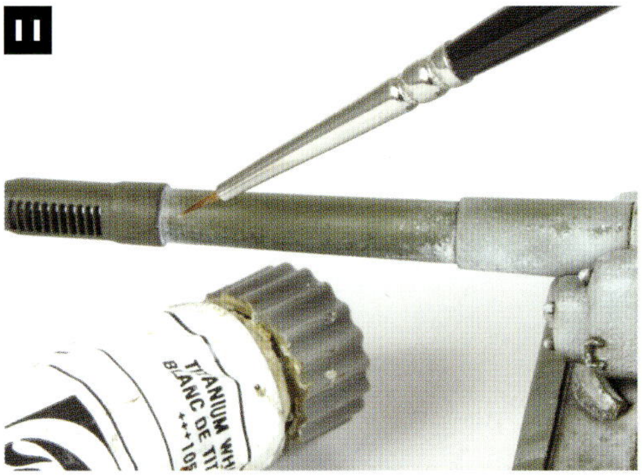

11. The same can be done with Titanium White oil paint. Anything goes…

12. A close up of the mantlet at this stage.

DUSTING

Time to move down to the lower hull. Although I wanted the model to look muddy from traveling through the wet winter landscape, it needed more than just the dark mud. When dirt dries, it turns to dust. So, first in order was to add some dusting to go underneath the fresh mud that would follow later. To create the dust color, I combined AK Interactive Dust Effects (015) with Dark Mud (023). Using a wide, flat brush, several filters were put on the lower hull, building up the dust gradually. Then, with a small round brush, I started adding more dust in specific areas, creating a more interesting look. Oil spills were then recreated around suspension parts using Vandyke Brown oil paint. The dusting was carried through over other parts of the model, concentrating it in logical places such as the rear fender, certain parts of the rear deck and the hull top, where the crew would drag up dirt on their boots. Always keep composition in mind, and try to make it visually interesting.

WET SPOTS, OIL SPILLS AND RUN-OFFS

The dust areas on the rear deck were carefully chosen, as I wanted to add some oil spills in particular places – and, as we know, oil spills attract dust. So the dust spots from before, or at least some of them, would now receive some Vandyke Brown oil paint simulating oil spills. Some smaller oil spills were created with Lamp Black oil paint, while further wet spots, be they oil spills or otherwise, were imitated by mixing gloss varnish with a little Vandyke Brown oil paint. I used Revell Gloss varnish (01) as well as Mig Productions Wet Effects and Damp Earth mixture (P409), as both gave good results. Basically, any gloss varnish could be used and tinted with an appropriate color.

Dirt etc. running down the sides of the hull was again simulated with Vandyke Brown oil paint. For the remainders of the whitewash, I used Titanium White oil paint.

1. The range of brushes used to create the dust effects on the model. For the dust itself, I used a mixture of AK Interactive Dust Effects (015) and Dark Mud (023).

2. Several filters of the mixture were added with a wide, flat brush.

3. Then, more dust build up was added in selected areas using a finer brush.

4. Using Vandyke Brown oil paint, fresh oil and grease marks were added.

1. Dusting was carried through to other parts of the model where it would accumulate naturally.

2. Close-up view showing the lower hull. The combination of dust and oil and grease usually works very well.

3. I had a few spots in mind where I wanted to add oil and grease spills. As oil and grease attract dust, those areas had already received the appropriate dusting beforehand. Here, I was working the other way round in adding them to the model, as it is easier to paint the dark stains over the lighter dust tones.

4. Crew drag up dirt and dust, so the roof was given the dust treatment as well. Here, the dust was concentrated where the crew walk.

5. Dust on the side of the vehicle was given a downward motion. Grease and oil stains will be refreshed afterwards.

6. Dust gets thrown up onto the rear of the vehicle.

7. A rather large oil spill was painted in one corner of the rear deck using Vandyke Brown oil paint. Details like this can add visual interest to your model.

8. Further oil and grease staining was carried out by mixing gloss varnish, here Revell Gloss (01), with a little Vandyke Brown oil paint. The gloss varnish adds a natural, wet, greasy sheen.

1. Any gloss varnish will do, basically. Here, I used Mig Productions' Wet Effects and Damp Earth mixture, tinted with a little Vandyke Brown oil paint.

2. Dirt running down the sides of the vehicle was painted on, once again, using Vandyke Brown oil paint.

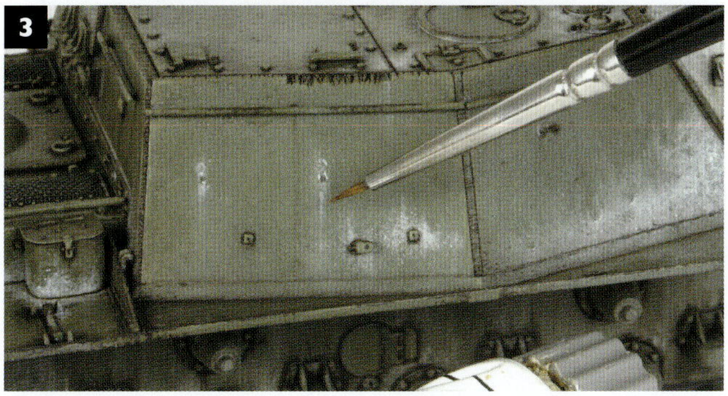

3. Titanium White was applied to simulate run off whitewash.

4. Here and there, a little more whitewash was added with Titanium White oil paint.

5 & 6. The grease and oil spills on the lower hull have been refreshed. The various layers add richness.

7. Close up of the rear deck at this stage. The contrast of oil spills and dust adds visual interest.

8. Here on the roof too, wet areas add variation to the look of the model.

Painting

WET MUD

Now with the dust in place, I could proceed with adding the wet mud. I had decided on smaller speckling on the lower hull and running gear, and more accumulated thick mud on the hull front and rear left side where the fenders were missing and mud would get thrown up by the tracks. For the speckling, I mixed Mig Productions Russian Earth pigments (P034) with AK Interactive Fresh Mud (016). This was then picked up with a brush and flicked onto the lower half of the model by pulling the brush along a wooden stick. Make sure you flick the mixture in the right direction – normally towards the rear for a forward-moving vehicle – otherwise the effect may look a bit odd.

To build up the wet mud on the fenders and rear left hull, I added the grainy pigments dry from the jar and then carefully fixed them in place with a little white spirit. Using too much liquid will make the grainy structure, imitating chunks of mud, disappear. Next, the mud required the same color as the speckling on the lower hull, so it needed painting with Fresh Mud (016). However, touching the fixed pigments with diluted paint trying to cover it from all angles made the chunky structure disappear. To solve the problem, I needed to fix the pigments more permanently. A little white glue diluted with water would do the trick and when carefully applied, it should not disturb the chunky structure. However, as surface tension of water will prevent it flowing as freely as (for example) White Spirit, I also added some washing-up liquid, which took care of that. With the pigments now firmly fixed in place, it was no trouble painting them.

On the left rear hull, the pigments were more dispersed, still revealing parts of the hull. Therefore, I first repainted that area with the AK dust mix (015 + 023) used on the rest of the model, after which the muddy chunks were picked out with Fresh Mud (016). Clean parts of the hull where then repainted with the 4 BO green base color. The mud splashes on the front upper hull were carefully built up with a rather dry Russian Earth pigments (P034) and Fresh Mud (016) mixture – no need to get out the white glue there.

WHEELS AND TRACKS

As per the lower hull, the wheels received the same dust and mud treatment. A little variation was brought into play by finishing the two drive sprockets in different ways, both in color and in weathering. It's always good to put variety into your model, as this will keep the viewer interested. Running surfaces of the road wheels, return rollers and idler wheels were colored with a soft lead pencil imitating bare metal, while the teeth of the drive sprockets were buffed up with a Karismacolor Silver pencil (949).

The metal tracks were given a sound basecoat with a Vallejo US Olive Drab (608) and Black (602) surface primer mixture overspray.

The weathering was begun by filtering the tracks with the AK dust mix (015 + 023). Then, both sides were dry-brushed with Vallejo German Camouflage Black Brown (822) to bring out the details. Where the wheels and tracks meet, the metal gets polished. So, to simulate this bare metal look, I used a soft lead pencil. To make sure I was working in a straight line, I used a ruler and a fine-tipped propelling pencil to mark the outsides. Superfluous deposits from the pencil were then cleaned off with a cotton swab. Next, the outsides were muddied up with the Russian Earth pigment (P034) and AK Interactive Fresh Mud (016) mix. Running surfaces were then restored to bare metal with a soft lead pencil. On the inside, I added some mud splashes by flicking the mud mixture with a brush and wooden stick (I should have done this before adding the bare-metal look). After touching up the bare-metal areas, once again a cotton swab was used for clean up. When the tracks were mounted on the model, more mud build up was added. A wet look was produced by dabbing the mud with Mig Productions Wet Effects and Damp Earth mixture.

Mud splashes on the lower hull were made by flicking a brush loaded with a dark mud mixture off a wooden stick. The splashes are directed towards the rear, where most splashes would be concentrated.

1. Fresh, wet mud on the fenders and rear left hull was built up by placing the grainy pigments straight from the jar. A little white Spirit was used to fix them in place. To fix the pigments more permanently so they could withstand painting with the appropriate mud color, I used a mixture of white glue, water and washing detergent. The detergent is used to break surface tension of the water so it will flow more freely.

2. The mud on the rear left was first revisited with the AK dust mixture (015 + 023).

3. Then the chunks of mud were painted with an AK Fresh Mud (016) and Mig Productions Russian Earth pigments (P034) mixture. Clean parts of the hull were repainted in the 4 BO green base color.

4. Mud splashes on the upper hull were painted on with the AK Fresh Mud (016) and Mig Productions Russian Earth pigments (P034) mixture. The pigments in the mixture add texture.

Below. The rear left side with fresh mud splashes above track level.

Drive sprocket after outlining with Vandyke Brown oil paint.

Road wheel after outlining with Vandyke Brown oil paint.

Dusting is done with the AK dust mixture.

The outlining/dusting stage is cleaned up by dry-brushing with the 4 BO green base color.

Vallejo German Camouflage Black Brown (822) was used for chipping.

For variation, both drive sprockets were finished differently. The right one was finished in a lighter tone and also received chipping with Lifecolor RAL 7008 GrauGrün/KhakiBraun (UA 212).

The left one was finished in a darker tint and received more dusting, as well as splashes with the dust color.

A silver pencil was used to polish the teeth of the drive sprockets.

Note the different finish on the drive sprockets. Variation adds interest.

1 & 2. Running surfaces of the road wheels were touched up with a soft lead pencil. The edges were given a metal shine with a propelling pencil.

3. The tracks were base-coated with a mixture of Vallejo US Olive Drab (608) and Black (602) surface primer.

4. A dust filter, mixed from AK's Dust Effects (015) and Dark Mud (023), was applied next.

1. Dry-brushing with Vallejo Model Color German Camouflage Black Brown (822) brought out the detail again.

2. Surfaces touched by the wheels were polished up with a soft lead pencil. A ruler was used to create a straight line.

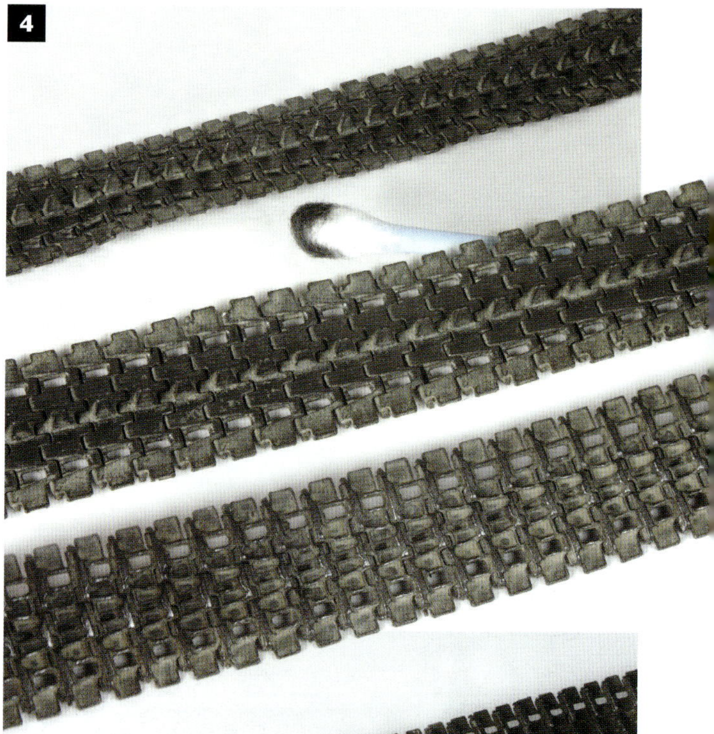

3. Various pencils were used to create the desired effects. The propelling pencil was mainly used in conjunction with a ruler to draw a straight line. The larger areas where then filled in with the green soft pencil, while the red pencil was used for touching up the guide teeth and running surfaces on the outside of the tracks.

4. Pencil dust was cleaned up with a cotton swab.

5. A wet-mud mixture made from Mig Productions Russian Earth pigments (034) and AK Interactive Fresh Mud (016) was added to the outer surfaces.

6. Metal surfaces where then touched up again using a lead pencil.

7. The inner surfaces were splashed with the mud mixture by flicking the hairs of a loaded brush with a wooden stick.

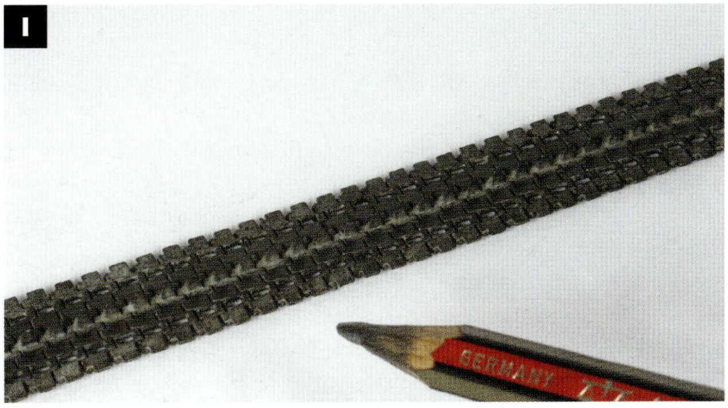

1. Polished metal surfaces were retouched with a lead pencil.

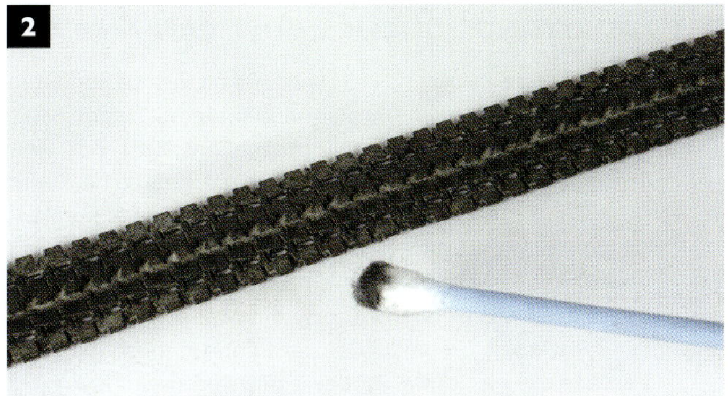

2. Pencil dust was once again cleaned up with a cotton swab.

3. The thick mud was then given a wet look by dabbing it with Mig Productions Wet Earth Effects & Damp Earth mixture.

Right. Rear view showing the wet tracks and splashed-mud effects.

4. The interior of the headlight was painted with Vallejo Air Chrome ((064).

5. A Punch & Die set was used to make a disk from black paper, which served to simulate the hole through which the electric wire for the lamp would enter.

FINISHING TOUCHES, FUEL CAN AND ACCESSORIES

The remaining work to be done on the hull consisted of finishing the headlight, fuel can and accessories. The interior of the broken headlight was first brush-painted with Vallejo Air Chrome (064). Then, with the aid of a Punch & Die set, a disk was made from black paper to simulate the hole in the rear of the light through which the wire to feed the lamp would enter. The electric wire itself was made from very thin copper wire.

Weathering on the fuel can was done in much the same way as the rest of the model. It only received a few extra rust streaks with Burnt Umber oil paint and AK Interactive Rust Streaks (013). For more interest, some handwritten chalk markings were added using a white pencil.

Metal parts on the pickaxe and the gun-cleaning rods were given a basecoat with Vallejo Model Color Black (950). The gun-cleaning rods were then dry-brushed with German Camouflage Black Brown (822) mixed with some Panzer Aces Highlight Ger. (Black) (337). Gradually, less of the Black Brown was used, finishing up with pure Highlight Ger. (Black). Shadows in between the rods and around tool holders were then produced using Lamp Black oil paint. By gently tapping with the side of a propelling pencil, a metal shine was recreated. Subsequently, some chipping was carried out using the German Camouflage Black Brown (822) and Chocolate Brown (872) mixture. To add further interest, a bit of rust tone was added with Lifecolor Rust Base color (UA 702) and a little Rust Light shadow (UA 703). Final metal highlights were added with the Silver Karismacolor pencil (949).

The wooden handle on the pickaxe first received a basecoat of Vallejo Model Color Buff (976), after which the wood grain was created using Raw Umber oil paint. I use the paint straight from the tube and paint on a wood grain pattern with a fine-pointed brush. Small corrections can easily be made with a brush moistened with white spirit. Here, the metal part in selected places was touched up with the German Camouflage Black Brown (822) and Chocolate Brown (872) mixture. As per the gun-cleaning rods, a bit of rust color was added, this time only using Lifecolor Rust Base color (UA 702). Again, final metal highlights were added with the silver pencil.

The spare track link was airbrushed with a basecoat of Vallejo Black surface primer (602) and Lifecolor Rust Dark shadow (UA 701). As mentioned above, it was varnished matt with Vallejo Air Matte varnish (059). Further local filters of Lifecolor Rust Base color (UA 702) and Rust Light shadow I (UA 703) completed the oxidized look. A little dusting and touching up of some edges with a propelling pencil finished it off. Selected edges and details all over the model were also given a bare-metal shine with the propelling pencil.

1. A layer of Vallejo Air Gloss Varnish (058) sealed the colors for further weathering.

2. For variation in color, the fuel can was airbrushed with the A. Mig 4 BO Russian Green (019) base color with a few drops of Vallejo Air Camouflage Light Green (006) added.

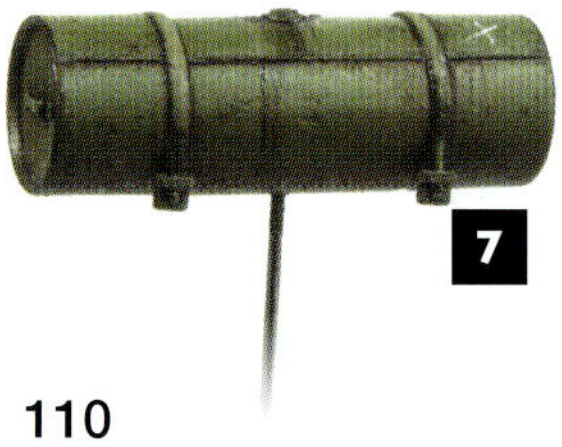

3 & 4. All details have been outlined with Vandyke Brown oil paint.

5. Chipping was done with a mixture of Vallejo German Camouflage Black Brown (822) and Chocolate Brown (872).

6. Rear view of the step 5 stage.

7 & 8. The finished fuel can with fuel spills, rust streaks and handwritten markings.

The fuel can was finished in a slightly different green color and received its fair share of weathering. I added the number 3 using a white pencil.

1

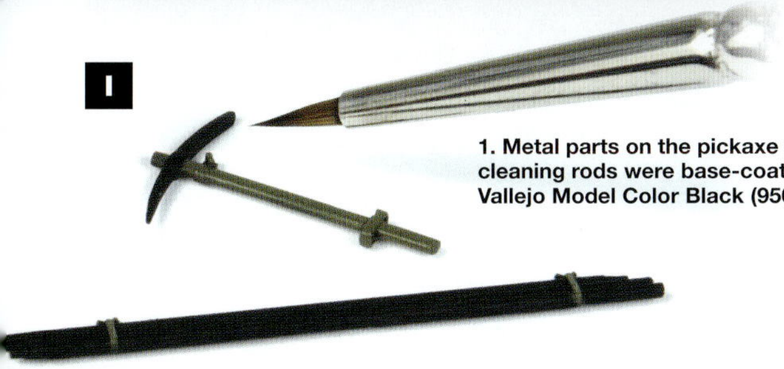

1. Metal parts on the pickaxe and gun-cleaning rods were base-coated with Vallejo Model Color Black (950).

2

2. The rods where then dry-brushed with a mixture of Vallejo Model Color German Camouflage Black Brown (822) and Panzer Aces Highlight Ger. (Black) (337). Gradually, less Black Brown was used, finishing up with pure Highlight Ger. (Black).

3

3. Shadows in between the rods and around tool holders were added with Lamp Black oil paint.

4

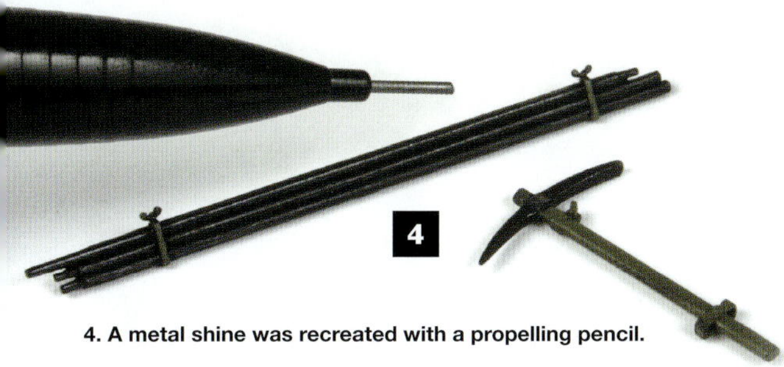

4. A metal shine was recreated with a propelling pencil.

5

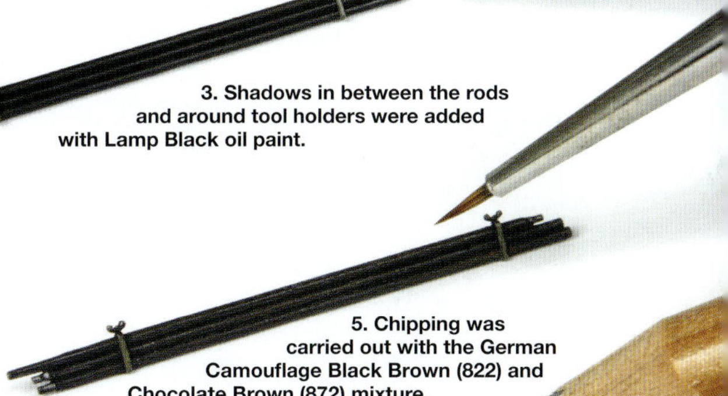

5. Chipping was carried out with the German Camouflage Black Brown (822) and Chocolate Brown (872) mixture.

6

6. A little interest was created by adding some light rusting with Lifecolor Rust Base color (UA 702) and Rust Light shadow (UA 703).

7

7. Metal highlights were added with a Karismacolor Silver pencil.

The finished rods on the model.

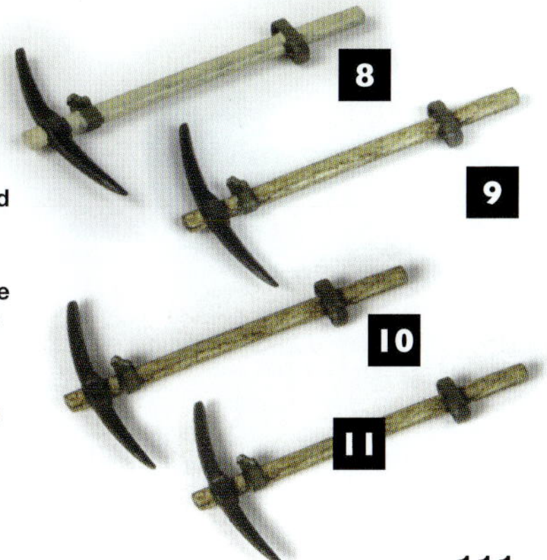

8 **9** **10** **11**

8. The wooden handle on the pickaxe was base-coated with Vallejo Model Color Buff (976).

9. Wood grain was then painted on with Raw Umber oil paint.

10. The metal part received selected filtering with a mixture of Vallejo German Camouflage Black Brown (822) and Chocolate Brown (872).

11. A little rust was added with Lifecolor Rust Base color (UA 702).

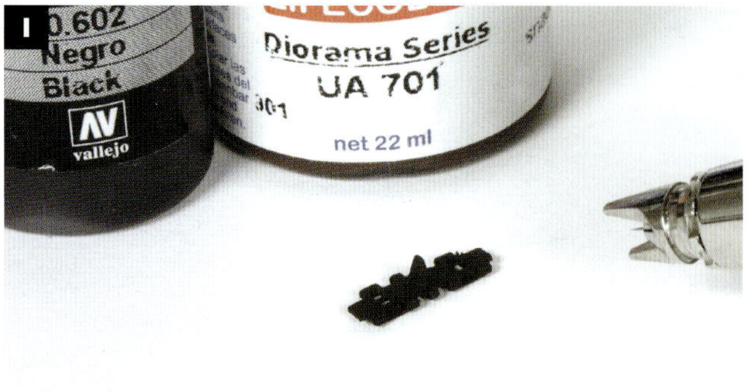

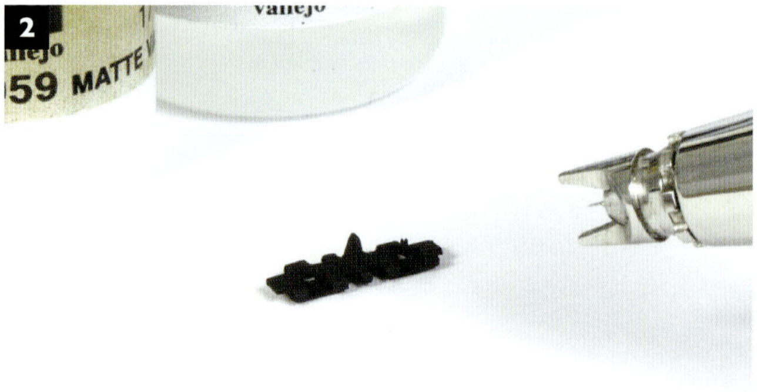

1. Vallejo Black surface primer (602) mixed with some Lifecolor Rust Dark shadow (UA 701) was used to airbrush the base coat on the spare track link.

2. This was then sealed with Vallejo Air Matt Varnish (059).

3. The spare track link before weathering.

4. Lifecolor's Dust and Rust set was used to add rusty tones. Here the more orange tints still need to be added, as well as some dusting and metal highlights.

The finished track on the model. The rusty tones add interest.

5 & 6. Details and edges were touched up with the side of a propelling pencil to simulate bare metal.

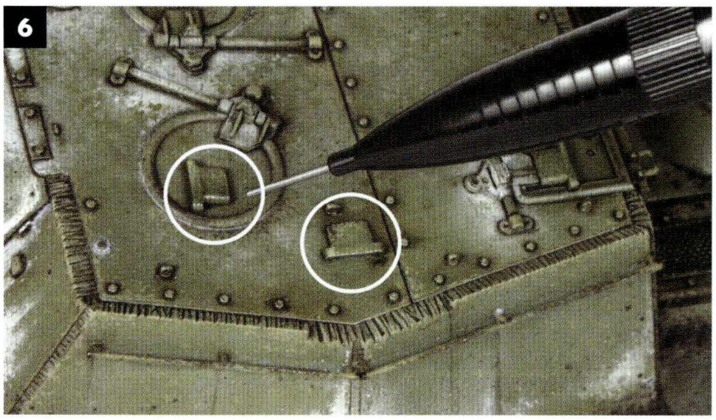

7. Mig Productions Black Smoke pigments (P023) were used to simulate soot deposits on the rear deck.

Above.
The holder for the towing cable was reworked and thinned to scale. Mud splashes on the front upper hull were brush-painted on.

Above. Note the mud thrown up on the front fenders and the damaged headlight.

Above. The missing fender is responsible for more mud build-up on the hull side. Observe the mud splashing on the lower hull.

Above. Overhead view onto the hull roof. The whitewash remains are situated in less accessible places.

Below. Overhead view of the rear deck. Dust and oil spills tend to go together.

Above. Weathering on the rear deck consists mainly of dust, oil and soot deposits. A mixture of whitewash remains, dust and oil spills adds variety and interest.

Above. The fuel tank in a slightly different shade of green has been quite heavily weathered. The pickaxe adds a bit of color to the monotone green base color.

Top. The gun-cleaning rods received their share of weathering.

048 N

Russian Infantry

Berlin, April 1945

Being an AFV modeler, I do like to embellish my models with a crew member or other figure, but I hardly ever get round to painting a figure for display purposes. So, when friend and fellow modeler Wim Van Hool asked me to paint his latest creation, a Russian infantryman, I felt that was the ideal opportunity to do exactly that. Wim also sculpted the GI figure for my late SdKfz 11 half-track, so I knew how much fun it would be to paint one of his creations.

The figure has been released by Mig Productions and depicts a Russian infantryman in late-war dress carrying a liberated Panzerfaust. It can be used in a variety of settings, and displayed on its own or in a vignette or diorama.

1/35

Mig Productions

- Mig Productions Russian Scrounger with Panzerfaust (no. MP 35-171), www.migproductions.com
- Balsa Wood and wooden strips
- Brass wire
- Cork
- Daler-Rowney System 3 – Acrylic texture paste
- Decadry dry transfers (no. 11 and 14)
- Evergreen Channel .100 (no. 263)
- Slater's Assorted Microstrip (no. 1001)
- Solder wire
- Tamiya Putty – basic type
- VP Cobblestone sheet resin (no. 1145)

ASSEMBLY

Excellently cast, the figure required only basic cleaning up. The head and left arm are separate, while the right one is cast to the body. Both hands are sculpted on the weapons they are holding, so no unrealistic or awkward positioning there.

For the ease of painting, I decided to paint the head and weapons separately and add them when painting had finished.

PAINTING THE FACE

Wim had based the figure on a photo he had found in a *Militaria* magazine. The pose differed, but the uniform and weapons were copied. It was also this photograph I used as a guide for painting.

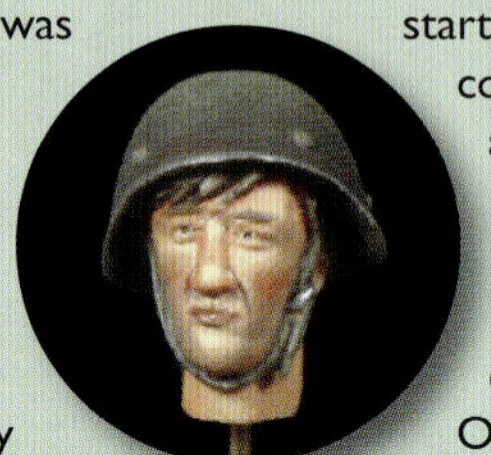

For a while now I've been using Vallejo paints for painting figures. Not being a figure painter, I still have a long way to go and my success varies, as I'm still trying to find the correct technique and color combinations. I've tried various mixes for painting skin tone, and although being reasonably pleased with my previous effort, I decided to try a different combination for this figure. As always, I started with the hands first, then the face and headgear, and then worked my way down to the boots.

Brown Sand (no. 876) served as a base coat for the skin. Initial highlighting and shading was done by adding Flat Flesh (no. 955) and Burnt Cadmium Red (no. 814) respectively. Deeper shadows were added with Flat Brown (no. 984), Leather Brown (no. 871) and German Camouflage Black Brown (no. 822). As the face still lacked some blush, I then added some local glazes with Scarlet (no. 817), which gave it a healthier look. I struggled with the face and started over a couple of times. In the end, I decided to be content with the effort thus far and opted for a different approach with the next figure. It's only when you paint the headgear that you get a really good idea about the finish of the face. For base coating the helmet, I used Bronze Green (no. 897), which I subsequently dry-brushed with Yellow Olive (no. 892), and Yellow Olive with some Khaki (no. 988) added, concentrating the lighter colors toward the top. The strap was painted with Russian Uniform (no. 924) and highlighted by adding some Green Grey (no. 886), while the edges where highlighted with some Yellow Olive (no. 892). The buckle was simply metalized with a silver Karismacolor pencil. Some minor weathering and chipping was carried out on the helmet using Raw Umber oil paint. The Karismacolor pencil was also used to add a sheen to the edge of the helmet.

THE COAT

Uniforms can change in color over time as they are worn and get dirty, bleached by the sun, etc. As I liked the color combination on the photograph I was using for reference, I tried to mix some paints to simulate it. For the coat, I mixed some Green Brown (no. 879) and Russian Uniform (no. 924). Before continuing with highlighting and shading, I first traced all the seams with German Camouflage Black Brown (no. 822), giving more depth to this typical feature. Then Khaki (no. 988) was used for highlighting, and Russian Uniform – as well as Russian Uniform with some German Camouflage Black Brown added – for shading. I tried to keep the color transitions subtle. Working in small areas at a time works best. Adding some Tamiya Flat Base to the paint helps to keep the colors matt, which is essential for a convincing result when it comes to fabrics.

Epaulets were simply painted Black (no. 950) with dark red piping (a mix of black and Scarlet (no. 817)). With the coat finished, I turned to the molded gun strap, belt and shirt. Contrary to the uniform where I started with a medium base color that was then highlighted and shaded, I now started with a very dark base color for the gun strap, which was then gradually lightened towards the top, creating a zenith light effect. The chosen base color was German Camouflage Black Brown (no. 822). For first highlights, I added some Flat Earth (no. 983). Further highlights were created by adding some English Uniform (no. 921) to the mix, while final highlighting was done with some Khaki (no. 988).

As I wanted to make things more diverse, I opted to do the belt in a different shade, giving it a leather appearance in contrast to the canvas gun strap. Starting with a darker base color, Black (no. 950), I again went for the zenith effect and

The contents of the Mig Productions kit. Both sculpting and casting are excellent. Only minor clean-up work is required.

highlighted with Chocolate Brown (no. 872). Final highlights were created with Orange Brown (no. 981). The belt buckle, ammunition magazine and buttons were also base-coated with black and then metalized with a lead pencil.

SHIRT AND TROUSERS

For the shirt, I started with a German Field Grey WW II (no. 830) and Green Grey (no. 886) mixture as base color. Working small areas at a time, I first finished the collar before starting work on the bottom part. For initial shading, I used straight German Field Grey, while adding some black for the darker shades. Highlighting was done with straight Green Grey.

It's important to get a nice balance in the colors of the different garments. They should go well together, yet be diverse enough to keep the figure interesting to look at. Sometimes, it can take a few try outs to find the correct color combination.

In this case, a base color of Yellow Olive (no. 892) and Russian Uniform (no. 924) was mixed for the trousers. For shading, Yellow Olive – the darker of the two colors – was used straight from the bottle. Highlighting was done with a mix of the lighter color, Russian Uniform, in combination with some Yellow Olive. For the highest highlights, I used straight Russian Uniform.

BOOTS

I always enjoy painting leather parts, so painting the boots was a fun thing to do. As with the belt, I started with a black base coat and used Chocolate Brown as a first highlight color. To get some variation with the belt, I this time used a mixture of Chocolate Brown and English Uniform for the final highlights.

PANZERFAUST

Time now to turn to the weapons. I tackled the Panzerfaust first and gave it a base coat with an Iraqi Sand (no. 819) and English Uniform mixture. Using the same techniques as on the uniform, I added some highlights with Dark Sand (no. 847). Then, to create some depth, I outlined all details with Chocolate Brown and later with Van Dyke Brown and Raw Umber oil paint. The reason for using some oil paint is that it is easier to blend for this sort of work. Raw Umber was also used to create some minor chipping.

MACHINE GUN

With rifles, I always start with the metal parts first. As with the ammunition magazine and buckles previously, the metal effect was created with a pencil over a black base coat. For the wood, I used an English Uniform base coat with a touch of Flat Earth. The wood grain was then painted on with German Camouflage Black Brown. Some final highlighting on a few edges was done with straight English Uniform.

Although all the painting was now finished, the figure looked a bit too clean.

What it needed was a bit of dust on the helmet, boots and trousers. To recreate this feature, I simply mixed some Naples Yellow and Raw Umber oil paint to get a nice dusty color, which was then painted and filtered on in the appropriate places.

The head and hands were painted separately. The details on the upper body are painted.

	Base	Highlight	High highlight	Shadow	Deep shadow	Glazes
Skin	Brown Sand (876)	Brown Sand (876) + Flat Flesh (955)		Brown Sand (876) + Burnt Cad. Red (814)	Flat Brown (984) Leather Brown (871) German Cam. Black Brown (822)	Scarlet (817)
Helmet	Bronze Green (897)	Yellow Olive (892)	Yellow Olive (892) + Khaki (988)			
Strap	Russian Uniform (924)	Green Grey (886)	Edge highlighted with Yellow Olive (892)			
Uniform	Green Brown (879) + Russian Uniform (924)	Khaki (988)		Russian Uniform (924)	Russian Uniform (924) + German Cam. Black Brown (822)	
Gun Strap	German Cam. Black Brown (822)[1]	German Cam. Black Brown (822) + Flat Earth (983)	German Cam. Black Brown (822) + Flat Earth (983) + English Uniform (921)	Khaki (988)		
Belt	Black (950)	Chocolate (872)	Orange Brown (981)			
Shirt	German Field Grey WW II (830) + Green Grey (886)	Green Grey (886)		German Field Grey WW II (830)	German Field Grey WW II (830) + Black (950)	
Trousers	Yellow Olive (892) + Russian Uniform (924)	Russian Uniform (924) + Yellow Olive (892)	Russian Uniform (924)	Yellow Olive (892)		
Boots	Black (950)	Chocolate Brown (872)	Chocolate Brown (872) + English Uniform (921)			
Panzerfaust	Iraqi Sand (819) + English Uniform (921)	Dark Sand (847)		Outlining with Chocolate Brown (872) and with Van Dyke Brown and Raw Umber oil paint		
Rifle wooden parts	English Uniform (921) (+ Flat Earth (983))	English Uniform (921)	Wood grain with German Camouflage Black Brown (822)			
Rifle metal parts	Black (950)	Karismacolor Silver pencil Lead pencil				
Dust	Naples Yellow and Raw Umber oil paint					

1 Originally, the color designated no. 822 was called SS Cam. Black Brown. Not only has the name changed (to German Cam. Black Brown), but so has the tone, as the new color is darker than the original. Personally, I hope the original color will be brought back into production.

The shirt and trousers painted.

Painting of the boots.

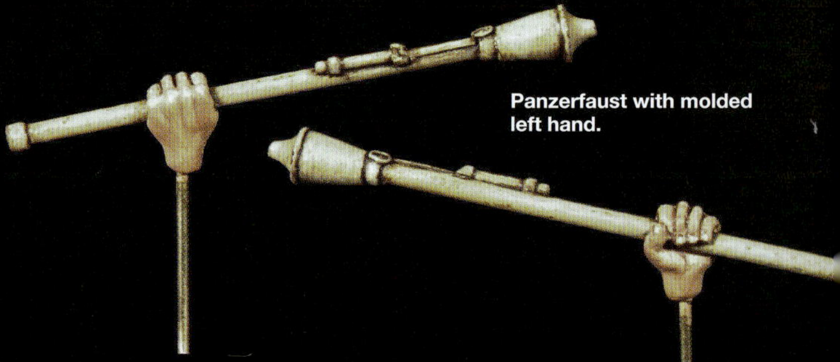

Panzerfaust with molded left hand.

The machine gun. The hand was sculpted on the weapon for a more realistic fit.

Here, the helmet has already received some dusting while the boots are still dust free.

The finished figure. The boots have now also received a coat of dust.

Base

CONSTRUCTION

Wearing late-war dress, the figure is ideal to be positioned on a base situated in Berlin at the end of World War II. What comes to mind for this scenario are ruined buildings with debris of bricks and steel, etc.

A feature I had wanted to use for a long time was a wooden spindle carrying cable. This setting would be the perfect opportunity to use it as a backdrop.

Before starting construction of the spindle, I first drew a rough scale drawing to determine the size and shape. Then, using strips of wood, I began to construct the spindle by gluing together two boards. When set, the two boards were glued on top of each other at right angles. Using a compass cutter the spindle was then cut out. Further detailing with bolts and a metal center was done with plastic card and a Punch & Die set. The middle section onto which the cable is rolled was made by gluing wooden strips around part of a plastic tube, which at one time served as a spool for sewing thread.

Plastic strip and profiles were used to create twisted metal beams. They would serve to create height and provide further backdrop for the figure. Bricks were made from a thin layer of cork, which was first coated with putty to diminish the roughness and get a more-to-scale effect. The bricks were then individually cut to size, and the remaining sides were again coated with putty and sanded.

The base itself was built up with wood to create some steps, and part of a resin casting representing a cobblestone street. A railing was soldered together from brass wire.

With the basic shape of the stairs, street and accessories finished, the composition of the vignette was tried out. Satisfied with the result, I then started to finish the stairs by coating them with filler. When set, they were sanded smooth and engraved. After adding the cobbles, it was time to get out the paint.

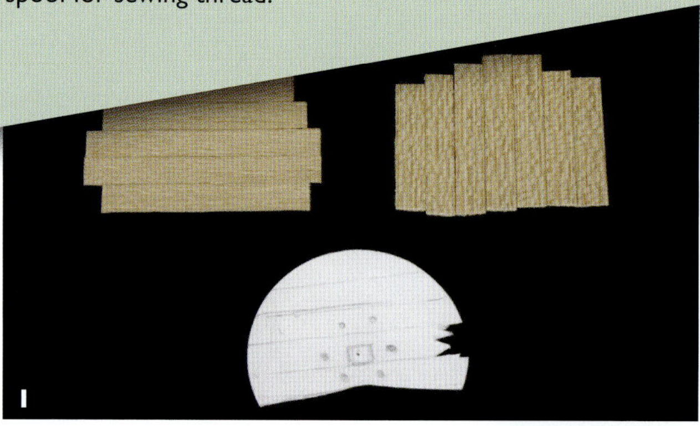

1. Two boards were made by gluing together lengths of wood. A paper template was drawn and cut out to determine the shape and size of the spindle.

2. The two boards were glued on top of each other at right angles. Then, using a compass, the spindle was cut out.

3. The metal center part and bolts were made from plastic card and using a Punch & Die set.

4. At the rear, the wooden strips were glued round part of a plastic tube of the appropriate diameter.

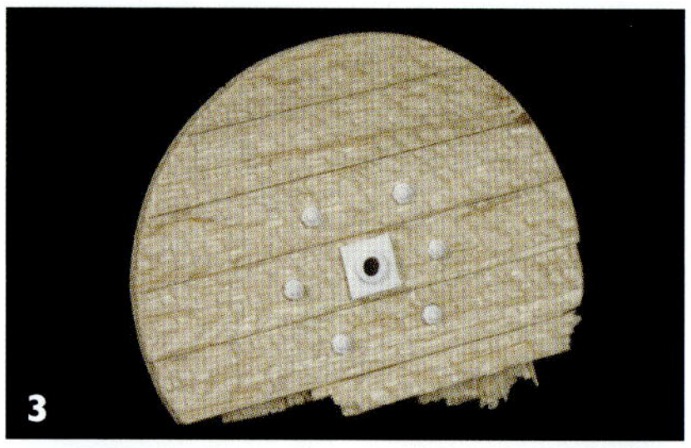

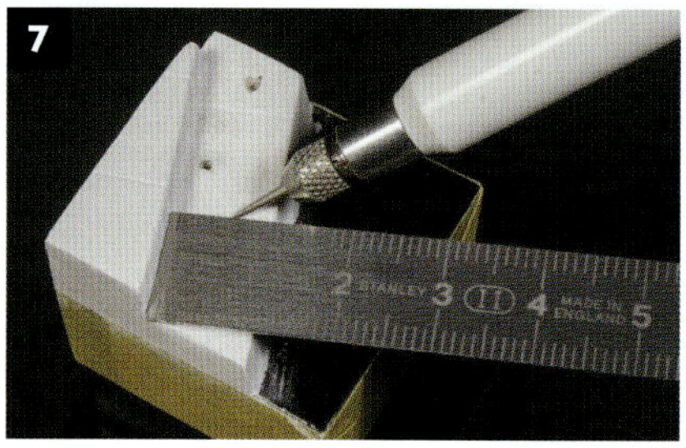

5. The base was made up of resin cobblestones and stairs made from wood. Two lengths of brass were soldered together to form the railing.

6. The wooden base for the stairs was coated with filler.

7. After sanding, the stones were scribed with a needle and ruler.

8. The cobbles were glued in place and the seams filled.

Painting

For painting, I opted to use Vallejo acrylics: they dry very quickly, so there are no waiting times in between the different layers of paint.

To create enough depth, I usually start from a dark base and then gradually add the lighter tones. This way, the majority of the shadows are already in place from the beginning. Here, Vallejo Air Black Grey (no. 56) formed the starting point. A combination of Model Air German Grey (no. 52) and Grey Green (no. 55) was then dry-brushed on, creating the first depth effect I was talking about. If you take a look at cobblestones, you'll notice that they don't all have the same color, but that there can be a lot of variation, ranging from very dark gray to even light beige. To add this variation, I used different colors (Luftwaffe Uniform WW II (no. 816); German Cam. Beige WW II (no. 821); Chocolate Brown (no. 872); and Khaki (no. 988), from the bottle and in combination, and picked out individual stones.

The stairs were base-coated with a combination of Luftwaffe Uniform WW II and German Cam. Beige WW II. A first dry-brushing was done with a mixture of German Cam. Beige WWII and Dark Sand (no. 847). In a second pass, Foundation White (no. 919) was added to give them a softer tone. To add more depth, the seams of the stones were then outlined with Van Dyke Brown oil paint using both filtering and dry-brushing techniques. Further staining was done by using Raw Umber oil paint, sometimes in combination with Van Dyke Brown. The last item to be painted on the base was the railing. After base-coating it with Andrea Black (no. AC-26), it was weathered and chipped with SS Cam. Black Brown (no. 822) and Burnt Cadmium Red (no. 814).

It's important to think about the different materials you will be adding to your composition and their respective colors. Variation is necessary, yet as discussed before with the figure, all colors need to work well together. For the metal profiles, I had a gray color in mind, but it needed to be different to the overall color of the cobbles. So, a different color combination consisting of Dark Sea Green (no. 868), Model Air Dark Sea Grey (no. 48) and Chocolate Brown (no. 872) was chosen. The Chocolate Brown was also used to filter some areas of the profiles and create a first rusting effect. This was then enhanced by combining it with Orange Brown (no. 981) for a more striking result. Some highlights and subtle variations were added to the gray areas with a combination of Luftwaffe Uniform WW II and Foundation White. Subtle stippling and filtering with Burnt Umber oil paint finished off the rust.

Again, to add variation in color, I decided to paint a smaller section of metal profiles in a brighter green color using Model Air Duck Egg Green (no. 009) and Pale Green (no. 095). Painting it in the gray color would make it almost invisible when lying on the cobbles. As previously, rust was added in a combination of chipping and filters.

1. Model Air Black Grey (no. 56) was used as a basecoat for the cobbles. They were then dry-brushed with a mixture of Model Air German Grey (no. 52) and Grey Green (no. 55)

2. Individual cobbles were picked out in different tones to add variation. The colors used were Vallejo Luftwaffe Uniform WW II (no. 816); German Cam. Beige WW II (no. 821); Chocolate Brown (no. 872); and Khaki (no. 988), both straight from the bottle and in combination with each other.

3. The stairs were basecoated with a mixture of Luftwaffe Uniform WW II (no. 816) and German Cam. Beige WW II (no. 821).

4. A first dry-brush run was made with a combination of German Cam. Beige WWII (no. 821) and Dark Sand (no. 847).

5. Further staining of the stairs was achieved with Raw Umber oil paint, sometimes in combination with Van Dyke Brown.

6. The railing and sides of the base were painted with Andrea Color Black (AC-26). This color is darker than the equivalent from Vallejo.

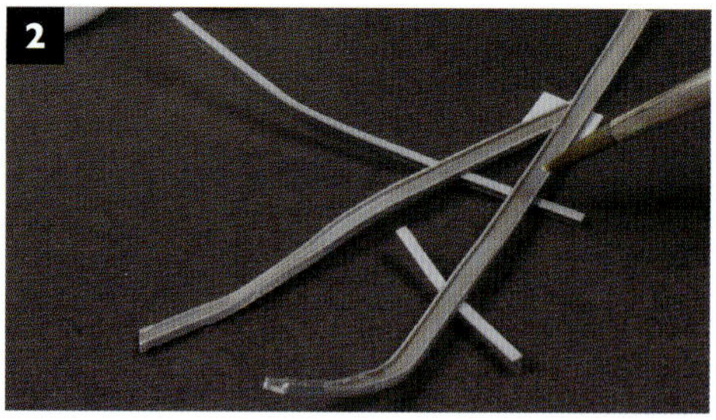

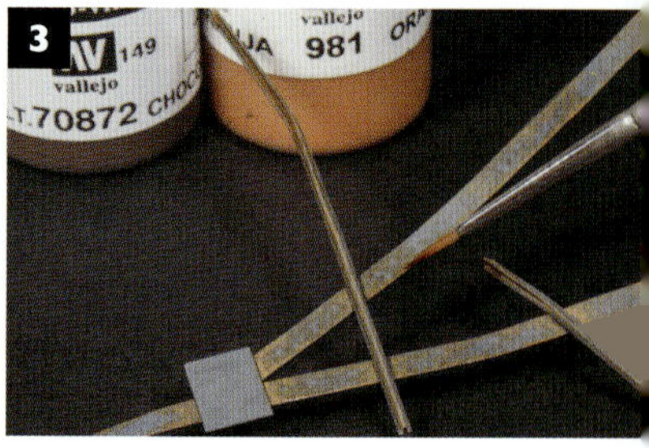

1. Plastic strip and profiles were used to construct twisted metal beams.

2. The metal profiles were base-coated with a combination of Dark Sea Green (no. 868), Model Air Dark Sea Grey (no. 48) and Chocolate Brown (no. 872).

3. Rust was added by filtering with Chocolate Brown (no. 872) and Orange Brown (no. 981).

4. The metal profile situated on the gray cobbles was painted with a mixture of Model Air Duck Egg Green (no. 009) and Pale Green (no. 095) to make it stand out.

5. As before, it was weathered with a combination of Chocolate Brown (no. 872) and Orange Brown (no. 981).

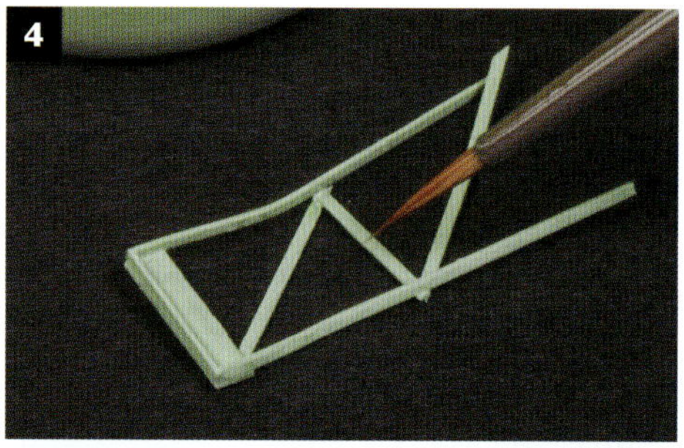

6. The base coat for the spindle was Burnt Cadmium Red (no. 814). Variation and highlights in the gray base coat were made with a mixture of Luftwaffe Uniform WW II (no. 816) and Foundation White (no. 919).

7. Chipping the paintwork to reveal the wood underneath was done with Iraqi Sand (no. 819).

8. A section of a board was taped off and painted white to take the black identification number.

9. Dry transfers were used to make up the number.

10. The metal parts were base-coated with Black (no. 950).

For the wooden spindle, I always had a deep red color in mind with a rectangle of white containing a black number. This would make it not too bright, yet it would go well with the color of the uniform of the figure. On the other hand, the color should be different enough not to look too similar to the bricks that would follow later on.

For the base color, I decided on Burnt Cadmium Red (no. 814). To create a zenith light effect, I then added Black (no. 950) and Orange Red (no. 910) to add shading and highlighting respectively. Of course, the position of the wheel slanting on the stairs had to be taken into account to get the correct horizontal transitions. Chipping the paintwork to reveal the wooden base underneath was done with Iraqi Sand (no. 819), sometimes in combination with German Cam. Beige WW II (no. 821). Part of a board was taped off to paint the white rectangle that would serve as the background for the black identification number. The number itself was made up from dry transfers. As the ciphers were rather glossy and therefore stood out too much compared to the matt white background, I gave them a coat of Andrea Matt varnish (AC-44) mixed with some Tamiya Flat Base (no. X-21). Adding the Flat Base makes sure the varnish dries matt – but don't add too much, as it may result in frosting. The pristine white rectangle was then chipped with Burnt Cadmium Red to reveal the base color.

Metal parts were base-coated with black and weathered with a combination of black, Chocolate Brown and Orange Brown.

To add depth, all planks were outlined with a combination of Raw Umber and Sepia oil paint. The paint was kept rather thick when performing this phase, while thinner mixes where used to outline the bolts and center part. Localized filters with Cadmium Red oil paint added more variation to the overall base color. Dust was simulated by filtering with a mixture of Naples Yellow and Raw Umber oil paint. To get a convincing result, it's best to build it up gradually in thin layers. The edges of the metal parts were then touched up with a pencil, resulting in a nice metallic sheen.

The rear of the spindle, which was to represent unpainted wood, received a base coat of German Cam. Beige WW II. Filtering, and dry-brushing with Raw Umber and Sepia oil paint added depth and staining. A combination of German Cam. Beige WW II and Iraqi Sand was used for highlighting and some chipping.

FINISHING

With all the separate items finished, the base could now be put together. The first item to be put on was the tall metal profile, as all the rest would be built up around it. To hold it firmly on the base, it was secured with a brass pin.

Some dried texturing paste was crushed and fixed to the base with white glue to represent small rubble. First, a mixture of Dark Sand (no. 847), Pale Grey Blue (no. 907) and Foundation White (no. 919) was painted on to simulate cement, followed by a mixture of Orange Brown (no. 981), Cavalry Brown (no. 982) and Hull Red (no. 985) simulating small pieces of bricks. The same colors were used to paint the bricks made of cork, which were then individually added to the base. Next, the bricks were filtered with the cement color mix to show the remainders of cement with which they were once mated together.

Although all elements were now present on the base, they still looked like individual pieces put together. What they needed was a layer of dust to unify them. The spindle received some extra dust with the Naples Yellow and Raw Umber oil paint mixture. Then, a more general layer of dust was added over the entire base with Mig Productions Light Dust (P027) and Brick Dust (P029) pigments. As the bricks were still missing some definition, I then used Cavalry Brown to touch up some edges and add some staining.

A final addition was some cable. By placing it over the metal profile and the wooden spindle, it again ties the different elements of the base together. The cable itself was made from soldering wire, which is easy to bend and shape. It was painted with Black and German Cam. Black Brown (no. 822) and dusted with the Naples Yellow and Raw Umber oil paint mix.

11. Weathering was done with a combination of Black (no. 950), Chocolate Brown (no. 872) and Orange Brown (no. 981).

12. The rear of the spindle was painted with German Cam. Beige WW II (no. 821) to simulate bare wood. Depth and weathering was created with a combination of Sepia and Raw Umber oil paint. German Cam. Beige WW II (no. 821) and Iraqi Sand (no. 819) were used for highlighting and chipping.

1. Dried and crushed texturing paste was used to make small rubble.

2. The tall metal profile for the background was added first and secured with a brass pin, then fixed to the base with white glue.

3. First, a mixture of Dark Sand (no. 847), Pale Grey Blue (no. 907) and Foundation White (no. 919) was painted on to simulate cement.

4. Then, a mixture of Orange Brown (no. 981), Cavalry Brown (no. 982) and Hull Red (no. 985) was painted on to simulate small pieces of bricks.

5. The base with all elements in place. The bricks were painted in the same manner as the small rubble. The cement color mix (Dark Sand (no. 847), Pale Grey Blue (no. 907) and Foundation White (no. 919)) was also filtered over the bricks. The spindle then received some more filters with Naples Yellow and Raw Umber to simulate dust.

6. Some Mig Productions Light Dust (P027) and Brick Dust (P029) pigments were used to tie all the elements together. Then, to bring out the bricks, some Cavalry Brown (no. 982) was used for touching up edges and adding some staining.

7. The finished base ready to take the figure. The cable was made with solder wire and painted with a mixture of Black (no. 950) and German Cam. Black Brown (no. 822).

As I had expected, due to my previous experiences with painting a GI on a half-track, the Russian infantryman was a real joy to paint due to Wim's excellent sculpting work on the folds. Also, constructing and painting the base, especially the wooden spindle, was a lot of fun.

References

PANZER I AUSF. A (PP.4–35)

Achtung Panzer no. 7: Pz.Kpfw. I/II Series and Variants, by Mitsuru Bitoh (ISBN 978-4499227735)
AFV Modeller issue 12 (September/October 2003)
Panzer I, by Janusz Ledwoch – Wydawnictwo Militaria No.10
Armor of the Deutches Afrikakorps, by Tom Cockle – Armor at War series no. 7021 Concord Publications (ISBN 978-9623616317)
Afrikakops: Rommel's Tropical Army in Original Color, by Bernd Peitz with Gary Wilkins – Schiffer Military History (ISBN 978-0764321405)
Internet:
Pictures of a Panzer I Ausf A. – Military Vehicle Technology Foundation: http://www.toadmanstankpictures.com/pzi.html
Detailed information on Panzer colors, including references to modeling paints, can be found at:
http://byrden.com/panzers/Colours/index.html

T-34/76 "CHTZ" (PP.36–61)

AFV Modeller issue 19 (November/December 2004)
T-34 In Action, by Steven Zaloga and James Grandsen – Squadron/Signal Publications – Armor No. 20
Beutepanzer Unterm Balkenkreuz: Russische Kampfpanzer, by Dr Werner Regenberg and Horst Scheibert – Waffen Arsenal/Podzun-Pallas-Verlag, Band 116
Photos sent to me by friends through e-mail.

PZKPFW VIII MAUS (PP.62–83)

Photos found on the internet.

SU-152 (PP.84–115)

Photos found on the internet.

RUSSIAN INFANTRY (PP.116–127)

Militaria magazine no. 238 (May 2005), "Fantassin, April 1945" (p. 41) – www.militaria-mag.com

Print Edition: ISBN 978-1-61200-7359
Digital Edition: ISBN 978-1-61200-7366

This book is published in cooperation with and under license from Sophia Histoire & Collections. Originally published in French as *Maquettes de chars 39-45. Allemands & Sovietiques*, © Histoire & Collections 2018

Translation by Alex Benvenuti
Edited by Nikolai Bogdanovic
Design by Myriam Bell Design
Models, photos and paintings by Mario Eens
Graphics by Morgan Gillard and Nathalie Sanchez

Printed in the Czech Republic by FINIDR, s.r.o.

Published in the United States of America and Great Britain in 2019 by
CASEMATE PUBLISHERS
1950 Lawrence Road, Havertown, PA 19083, USA
and
The Old Music Hall, 106–108 Cowley Road, Oxford OX4 1JE, UK